DISCARD

# THE PSYCHIC THREAD

# THE PSYCHIC THREAD

*Paranormal and Transpersonal Aspects of Psychotherapy*

## Elizabeth E. Mintz, Ph.D.

*National Psychological Association for Psychoanalysis
New York City*

*in consultation with*

## Gertrude R. Schmeidler, Ph.D.

*Professor Emeritus, Psychology
Department, City College, City
University of New York*

 **HUMAN SCIENCES PRESS, INC.**
72 FIFTH AVENUE,
NEW YORK, N.Y. 10011

Copyright © 1983 by Elizabeth E. Mintz
Published by Human Sciences Press, Inc.
72 Fifth Avenue, New York, New York 10011

Printed in the United States of America
3456789 987654321

**Library of Congress Cataloging in Publication Data**

Mintz, Elizabeth E.
  The psychic thread.

  Includes bibliographical references and index.
  1. Psychotherapy.  2. Extrasensory perception.  I. Schmeidler, Gertrude
Raffel.  II. Title.  [DNLM: 1. Psychotherapy.  2. Parapsychology.  WM 420
P97302]
RC480.5.M56 1983        616.89'14        LC 82-15716
ISBN 0-89885-139-4

*Miracles do not happen in contradiction to nature,*
*but only in contradiction to what we know of nature.*

—St. Augustine

*Remembering—*

Alex, Morty, Jim, and Leo

Appreciation is due to the following friends and colleagues who provided me with some of the experiences recounted in this book, although not all of them agree with my inferences.

Helga Aschaffenburg, Bernard Berkowitz, Mildred Newman Berkowitz, Patricia Blumenthal, David Blumenthal, Frank Donnelly, Martin Johnson, Joan Kauffman, Richard Kitzler, Noemi Matthis, Dagmar Morrow, Marjorie Newstrand, Betty Phillips, Kent Poey, Elaine Rapp, Rea Rabinowitz, Shirley Schechter, Elizabeth Thorne, Montague Ullman, Bradford Wilson, Eleanor Zimmerman

# CONTENTS

# PREFACE

This book is primarily addressed to the practicing clinician. It discusses the psychodynamic significance and therapeutic management of paranormal and transpersonal experiences reported by the patient or taking place in the therapeutic situation (for example, apparently-telepathic communication between therapist and patient).

The clinical data presented here is drawn from personal observations by myself and various colleagues; it cannot be regarded as scientifically acceptable evidence. However, rigorously controlled research has yielded findings which, for some of us, constitute satisfactory proof that paranormal phenomena can and do occur.* Acceptance or rejection of this conclusion seems to depend upon temperament and personal philosophy, not upon impartial evaluation.

Transpersonal or mystical experience, in contrast, is not subject to experimental evaluation. It may represent pathology, naïvete, or valid glimpses of a reality far beyond the senses or the

*Since this is my personal bias, it is fair to refer readers to a group of skeptical reviews in *Contemporary Psychology* 26, 1, (January 1981).

limited world of reason. Just as it is not my purpose to offer "proof" of paranormal occurrences, neither is it my intention to maintain that a transpersonal approach to life is necessarily associated with deeper happiness and greater social usefulness. Mystical experiences do occur, sometimes to people respected by society, sometimes to people generally regarded as psychotic. My focus is not upon the philosophical or spiritual implications of such experience, but is again primarily upon its therapeutic management.

The burgeoning interest in Eastern mysticism, the popularity of films and books dealing with the supernatural, and the growing interest in nontraditional healing all indicate a hunger for experiences that transcend the materialistic and mechanistic viewpoint. Unless responsible practitioners begin to regard the paranormal and transpersonal dimensions of human life as a legitimate concern of psychology, I venture to predict an enormous influx of untrained, potentially dangerous, profit-seeking psychic entrepreneurs. They are appearing even now, sometimes terming themselves spiritual leaders or psychic healers, but actually engaged in wild psychotherapy without training in any recognized discipline.

A personal introduction may be appropriate. I come from thirty years of practice as a psychotherapist, with a conventional background in clinical psychology and psychoanalysis, and with considerable exposure to the Gestalt approach and other contemporary viewpoints. I do not regard myself as psychically gifted, nor do I consider myself a mystic, although I deeply respect transpersonal values. And while I do not essay to persuade anyone to believe either in paranormal experiences or in the mystical world view, I do wish to suggest that these be regarded as aspects of the human condition that deserve our respect and consideration.

# INTRODUCTION

Two areas of human experience relatively neglected by many clinicians and theoreticians are of great importance to psychotherapists, both on a practical level and in the understanding of human personality, i.e., the transpersonal and the parapsychological. These terms are often confused, and do indeed in some respects overlap. However, if we wish to explore these two frontiers of psychology it is necessary to begin with a working distinction between them.

Parapsychology is the study of interactions between the human mind and the external world that cannot adequately be explained by what we now understand about the laws of physiological psychology and physics. These interactions include telepathy, precognition, clairvoyance, psychokinesis and psychic healing, all frequently grouped together under the rubric of psychic occurrences or paranormal phenomena. The acceptance of parapsychology as a legitimate branch of science does not imply belief in the occult or the supernatural, or even in spiritual values. It is a field of investigation, formally recognized as such in 1969 by the acceptance of the Parapsychological Association as an affiliated society of the American Association for the Advancement of Science.

Data regarding the occurence of psi phenomena under laboratory conditions has been accumulated by respected scientists. Outstanding figures in various conventional fields such as physics, biology, astronomy, and even engineering have indicated their acceptance of the paranormal.* It has been said that if the evidence for any other set of phenomena were as convincing as the evidence for the existence of psi, we would accept it as naturally as we now accept the laws of gravity and thermodynamics. Scientists are reluctant to accept the data, (although the total statistical data is impressive) partly because individual experiments are difficult to replicate, and partly because such an acceptance involves a revision of the accepted structure of classical physics—including our concepts of time and space—although these concepts appear far more complex now than in Newton's time.

My personal conviction, and one that is shared by many noted psychotherapists (Freud, Jung, Assagioli, Fodor, Ehrenwald, Eisenbud, Frank, Maslow, Pierrakos, LeShan, Dean, and many others), is that psychic phenomena do take place in therapy and may even be an integral part of the therapeutic process. Evidence for this naturally comes from specific clinical observations rather than from controlled laboratory experiments. But as psychotherapy itself is essentially a very complex and subtle set of interactions between two people, it cannot be explored and replicated by the same methods used with phenomena belonging entirely to the hard sciences. After all, Freud's formulation of the laws governing relationships between conscious and unconscious aspects of the mind were not made in a laboratory, but in his consulting room.

Fortunately, the possibility that psychic phenomena occur in therapy can be explored on a hypothetical basis even if we prefer to reserve final judgment. As therapists, we can inquire as to

*A questionnaire sent out by Tornatore[1] to randomly chosen members of the American Psychiatric Association indicated that, of 609 respondents, 79 percent either strongly believed in the occurrence of psychic phenomena or accepted their occurrence as possible. However, it should be noted that the 2,400 members who did not respond may well have been people who did not consider the question worth exploring.

under what circumstances these seemingly paranormal phenomena occur, what they can contribute to our understanding of psychotherapy, and—especially—what the responsibilities are for the therapist in their evaluation and management.

In contrast to psychic phenomena, our concept of the transpersonal dimension of human experience is not based on observation and experiment, but is based only upon direct, subjective experience. If, after examining the evidence, we say "I do not believe in the existence of paranormal events," we are questioning the validity of a body of data. But we are unable to say, "I do not believe in the existence of transpersonal experiences" because these experiences are as subjective as love or the enjoyment of beauty or music. We can only say, "I, personally, have never experienced any transpersonal feelings." This dimension is related to poetry rather than to science, to religion rather than to research. A definition has been offered by Vaughan, who writes:[2]

> The transpersonal level corresponds to the stage of self-transcendence, where the individual no longer experiences himself as separate and isolated, but as part of something larger. . . . The individual in relationship to the universe comes into focus and the underlying unity of all life may be experientially realized.

The Statement of Purpose from the *Journal of Transpersonal Psychology* also suggests the quality of this approach:

> The *Journal of Transpersonal Psychology* is concerned with the publication of theoretical and applied research, original contributions, *empirical* papers, articles and studies in meta-needs, ultimate values, unitive consciousness, peak experiences, ecstasy, mystical experience, B values, essence, bliss, awe, wonder, self-actualization, ultimate meaning, transcendence of the self, spirit, sacralization of everyday life, oneness, cosmic awareness, cosmic play, individual and species-wide synergy, maximal interpersonal encounter, transcendental phenomena; maximal sensory awareness, responsiveness and expression; and related concepts, experiences and activities. As a statement of purpose, this formulation is

to be understood as subject to *optional* individual or group interpretations, either wholly or in part, with regard to the acceptance of its contents as essentially naturalistic, theistic, supernaturalistic, or any other designated classification.

To further highlight the differences between these two approaches to human experience we may consider the description of a recently developed laboratory device in which subjects, making tens of thousands of trials, attempt to influence which target will be randomly selected by a machine; results are then evaluated by sophisticated statistical procedures that enable a comparison between the accuracy of these results with the results that would have been obtained by chance alone.

> An electronic apparatus displayed to the subjects a group of four small light bulbs, each with a pushbutton adjacent. Pushing any button would cause one of the lamps to light; *which* one was determined by a highly random physical process, the disintegrating of an atom in a bit of radioactive strontium. In a first series, the subject was asked to try to push the button next to the lamp that would then light, thus automatically registering a "hit." A total of 63,000 trials by three subjects in this series yielded highly significant results ($P = 2 \times 10^{-9}$); i.e., one possibility in 500 million that the score was due to random events.[3, p. 12]

Clearly, this type of research implies no commitment to belief in supernatural suspension of the natural laws of physics, but does imply the hypothesis that the interaction of human experience and human reality obeys laws we do not yet understand. Conversely, the validity of the transpersonal dimension of human life rests primarily upon the reports of men and women who have undergone mystical experiences which, as William James has pointed out,[4] show impressive similarities from one individual to another, from one culture to another widely different culture, and even from one millenium to another.

Thus, there is consensually validated evidence for the occurrence of psychic phenomena, while transpersonal experiences, although deeply moving for most of those who have undergone them, are essentially related to personal spiritual values.

Nevertheless, even with these reservations a closer scrutiny of psi phenomena suggests certain hypotheses that have a clear relationship with the mystical experience. This is especially true of clairvoyance and precognition, which seem to require more fundamental alterations in our concept of reality than does the phenomenon of telepathy.

The occurrence of telepathic communication between two living people is, for most of us, relatively easy to accept. Decades ago, when this phenomenon was investigated by card-guessing experiments, first by Rhine and later by other research workers, it was apparent (at least during the later years of the laboratory work) that every precaution had been taken against contamination of the guesses by subliminal sensory cues, that the directors of research made every effort to maintain high standards of integrity, and that the statistical evaluation of the data was impeccable.* Superficially, the explanation for telepathic communication seemed easy. Electrical charges are involved in brain activity, and a thinking brain can readily be viewed as a source of electrical emissions that could be perceived by another brain under appropriate circumstances. All this seemed hardly more remarkable, to many of us, than television.

This interpretaton of the data is quickly demolished by other data, equally impressive in terms of experimental precautions and statistical evaluation, which indicates that statistically significant accuracy in card-guessing can also occur when no human agent is aware of the order of the cards (clairvoyance) or when selection of the target card has not yet been made (precognition).† These experiments imply not merely the possibility of astounding unexplored capacities of the human mind and an entirely new conception of the way in which mind interacts with

---

*Chapter 1 includes a more detailed description of these experiments.

†Clairvoyance refers to knowledge about objects of events obtained without sensory data and without involvement of any human agent; precognition refers to knowledge of future events.

space and time, but even a new vision of the basic nature of time, space, and energy.

As LeShan has convincingly argued,[5] these new conceptions converge astonishingly with contemporary physics, which requires us to accept a nonlinear picture of causation and a post-Newtonian picture of space and time. They converge also with the experience of mystics, who feel—at least at the moment of the mystical enlightenment—that they are one with mankind and the cosmos, and that time and space are irrelevant.

Again, what are the implications of these concepts for the practicing psychotherapist? It is certainly not our task to try to develop mysticism or even to encourage Maslovian peak experiences in our clientele; even less it is our task to persuade them to accept the occurrence of paranormal events. However, unless we choose to regard our patients as stimulus-response automata who can be manipulated into better social adjustment, we should perhaps recognize that paranormal and transpersonal dimensions of human life may be not only valid but valuable.

*Chapter 1*

# THE NATURE OF PSI

*For us who are convinced physicists, the distinction between past, present and future is only an illusion, however persistent.*

—Einstein

It is unfortunate that for many people scientifically validated phenomena such as telepathy are still confused with vampires, werewolves, and various superstitions associated with Grade C movies. Even psychotherapists, who often have the opportunity to observe paranormal occurrences, may regard data on extrasensory perception (ESP) as a mixture of coincidence, poor research methods, muddy thinking, and possibly even deliberate or unconscious fraud.[1] In contrast, this same data on extrasensory perception, psychic healing, and other paranormal phenomena is viewed as convincing by a galaxy of highly accredited physicians, psychologists, physicists, and other scientists, including such luminaries as William James, Sigmund Freud, C. G. Jung, and the late Gardner Murphy, one of the most highly respected American psychologists.

Data about paranormal phenomena comes from two sources: experiments and anecdotal evidence. It seems that any unbiased person willing to examine laboratory data, such as the scores obtained by literally thousands of subjects in variations of the card-calling method developed by Rhine* and evaluated by the most rigorous statistical methods, can hardly fail to acknowledge the existence of extrasensory perception. This data, however, utilizes great numbers of subjects and enormous numbers of guesses, and it is never possible to be sure that a specific subject will guess a specific card correctly.

Anecdotal evidence is more difficult to evaluate because the factors of human error and the possibility of wishful thinking are difficult to rule out. Consider, for example, a patient who enters his therapist's office and excitedly describes his unexpected receipt of a family heirloom from his Uncle Sherman—just as he had dreamed of it three days before! This dream could legitimately be regarded as precognitive, by scientific standards, if it could only be established that:

1.   The patient had informed several people about the dream before receiving the watch from Uncle Sherman, and
2.   The patient had no reason to expect that Uncle Sherman would present him with the watch, a factor all but impossible to rule out.

*The Rhine or "Zener" cards consist of twenty-five cards evenly divided into five geometrical symbols (cross, circle, square, star, and wavy lines). This deck can be used to test for telepathy, in which testing a "sender" gazes at a series of cards that have been placed in random order, and a "receiver," physically screened from the sender or even many miles away, attempts to guess intuitively the symbol the sender is viewing. In tests for clairvoyance, the cards are placed in order by a mechanical device but are not viewed by any human being. Tests of precognition can also be made by requiring the subject to foresee the order of a deck that has *not yet* been placed in order; the ordering is done later by mechanical shuffling or by the use of a table of random numbers.

This method has the great advantage of accumulating data that can be statistically evaluated; chance alone would give correct guesses on five

Fortunately, it is not the therapist's task to determine whether or not the apparently precognitive dream was actually an instance of extrasensory perception; it is his task only to explore the meaning of the gift to the patient. Even if the therapist judges that the patient is probably giving a correct report of what happened, the possible precognitive element in the dream is of clinical importance only in implying that Uncle Sherman's gift had some special significance.

Anecdotal evidence, however, is cumulatively impressive.* Many of the experiences reported by people from widely different walks of life, of widely varying personality types, and from all parts of the United States and Europe show certain striking similarities. For instance, there is a multiplicity of stories (many well-supported by corroborative evidence) in which an individual

---

out of the twenty-five cards. When actual scores are compared with scores that would occur by chance, it is possible to work out a probability quotient that indicates the likelihood of some factor other than chance at work. This statistical method, familiar to every sophomore student of Psychology I, in many experiments has yielded a probability quotient which indicates that odds against the obtained results (usually evaluated in terms of the total group of percipients in a large-scale experiment) having been obtained by chance alone may be as great as 100 million to one.

For readers who wish to explore this field further, many excellent references are available, including data in which personality variables associated with high scores are identified.[2,3,4] A serious review that opposes the psi-hypothesis is offered by Hansel,[5] who stresses the possibility that data may have been collected with inadequate experimental safeguards, or may have been distorted by unconscious bias or even deliberate falsification.

*Readers who wish to examine this data further are referred to the early classic of Gurney and Myers;[6] to a later work by Tyrrell;[7] and to a current volume by Louisa Rhine.[8] Gurney and Myers were Cambridge scholars in the humanities; Tyrrell was a radio engineer who turned to psychic research; and Dr. Louisa E. Rhine, wife of the late J. B. Rhine, is a highly accredited scientist in her own right. These writers present corroborative evidence and try to distinguish well documented cases from those which depend only on hearsay or on questionable memory.

reports seeing the apparition of a geographically distant friend or relative close to the time of the friend's death, sometimes within the same hour. There are also many stories of disasters averted by some kind of precognitive "hunch" or warning. None of these anecdotes in themselves can constitute *proof* of psychic phenomena, but taken cumulatively, they not only bulwark the psi hypothesis, but suggest some tentative answers to questions of primary interest to the practicing clinician: Under what circumstances does extrasensory perception occur, and what is its significance to the individual who experiences it?

Both laboratory evidence and anecdotal data strongly suggest that psi phenomena are more likely to occur when some basic human need is served by their occurrence. This is hardly surprising. Classical psychoanalysts see libidinal strivings as the basic determinants of feeling and behavior; behavioral psychologists think in terms of positive and negative conditioning and reinforcement; humanistic psychologists emphasize self-actualization as the goal toward which we all strive; and every school of thought, in one way or another, recognizes the primary importance of motivation.

Even in the relatively content-free laboratory experiments with the Zener cards, motivation emerges as important. As a group, subjects who believe in the possibility of paranormal communication score higher than chance in card-calling experiments, perhaps because they are not afraid of being receptive to intuition, but perhaps also because they wish to provide evidence for their belief. Subjects who deny the possibility of psi communication score significantly *lower* than chance, presumably because they also wish to provide evidence for their point of view.[9,10]

Motivation appears more dramatically in anecdotal instances of spontaneous telepathy or precognition in which the percipient seems to have paranormal warning of a threat to the life or well-being of himself or another person and is consequently able to avert the danger. Anecdotal evidence cannot meet rigorous scientific standards since the episodes occur spontaneously and cannot be replicated, but the reports of such incidents are numerous and striking. For example, Heywood[11, p.241] describes two such incidents:

The percipient . . . was about to set out for work and did not want to be late when she felt an urge to go down to her landlady's basement kitchen and take in some clothes from the garden lines—clothes which she knew could very well wait. The urge was so overwhelming that she gave in to it, hurried downstairs, and saw her landlady sitting at the kitchen table, waving a glass and surrounded by empty beer bottles. But she also heard water splashing in the bathtub with the tap turned off, and hastened across the room to find out why. The landlady's ten-month-old baby was in the tub, completely submerged except for his feet which were splashing the water. The drunken mother said, "Oh, I was giving baby a bath and forgot about him. . . ." The percipient applied first aid and the baby was saved.

A Mr. C. was in the habit of visiting friends forty miles away at week-ends only, but suddenly . . . he felt he had to go there *at once*. So without even fetching nightgear from his hotel, he took the first possible train, thinking "This is the craziest thing I have ever done in my life." But he was wrong. On his arrival he found his friend's house in darkness. . . . Then he saw someone lying on the ground. It was his friend's wife. She had had a stroke. Her husband was away, and if Mr. C. had not followed his hunch there would have been no one to help her.

Both of these episodes, which seem to go far beyond what could be explained by chance alone, can be accounted for by the hypothesis of telepathy. We may conjecture, for example, that in the first episode the percipient became telepathically aware of the baby's terror, or that the mother—even in her drunken state— was unconsciously aware of her baby's peril and sent out an unconscious cry for help. We may conjecture, also, that in the second episode the woman became aware of her need for help before she waxed unconscious, and Mr. C. picked up this need telepathically. Both these hypotheses, of course, are in utter violation of common sense; if there were not so many similar anecdotes reported by respected observers, we would have to regard both the episodes and the explanatory hypotheses as unbelievable.

Similarly, we can only conjecture as to possible motivational factors in the most frequently reported of all spontaneous paranormal phenomena: the apparition of a beloved person, seen either as a sensory vision or in a dream by a friend or relative, usually at the moment of the beloved's death or sometimes shortly before or shortly afterwards. It seems conceivable that these apparitions are made possible by the emotional rapport between the dying person and percipient, and that on both sides the motivation may be a reaching out by the dying person—perhaps a wish to be close to another person at the moment of death—which somehow sets up in the percipient a resonance of the same wish for closeness. This, of course, is the purest conjecture. It would be interesting to know a great deal more about the personal relationships of the two communicants in these circumstances, but such intimate material is rarely revealed to interviewers and might even involve unconscious factors on the part of the percipient.

For most of us, precognition is far more difficult than telepathy to reconcile with the safe and sane, familiar world of sensory observation and mechanistic law. Our taken for granted distinction between present and future events is shaken, since individuals seem to "know" about events that have not yet occurred. Yet for precognition also, anecdotal evidence is well-supported by laboratory experiments and statistically tested mass observations. Evaluated on a group basis, subjects using the Zener cards are able to guess ahead, predicting well beyond chance, the order of cards in a deck that has not yet been mechanically sorted.[12] At the Maimonides laboratory, a gifted "sensitive" was able to predict—with an accuracy which, according to the statistical formulation of probability, could have occurred by chance only once in five hundred times—which of two colored lights would next be lighted by an electronically controlled random number generator. Other work at Maimonides also lends credibility to the age-old belief that dreams may be premonitory; the same "sensitive" predicted the content of pictures that were selected, through an elaborately controlled random number system, the day *after* his dream had been recorded.[13] There is also statistical evidence that the number of cancellations for train trips on which catastrophe occurs is greater than the average number of cancellations for trips which are uneventful.[14] It is as if at least some of the travellers who decided to cancel had precognitive awareness, conscious or unconscious, of the impending danger.

Here, too, anecdotal evidence about the spontaneous occurrence of precognitive "warnings" may show one of the strongest motivations of which human beings are capable—the wish to save the life of a beloved person, an emotion especially strong between mothers and children. A case reported by Louisa Rhine[8] has been corroborated in a way that meets ordinary standards of credibility, although (since in this case the husband was the only witness) it cannot meet scientific standards.

A woman awoke from a nightmare in which she saw her baby, lying in its crib in the next room, crushed by a huge ornamental chandelier which, in actual fact, was suspended from the ceiling above the crib. In this nightmare, the mother saw a clock that was actually in this room; its hands pointed at 3:45. So vivid was the dream that the young mother got out of bed, went into the next room, picked up the baby, and put it back to sleep in her own bed. Her husband awakened, and teased her about her superstitiousness. Later that night they were awakened by a crash from the adjoining room. The chandelier above the crib had indeed fallen, and the clock read 3:45.

Despite the spine-chilling impact of such anecdotes, which not only challenge our concept of time but raise basic metaphysical questions about the very nature of reality, the clinician must realize that dreams, hunches, and premonitions are completely unreliable. Even sensitive, intuitive people make mistakes in job choices and in personal decisions, contract disastrous marriages, get caught in fires and earthquakes and explosions. Moreover, most people frequently have unexplicable premonitions that carry a strong feeling of certainty—but that do not come true.

Moreover, the motivation is not necessarily positive. Purposefulness of quite a different kind may appear in poltergeist phenomena, which seem more bizarre to most of us than even precognition, but for which well-corroborated anecdotes exist.

The word *poltergeist* means "noisy spirit." It was formerly believed that certain houses were haunted by goblins or evil spirits that caused inexplicable fires, objects falling and breaking for no apparent reason, showers of stones falling from nowhere, and the mysterious movement of objects from one place to another without human agency. It is difficult to believe that such events are not imaginary or fraudulent, especially since careful investigation has shown that *some* happenings of this type are indeed a fraudulent attempt, usually by an adolescent, to attract attention and frighten the adults. However, reputable investigators have found striking common denominators in these occurrences.[15,16,17] Typically, at least one family member is in serious emotional conflict. Most often, it is a rebellious adolescent whose natural sexual strivings are frustrated by parental or social taboos, or by personal immaturity. Sometimes, also, a religious conflict is found in such households, which are often headed by parents of widely different religious orientation.*

Some parapsychologists who have studied the poltergeist phenomenon think that intense, repressed hostility is somehow converted into psychokinetic energy that actually affects the environment and makes life uncomfortable for the other family members. In contrast to the majority of people who may possess gifts for clairvoyance, telepathy, or precognition, originators of poltergeist phenomena usually are described as emotionally primitive, not above average in intelligence, and unable to express their feelings directly. If, indeed, repressed hostility is the source of the alleged poltergeist phenomena, its effects are thought to take place by means of the above mentioned psychokinesis, the influence of the mind on the physical environment.

A colleague describes a case that suggests poltergeist phenomena, although scientific weight cannot be provided for the hypothesis. He was consulted in a clinic by a relatively uneducated woman who was depressed by genuine family problems. She expressed the fear that she was "going to pieces," as indicated by a feeling that her environment was playing tricks on her; things were not where she remembered having put them, her hairbrush twisted in her hand "as if it did it by itself," and a perfume bottle that was apparently in a secure place on the bathroom shelf had fallen of its own accord. The clinic's medical director feared an incipient or ambulatory psychosis, and pre-

*Personal communication, Laura Knipe, secretary of the American Society for Psychical Research.

scribed tranquilizers that did indeed reduce the woman's anxiety, but her odd complaints continued.

My colleague had read of poltergeists. Although he was skeptical, he recognized in his patient's description of her thirteen-year-old niece, who was living with them, the type of adolescent usually involved in the reports of these occurrences. She was moody, sulky, isolated; she stayed alone in her room with the radio and comic books: she was resentful that family circumstances made it necessary for her to live temporarily with her aunt's family, and she obviously disliked her aunt. As for seeing a "shrink" herself, she totally rejected the idea.

My colleague decided—a decision that would have been clinically sound even without suspicion of poltergeist activity—to focus upon the antagonism between aunt and niece. With persuasiveness and tact, he managed to help the aunt perceive the niece as an unhappy, lonely girl, and to encourage her to find activities more normal for someone her age. No miracle took place, but the aunt and niece grew less antagonistic, the girl began to move toward friendships, and the patient ceased to complain about the peculiar behavior of objects in her home, behavior she had never seen as supernatural but as rather an indication of her own disturbed condition. My colleague, wisely, did not discuss with his patient the possibility of poltergeist activity; this would have frightened and bewildered her.

Poltergeist phenomena are not the only evidence for psychokinesis, nor is repressed hostility a necessary condition for its occurrence. Laboratory experiments, in which the motivation is presumably a combination of the subject's wish to demonstrate psychic power and a wish to please the experimenter, also suggest that mind can exert a direct influence over matter. Although it has been alleged that some of these experiments could be duplicated by a highly skilled magician, others have been conducted under carefully controlled conditions. An example is the evidence that certain people are able to perform such feats as raising the surface temperature of bakelite fragments, or influencing the fall of mechanically thrown dice.[18]

Motivation, then, is evidently a key factor in the occurrence of psi phenomena. Another factor, where two communicants are involved, as in telepathy, appears to be the relationship between the two people. The vast majority of spontaneous incidents of telepathy or precognition occur between people who are related by love, friendship, or family ties, and there are a great many convincing examples, as cited in the following chapters, of apparent telepathic communication between therapist and patient.

The hypothesis that a close personal relationship between two communicants is likely to facilitate telepathy or precognition, like other hypotheses drawn from anecdotal data, is supported by laboratory evidence. It has been found, for example, that five-year-olds pick up telepathic messages from their own mothers (who are of course separated physically from the child so there is no opportunity for the unconscious transmission of familiar subliminal sensory cues) more readily than from the mothers of other five-year-olds.[19] Twins appear to be particularly in tune with one another telepathically.[20] It has also been found that pairs who appear particularly congenial, as measured by Rorschach tests, do better in telepathic tests than pairs who appear uncongenial.[21]

Of special interest to the clinician, who may sometimes be uncertain as to whether a patient is reporting bonafide psychic experiences or whether he is suffering from delusions or wishful thinking, is the question of what personality traits are likely to be associated with experiences of telepathy, clairvoyance, or precognition. This question is related to basic considerations of the nature of psi. Here we find a number of widely different viewpoints, each of which is supported by outstanding students of human nature and to a greater or lesser degree, by empirical data.

One such viewpoint holds that information obtained through psychic channels simply represents an archaic, primitive way of relating to the environment that has gradually diminished among civilized people, and is now found principally among young children and (as anthropological evidence strongly demonstrates) among non-industrial societies usually regarded as "uncivilized," i.e., American Indians, Eskimos, and tribes dwelling in jungles or the desert wilderness in Africa and the South Pacific.

Freud, who in his later years came to accept extrasensory communication as either a certainty or a strong probability, held this point of view. He writes:

One is led to conjecture that this may be the original archaic method by which individuals understand one another and which has been pushed into the background in the course of phylogenetic development by the better method of communication by means of signs apprehended by the sense organs.[22]

An analogous position is taken by Ehrenwald, a psychiatrist who has made meticulous records of apparently telepathic communication between himself and his analysands.[23] He sees mother-child telepathy as a normal means of communication; a sensitive mother can not only interpret subtle cues as to when her baby needs attention, but can sometimes be aware of its *specific* needs by extrasensory channels. However, as the child's sensory organization and nervous system become mature, its ego boundaries grow clearer, the child identifies himself as a separate being, and the telepathic bond gradually dissolves.

Students of psychoanalytic theory will recognize in this formulation a clear analogy of Margaret Mahler's description of the process of separation and individuation in child development. If the growing child is not able to dissolve the early symbiotic bond with mother and experience himself as a separate individual, he will at best become a neurotically dependent adult and at worst a schizophrenic. A corollary of this position is that telepathic communication, perhaps, is more likely to occur in therapy when the patient (or, possibly the therapist) is in a stage of regression and dependency.

The implication, then, is that telepathic ability and other paranormal powers are essentially primitive traits, indicating either regression or immaturity. In support of this hypothesis, Ehrenwald adduces several well-documented studies, including the story of Ilga, a nine-year-old girl with a severe reading disability who was nevertheless able to read material that her mother, concealed behind a curtain, was simultaneously perusing; and a similar account of a blind boy who could read oculists' charts when in the presence of his mother.

Like Ehrenwald, other students of parapsychology see telepathy and other paranormal abilities as part of human genetic endowment, but do not necessarily share his opinion that their persistence into later life may imply pathology or immaturity.

Schwartz, a psychiatrist who for years noted instances of tele-pathic communication between himself and his wife and their two young children, believed that the clarity and frequency of the telepathic episodes was positively related to the maturation of the children. He writes:

> The overall increase in frequency of telepathic episodes seems to correlate with Lisa's growing awareness of her environment and her differentiation in interpersonal rela-tionships, as well as her parents' developing awareness and interest in such phenomena. . . . These increased telepathic events also reflect the increased complexity of her expand-ing vocabulary and the development of various mental mechanisms.[24, p.95]

We may perhaps conjecture that in the Schwartz family, where there seems to have existed a good deal of warmth and rapport, the telepathic abilities of the children were not only stimulated by closeness to their parents but were strengthened by the obvious fact that these abilities were not merely accepted but were also valued.

Other writers[25,26] also believe that psychic abilities occur naturally among children. Pearce, however, thinks that these abilities are stage-specific and diminish gradually from about the fourth year of life, especially if the parents tend to discourage their manifestations. Here, as so often in the whole area of para-normal phenomena, the evidence is contradictory. Eileen Gar-rett, Rosalind Heywood, and others whose psychic gifts were repeatedly demonstrated under carefully controlled conditions all report having had telepathic, clairvoyant, or precognitive ex-periences as children; these experiences were regarded by adults around them with disfavor, but, nevertheless, their psychic gifts survived and developed.

A very different hypothesis regarding psychic ability is that it represents a further step along the evolutionary ladder, and is generally associated with altruism, mysticism, and spiritual and religious values.[27,28]

From the East come many reports of yogis, swamis, and other advanced spiritual leaders who are believed by their followers, who today include many Westerners, to have achieved high spiritual* development and who have demonstrated various psychic abilities under controlled conditions, including voluntary control over such bodily functions as heartbeat and temperature. Such individuals may also possess striking telepathic and clairvoyant powers.

In the West, there are several examples of psychic healers, including mediums who enter the trance state and prescribe treatment, who identify strongly with mystical or religious tradition, and who have also given impressive evidence of extrasensory powers. Among them is the late Edgar Cayce, derogated by some who see his followers as cult devotees, but whose prescriptions for ill patients, offered while he was in a trance condition, were very often found efficacious by the physicians who sought his help in consultation.[29] Cayce, a practicing Christian, believed that his abilities came directly from God.

There may be a relationship between psychic gifts and spiritual development, but the data is contradictory. A Dutch psychic, Dykshoorn, writes that although he is deeply religious, he views his psychic powers (documented by laboratory evidence and even utilized by the Dutch police in solving crimes) as a natural gift that has nothing to do with his level of spiritual development.[30] He regards his paranormal talent as an ability that is essentially value free and may be used either destructively or helpfully, just as high intelligence may be used either destructively or in the service of humanity.

Another hypothesis as to psychic ability, which seems to fit well with our admittedly contradictory and incomplete data, is that it is to some degree possessed by all human beings, perhaps distributed in the familiar bell-shaped curve, but ordinarily blocked from awareness by our need to pay attention to the world's practical demands, and perhaps also blocked by the social

*Throughout this book, the word "spiritual" is used to denote high ethical development, devotion to humanitarian rather than materialistic values, and aspiration toward religious or mystical experiences. It is not used to refer to the existence of "spirits" as discarnate entities that may or may not be regarded as the immortal part of deceased human beings.

anxiety and disapproval with which paranormal phenomena are frequently received.

Laboratory studies, cross-cultural observations, and anecdotal evidence certainly give no consistent picture as to the kind of person likely to exhibit paranormal powers. They seem to occur among African bushmen, Eastern mystics, and highly educated Westerners. In our culture they may be associated with high intelligence or low intelligence; with excellent social adjustment or pathological symptomatology; with altruism and a high degree of spiritual development or an interest in financial profits.[31]

However, if psi-ability is to some extent present at all times in the unconscious minds of all human beings, we must ask ourselves this question: Under what circumstances and in what kind of people is this ability most likely to break through into consciousness? Here, as elsewhere, our speculations are partially supported by hard data from the laboratory.

We have already seen that motivation may be crucial in bringing about psychic phenomena; we have also seen that personal ties between the communicants may be a factor. The circumstances seem to contribute to the breakdown of the barrier that ordinarily stands between our consciousness and whatever deep level of the unconscious mind is psychically in touch with other individuals and (as mystics claim) perhaps with the entire universe. We may think here of Jung's concept of the "*collective* unconscious" as a deep stratum of the unconscious mind that lies below the *individual* unconscious, the personal repository of repressed memories and unacknowledged drives as explored by Freudian psychoanalysis.

If we now return to the individual who, either in a laboratory experiment or in a spontaneous experience, gives evidence of psychic ability, we find that he or she usually bears no resemblance to the stereotype of the withdrawn, dreamy, impractical mystic, and is equally removed from the wild-eyed flamboyant eccentric (for example, Noel Coward's character of Madam Arcati in his play *Blithe Spirit*). Psi ability is occasionally associated with eccentricity and social deviation, but anyone who reads the autobiographies of such noted psychics as Eileen Garrett[34] or Rosalind Heywood[11] or the writing of Lawrence LeShan, a highly accredited psychologist who trained himself to become a psychic healer,[35] can doubt that they are in the presence not only of exceptional intelligence but of exceptional sanity.

Data obtained through Rorschach tests and use of the Zener cards suggests that, in general, people who scored high on ESP tests were friendlier, more outgoing, and better adjusted than those who had low scores. Even more striking, in the study that indicated that people who believe in the possibility of extrasensory perception score significantly higher as a group than people who deny this possibility, was the finding that well-adjusted believers score higher than poorly adjusted believers, while well-adjusted skeptics score significantly *lower* than poorly-adjusted skeptics.[9] If we assume that well-adjusted people are, in general, better able to use their natural abilities, it seems logical that they can make better use of psi to influence their scoring in their preferred direction.

In a research project at the Newark College of Engineering, it was found that company presidents who made outstandingly high profits relied more on ESP (hunches, guesses, presentiments) than presidents who made lower profits. Among 67 company presidents who responded to a questionnaire, 48 not only believed in the existence of ESP but stated that they used it in making decisions.[31]

Here, too, our evidence is not consistent, nor does it apply to every individual. The Zener card tests were conducted with large groups of people, and there were individual exceptions to the mass statistical findings. As reported in subsequent chapters, people with severe personal problems may have paranormal experiences. The practicing therapist may see people who enter therapy in part because they are undergoing psychic experiences that alarm and overwhelm them; people who are socially withdrawn or confused and try to develop their psychic gifts as an escape; or people who have a mixture of delusional beliefs and extrasensory awareness.

It would seem, then, that certain qualities—say, high motivation and personal openness—may enable the individual to be receptive toward input from the external world obtained by extrasensory means (telepathy, clairvoyance, precognition) or may enable him to affect the external world by extrasensory means (psychokinesis, psychic healing). Perhaps there are other factors difficult to explore, such as electromagnetic fields, weather conditions, astrological conditions, and space-time-observer relationships that have to do with quantum mechanics and lie within the domain of physics.*

Even more challenging, if we accept the hypothesis that psi is a latent human ability that is always potentially present and that becomes active only under certain conditions, we must as scientists eventually accept the task of identifying conditions under which it does *not* occur. Laboratory research suggests that certain personality traits, such as rigidity in thinking and emotional defensiveness, are inimical to the operation of psi.[4] And, as every psychotherapist knows, these traits also constitute barriers against contact within the unconscious.

It may be, then, that we are always in unconscious extrasensory interaction with the environment. A remarkable experiment by Charles Tart, a research psychologist, supports this possibility.

Subject A, placed in a sensory isolation chamber, was hooked up with a polygraph machine that registered brain waves, heart rate, pulse rate, and other physiological measurements. Subject B was placed in a second isolation chamber. The first subject, A, was informed that B was to be given periodical electric shocks (unpleasant but not injurious) at random intervals, and was asked to discern telepathically when these shocks were administered.

Here is the result: Subject A had no conscious awareness whatsoever of the moments when the shocks were given. But his body knew. His polygraph readings showed strong, significant changes at the times of shock. The only implication possible is that, on an unconscious telepathic level, A knew when B was being shocked.[10] This finding lends very strong support to the hypothesis that telepathy, and perhaps other paranormal processes, may occur below the level of awareness, but can reach the conscious level under certain conditions.

*Readers interested in this area are referred to *Mind and Matter,* by Erwin Schrodinger, a physicist who developed some of the basic equations of quantum mechanics; *The Tao of Physics,* by Fritjof Capra; and *The Dancing Wu-Li Masters* by Gary Zukov.

These conditions, of which motivation is probably most important, seem also to include a *willingness* to receive the paranormal messages originating in the environment and unconsciously perceived. This would account for the well-known finding of parapsychologists that precognitive information is most frequently received in dreams, when we are in a passive and receptive state. It would explain why children and primitive people, whose logical defenses against breaks in the safe fabric of conventional sensory reality are less well-developed, are more likely to have paranormal experiences. It would explain why people who accept the possibility of extrasensory perception do better on the Zener cards than people who deny the possibility. It would account for the positive relationship between paranormal abilities, as shown on the Zener cards and in the Maimonides dream experiments, and an open, accepting attitude toward life.

It would further account for the remarkable capriciousness of psi phenomena in general, which is evident even from the limited data offered above. Psi messages may appear as an inexplicable urge to take a specific action which, on the surface, seems irrational, as with the woman who saved the life of her landlady's baby. They may break through in clear, specific images, as with the mother who rescued her child from being crushed by the chandelier. They may come as premonitions or hunches, both anecdotal and experimental. And, like most of the communications from the unconscious, including dreams, they frequently reach consciousness in altered form, disguised by symbolism and other defenses familiar to students of psychoanalytic theory.*

Even when the message itself seems relatively clear, psi operates capriciously. Apparently precognitive or telepathic hunches may be untrustworthy, regardless of a sense of subjective convic-

*The best source for readers who wish more information about the way in which paranormally perceived material may be altered as it enters consciousness is Devereaux,[1] *op. cit.* who, beginning with Freud, has collected accounts from various psychoanalysts. These psychoanalytic studies have the special advantage of offering enough information about the communicants, in these cases patients and their analysts, to provide some idea of the particular circumstances and individual personality characteristics that may have governed the paranormal experiences.

tion, and, moreover, their appearance at time of need fails more often than it occurs.* Eileen Garrett once participated in an experiment with psychometry, obtaining information about an absent and unknown person through touching some object the absent person had previously handled or possessed. Holding a number of small personal objects in succession, she was able, to the satisfaction of the scientists conducting the experiment, to offer correct information about their previous owners. On one object she failed completely. However, her description of the physical and psychological traits of the person whom she described turned out to tally almost precisely with a description of a laboratory assistant who had also handled the object.[35, pp. 30–32]

Yet one more contradiction found in our consideration of the nature of psi is that in most instances of spontaneous paranormal perception the experience occurs involuntarily; yet on the other hand, certain experienced psychics are able to enter *voluntarily* into an altered state of consciousness during which they have access to messages from their unconscious minds. Edgar Cayce, for example, "went to sleep;" Eileen Garrett was able to enter the trance state at will; and subjects in telepathic experiments usually do better when they place themselves in a relaxed, receptive state of mind rather than concentrate effortfully on the experimental stimulus.

From this overview of data and theories on paranormal phenomena, we may glean certain formulations of special importance to the practicing clinician that will be developed further in ensuing chapters.

1.  Paranormal communication appears to exist and may be of importance in the relationship between therapist and patient.
2.  Psychic experiences may occur in almost any type of personality and are not necessarily a sign either of pathology or of high spiritual development.

*LeShan has remarked dryly that the development of telepathy is useless; the telephone is infinitely more reliable. The *study* of telepathy is, however, extremely useful in extending our knowledge of human personality.

3. Motivation is of great importance in paranormal events; a paranormal experience usually denotes strong feeling, possibly repressed.
4. Psychic experiences, such as telepathy and precognition, are highly unreliable. They cannot be dismissed altogether, nor can they be relied upon as a guide to behavior. Here, as everywhere in effective and responsible psychotherapy, the therapist's attitude and his choice of interventions must be based on the psychodynamics of the individual patient.

*Chapter 2*

# IN THE CONSULTING ROOM

## PSI Probable and PSI Improbable

*It seems to me that one is displaying no great trust in science if one cannot rely upon it to accept and deal with any occult hypothesis which may turn out to be correct.*

—Freud

It is the beginning of a therapy session. The therapist,* a classically trained psychoanalyst, sits behind the couch. The patient, a young advertising executive, is describing a dull party he recently attended, offering an ironical description of the canapés

"Hot shrimps with curry sauce, those greasy little puffy pastries. . . ."

The analyst is not displeased that, even though it makes the therapeutic sessions somewhat dull, this patient uses most of his

*This incident, like many others reported in this book, comes from one of several colleagues who, for the protection of their patients, wish their names to be cited only in the general acknowledgement. Other incidents have been drawn from my own practice and from the literature.

analytic time in speaking of dissatisfaction with his work, his social engagements, and his life in general, which more and more seems meaningless to him. The analyst hopes that as his patient becomes more deeply aware of his dissatisfaction, he will gradually understand its roots, and will find ways to change his life-style. Nevertheless, the party bores the analyst as it had bored his patient, and part of his mind is vaguely aware of a tune that has been running through his head since the beginning of the session. "Da da da *da* da *da* da. . . ."

" . . . and there was just one interesting woman there. She was talking about music. Mozart is her favorite and I thought she must be intelligent. I took her number, I'll call her when I have time, maybe when I break off with Alice . . . "

Mozart. Now the analyst identified the tune that had been haunting him. It was from the opera *Don Giovanni,* the exquisite song in which the Don attempts to seduce Zerlina. *La ci darem la mano . . . Come, give me your hand.*

The analyst thought, "An odd coincidence." The patient continued to talk about various women he had met lately, and the analyst dismissed the coincidence and said, "The parties sound very much alike. So do the women, at least you talk about them as if they were all the same. . . ."

Some weeks later, the analyst attended an informal seminar on the technique of listening. The group discussed the suggestion of Reik,[1] that if the analyst can focus on his patient and at the same time allow his own thoughts to float into consciousness, these thoughts will usually provide a clue as to what the patient is not saying, perhaps even to what the patient does not yet consciously know about himself.

As an exercise, the analyst traced the relationship of Don Giovanni's song to the dynamics of his patient. Like Don Giovanni, the patient had sexual relationships with many women, but was satisfied with none.

But why did the seduction song from Don Giovanni begin to haunt the analyst *before* the patient mentioned Mozart? To the analyst's recollection, the composer had never been mentioned by this patient before, nor was the song mentioned during the session.

As a further exercise, the analyst required himself to free

associate, and recognized that the song had a personal significance, not only for the patient, but for himself. Although his marriage is usually pleasant and sometimes happy, this middle-aged professional man is beginning to feel slightly restless. He sometimes fantasizes that it would be wonderful to have an extra-marital romance.

But the analyst cannot see himself as a Don Giovanni. A sexual adventure would be unfair, he thinks, to his wife and to his fantasized sweetheart; he would derive from it no more genuine satisfaction than the Don derived from his endless list of conquest.

In effect, the analyst was saying, "I would rather like to be a Don Giovanni, but on the whole it's better not to be one." The patient was saying, "I am a Don Giovanni, but it does not satisfy me." The similarity of these deep-lying conflicts may well have created in the analyst a sensitivity that made paranormal communication possible.

Another hypothesis, of course, is also tenable. The patient may have been humming the tune from *Don Giovanni* in the waiting room, indirectly expressing his unconscious conflicts, and the analyst may have picked it up subliminally. Alternate explanations for apparent paranormal phenomena must always be considered. And even the most dedicated therapist may have thoughts and associations that have nothing to do with the patient but come entirely from his own personal preoccupations.

Such occurances as the *Don Giovanni* episode are common in psychotherapy, although they are usually dismissed as coincidental. It is not necessary to accept these episodes as final *proof* that paranormal communication may take place between therapist and patient. But, as Eisenbud suggests,[2] we may profitably accept the paranormal hypothesis *as a working hypothesis,* just as other theories have been accepted tentatively in the course of scientific exploration.

In practice, this does not imply that any thought occurring to the therapist is relevant to the therapeutic situation. Perhaps the therapist's mind may be wandering toward his own concerns. The therapist then has the task of deciding whether his thoughts and fantasies are genuinely related to the task at hand, or whether they are intrusions from his personal needs and tensions.

Perhaps the greatest value in the analyst's recognition of the possible paranormal element in this episode was that it emphasized the importance of a central conflict of which the patient himself was just becoming aware. By his own self-exploration, the analyst was also warned and armed against the dangerous possibility that his own life situation might color his work with this particular patient, and was able to avoid an unconscious identification which might have been detrimental to the therapeutic work. Furthermore, in the subsequent course of this analysis, it turned out that the patient was familiar with the opera, and the character of the Don became for both of them a meaningful and convenient representation of the patient's Donnish behavior.

Should the therapist have shared with the patient his probably-paranormal experience? He did not do so, and this decision seems correct. Trained in a school that holds personal revelations as usually inappropriate for a therapist, he would have been uncomfortable in sharing the personal element in the episode. And if he had shared the haunting melody as indicative of an intuitive or paranormal understanding of the patient, he could well have elicited the feeling, "My God, this guy knows my thoughts before I think them!" which might possibly have led to paranoid fears, toward which this particular patient had some predisposition.

As the evidence for paranormal phenomena continues to accumulate, practicing therapists will increasingly face the task of thinking through what attitude to take when these phenomena emerge in the course of therapy.* Some therapists, especially those who have been trained in one of the more conventional traditions, dismiss paranormal material as fantasy, coincidence, or evidence of delusion. At the other end of the spectrum, there

---

*I recently discussed this question with an experienced, highly respected psychoanalyst who categorically said, "I don't believe in this." I asked her what she would do if a patient brought in material in which the existence of telepathy or recognition seemed unquestionable, as in the case of Liana (presented later). She laughed and said "I wouldn't listen." Her joking remark perhaps does represent the position of some therapists, which to some of us seems the exact reverse of a genuinely scientific attitude.

seems today to be a tendency on the part of less rigorously trained therapists to become fascinated by the psi phenomenon and focus on it while neglecting other processes conducive to therapeutic progress.

A wide variety of apparent psi phenomena, ranging from those that present convincing evidence as to the operation of psi to those that could be accepted as such only by the most credulous, do appear in therapy. Patients present dreams and fantasies which subsequently come true; patients present experiences which they believe to be psychic but which seem to arise entirely from imagination or misinterpretation. Patients recount dreams about the therapist which indicate information that could not have been obtained through the usual sensory channels; patients recount dreams about the therapist which appear to be based on transference alone. Therapists dream about their patients, and sometimes these dreams are difficult to explain without invoking precognition or telepathy; more often, such dreams arise from therapeutic intuition or from countertransference. In deciding whether or not to discuss the possible emergence of psi, the therapist can be guided by the same consideration that motivates him in making other decisions: Will it be helpful to this particular patient, at this point in time?

Here are examples, beginning with a case in which I decided that the most effective therapeutic procedure was to discount altogether the possibility of psi, ranging in order of probability to a case in which the therapist was literally unable, in the face of the data, to retain her conviction of the nonexistence of the paranormal.

The story of "Carmen," a second-generation Puerto Rican woman,* clearly shows how an unacknowledged or dissociated part of the self may be projected into the fantasy of an evil spirit.

Carmen came into my office under unusual circumstances. She had telephoned the psychology department of the City College of New York after reading a newspaper article on laboratory research in extrasensory perception, and had asked for someone who could help her. She insisted that she did not wish to be

---

*According to custom, pseudonyms will be used for all patients mentioned; they will be signalled by the initial use of quotation marks.

referred to a clinic, succeeded in getting through to the psychology department, and was ultimately referred to me.

Even before she was able to state her problem, Carmen seemed to be an interesting woman. In her late twenties, she had gone beyond her very underprivileged background and had been able to establish herself professionally as a skilled beautician. After perhaps twenty minutes, she felt sufficiently at home to tell me why she wanted help.

"There is a spirit . . . the spirit of my husband . . . comes to me."

Carmen's diction was ordinarily flawless, but under this stress, she was halting. Her story emerged in sections. The spirit, she said, came to her and she was frightened. She often sensed his presence, sometimes she almost saw him, and she knew he wished to do her harm.

At first, naturally, I assumed that her husband was dead. Assumptions in psychotherapy are often unsafe, and it soon emerged that Carmen's husband had left her some months before and was now living in another city with another woman.

"Is there any special time when you're more likely to sense the presence of your husband?"

This was the right question. Carmen was living with a boy friend, and when they were in bed together the spirit of her husband seemed to hover near the ceiling, across the room. Sometimes she perceived him as a black cloud, but usually she only sensed his presence. Her boy friend had begun to feel it too, and he was also frightened.

The dynamics seemed clear enough. Carmen, like many more sophisticated people who choose social or political figures to represent their own projected guilt or anger, had constructed a demon. And she had come to a psychologist for help, although without recognizing that her problem was psychological, because other avenues of help were not acceptable to her. She was Catholic, but not especially devout, and feared that if she talked with a priest he would forbid her to continue living with her boy friend. A cousin had advised her to consult a spiritist or witch, but Carmen was proud of her educated, Americanized point of view, and rejected this suggestion. As she had not the slightest fear that she was unbalanced, she did not think of a psychiatrist. The newspaper article, which gave her the erroneous impression that the City College researchers were concerned scientifically with spirit appearances, offered this naive but intelligent woman a perfect solution.

Except for her anxiety about her husband's spirit, which was natural in view of her ethnic background, Carmen did not seem psychologically disturbed. She would almost certainly have refused referral to a clinic, nor did I think she needed long-term treatment.

What to do? I decided to appeal primarily to Carmen's intelligence and common sense, but at the same time to utilize psychological concepts that could be presented in a form that might also reach the primitive, superstitious ideas Carmen had unconsciously retained from her upbringing. In three sessions (Did I unconsciously choose *three* because it is considered a magic number?) I repeated several basic points over and over.

First, it was important that her husband was alive. (Although I do not believe that spirits of the dead come back to visit the living, many people do believe this and it may possibly be so.) I told Carmen that it is not usually possible for a living person to send out his spirit at will. Bulwarking myself with authority, I added that "most other doctors agree with me."

Next, I suggested to Carmen (somewhat illogically, in view of my first point) that when she and her boy friend sensed the presence of her husband, they should simply ask him to go away. I did not suggest any quasi-religious or magical rituals because this would have reinforced the superstitious side of Carmen's nature by putting me into the position of claiming occult powers. I suggested that they say to him politely, either aloud or in their heads, "Look, you're happy with your woman, and we're happy with each other. Please go away and leave us alone.*

Finally, in the most simple and direct words I could find, I

---

*The technique of getting rid of a ghost or demon by telling it to go away is in the best occult tradition; in traditional exorcism, the evil being is ordered to depart. A similar technique is sometimes used in modifications of psychodrama, where, for example, a patient may be asked to say to a visualized image of his father or mother, "Go away, don't bother me, I'm grown-up now!"

tried to explain to Carmen that even though most people would consider her fully justified in having a boy friend, I believed she felt guilty about it "in her secret heart." I explained that we sometimes have feelings we don't know about, and later used the word "unconscious," which she seemed to understand. She was unconsciously guilty, felt that she should be punished, and imagined that the spirit of her husband wanted to punish her.

The word "imagine" was successful. Carmen's face lit up. She said, "You mean I'm just imagining he's there?" At the beginning of our third session, Carmen reported that the dark cloud had appeared again, "but dimmer," had been asked to go away, and since then had never reappeared. There is no follow-up on Carmen, but she seemed relaxed after our final session, and her boyfriend—who always sat in the waiting room when she came to my office, although we had never spoken—offered me a smile with a big handshake.

My therapeutic approach, of course, lacked logical consistency. On the one hand, I persuaded Carmen that the spirit was imaginary; on the other hand. I told her to order it to go away. This latter procedure was an effort to get Carmen to mobilize her own energies against the "apparition," which I still consider as imaginary. Nonetheless, since in this field it is always fair to consider alternative hypotheses, it is not impossible that Carmen's estranged husband was thinking of her angrily and vengefully, and that she had picked up these feelings through telepathy. In that case, we might speculate that by ordering him to go away, she closed the telepathic channel.

Next is an example of a dream for which there is hardly a shred of evidence for precognition, but which I approached as if it might be precognitive on the basis of my own intuition and my knowledge of the patient, who was exceptionally intuitive and who without anxiety suspected that she might be psychic.

"Jeanette," an intelligent and vital woman in her early forties, tells me a nightmare. Having uttered the word "nightmare," she stops to laugh because it is indeed a dream about a mare. She is attempting to mount a white horse, but the horse goes wild and attacks her, trying to crush her against the stable wall.

She has been taking riding lessons, which she enjoys, although she is slightly nervous in the saddle. She recognizes the wild dream horse as Willow, a mare she describes as "sort of skittish," but which is considered safe. Since Jeanette finds the Gestalt empty-chair technique congenial, I ask her to speak alternately as herself and as the white horse. Here is the dialogue:

> Jeanette (as herself):    Why do you want to crush me?
> Jeanette (as Willow, in the empty chair):    I'm going to crush you—I'm going to push you right against the wall and hurt you.
> Jeanette (as herself):    But why do you want to do that?
> Jeanette (as Willow):    Because you're not supposed to have fun—you ought to be crushed because you're having too much fun.
> Jeanette (as herself):    You're a nag!

We both break into laughter, not only at the pun, but because the word "nag" fits in directly with the therapeutic work we have been doing. Jeanette is enjoying life more and more, but has difficulty in accepting her right to enjoyment without guilt because of the introjected influence of her depressed, nagging mother. We have been exploring her tendency to pay for her fun by periods of guilt and depression.

This tendency comes to light once more when Jeanette (she is a writer, and it is not surprising that puns arise from her unconscious in dreams) suddenly recognizes another implicit pun in the word "Willow," which suggests "will to be low," in the sense of choosing to be periodically low in spirits.

Jeanette is now requested to have a dialogue with her mother, using the empty chair again. It proceeds along lines familiar to anyone who knows the Gestalt dialogue technique, a technique that almost invariably moves toward health.

> Jeanette (as herself):    I've got a right to have a good time.
> Jeanette (as mother, nagging):    Oh, no you don't. I'm miserable and you're supposed to be miserable too.
> Jeanette (as herself):    I will so have a good time!

Jeanette (as mother):    You mustn't.
Jeanette (as herself, very firmly and loudly): I WILL!

According to the usual therapeutic standards, this episode has come to a gratifying conclusion. Jeanette's symbol of the "nag" to represent her mother is readily understood on the basis of what emerged in the Gestalt dialogue. There is no reason here to invoke a paranormal hypothesis. But in view of the fact that Jeanette and I have already done a great deal of work on her introjected nagging mother, the intense nightmare quality of the dream seems out of proportion.*

In line with my conviction that it is often helpful for the therapist to share his thinking with the patient, I tell Jeanette that, to me, the intensity of her dream panic still seems unaccounted for. Perhaps the dream carries a warning. Although she is unfamiliar with horses, Jeanette may have sensed in Willow a potential dangerousness that was not picked up even by the experienced stable manager. There is, finally, the possibility that the

---

*To account for the nightmare element in this dream, other hypotheses may legitimately be considered. We can conjecture that Jeanette's slight nervousness with horses covers a deep unconscious panic that broke through directly into the dream, but nothing about her character structure or her work in the session substantiates this. We can speculate that Jeanette unconsciously plans to bring about a self-punitive accident by provoking the horse, but again this notion does not fit in with the character of Jeanette, who does not tend to provoke self-punitive accidents.

In Freudian symbology, the horse is often seen as a symbol of male sexuality, but again there is no evidence that Jeanette fears the phallus. Any symbol may have an idiosyncratic meaning, depending on individual life experience. In classical psychoanalytic thinking the snake, for example, is seen as a masculine sex symbol. It may also connote temptation or wisdom (as in the Garden of Eden); it may be a symbol of infinity (the Worm Ouroboros, with its tail in its mouth); or refer to an awakening of psycho-physical energy (in Yoga, the Kundalini serpent power). It is usually unsafe to interpret the symbolic meaning of a dream without evidence from the dreamer, although it is useful to be familiar with psychoanalytic and mythological dream symbolism.

dream may have been a precognitive warning. Since Jeanette is interested in psychic phenomena and is not at all afraid of them, I do not hesitate to mention both these possibilities. I suggest to Jeanette that she should ask the stable manager not to assign Willow to her again, and Jeanette readily agrees.

It is my tentative impression that, when possibly-paranormal elements in a dream are dealt with therapeutically, the dream often has a special impact on the life of the dreamer. Jeanette decided to give up her riding lessons altogether. She recognized that she did not really enjoy them, and that she had been taking the lessons as part of her rebellion against her mother's taboos, a rebellion that was essentially healthy but which at times became compulsive and feverish. Since she was in general an active and adventurous person, whose life included joyous physical activities, this decision was basically self-fulfilling rather than self-denying. She decided to examine her priorities, and drop from her busy schedule any leisure activity she did not genuinely enjoy.

With another patient, "Barbara," I deliberately chose to ignore the paranormal aspect of her experiences, perhaps mistakenly. In her mid-sixties, with her children grown and with few interests other than the decorating and redecorating of her expensive home, Barbara's world was abruptly shattered. Her husband, living out a soap opera cliché, fell in love with a younger woman. Furious, confused, and terrified, Barbara sought therapeutic help.

She was a difficult patient. She did not seem to want personal growth or insight; she wanted ways to "win her husband back," something I was naturally unable to give her. Her husband was willing to maintain the semblance of a marriage, and to provide for her luxuriously, but he was never home. He responded to Barbara's demands for companionship by pleading necessary business trips, and Barbara was totally obsessed with trying to get evidence of where he actually went on weekends, suspecting—no doubt correctly—that he was away with her rival.

My therapeutic goal was to help Barbara develop interests and activities that would make her life more rewarding, even in the travesty of her marriage, and would give her some emotional nourishment in the event of a divorce. But I could not shake her preoccupation with her husband's infidelity. She would, for example, spend a typical therapeutic session telling me that although he had claimed he was going to a conference in Cincinnati, she *knew* he was in Florida with his sweetheart. She even guessed the hotel in Florida where he might be (an elegant hotel where they had once been guests) and confirmed her hunch by telephoning him there and finding out that he was indeed registered.

Barbara took these episodes, of which there were several, as evidence that she was psychic, but she seemed interested in this ability only insofar as it might enable her to keep track of her husband. The climactic incident occurred when, on a Saturday when he had told Barbara that he had office business, she suddenly had a strong conviction that he was buying gifts for his sweetheart at a French boutique near their suburban home. She jumped into her car, drove to the boutique—and sure enough, there he was, with two salesgirls modelling capes for him! He protested that the cape was to be a special gift for his sweetheart's overtime work (she was one of his assistants); Barbara made a scene in the boutique, and when she told me about it, the impressive paranormal quality of the incident was lost in her flood of indignation. Vainly I tried to persuade Barbara that she had been acting against her own best interests. She left the session still in the same fine, self-righteous rage, and shortly afterward left therapy, complaining to a mutual acquaintance that she had been depressed by the haphazard color scheme of my office.

Perhaps Barbara would have felt more rapport had I acknowledged the seemingly paranormal aspect of her experiences. With encouragement, she might even have developed an interest in parapsychological research (she was an intelligent woman) and found an interest other than her obsessive jealousy. Or, possibly, she might have become paranoid and taken every jealous thought as a supernatural message. It was this possibility that deterred me; in retrospect, I think I was mistaken.

The advisability of a therapist's willingness to entertain the possibility of ESP, if only as a hypothesis, is shown by a striking series of precognitive dreams, provided by Dr. S., an experienced analyst whose outlook and techniques are conservative, and who is by no means temperamentally disposed toward an interest in psychic phenomena.

The patient, "Liana," was painfully obsessed with a former lover, with whom she had lived for two years, and from whom she was now separated. But she could not separate emotionally, although she knew there could be nothing for her except grief and danger if they were reunited. He was a drug addict, and Liana had shared the addiction while they were together, although she had become drug free with the help of her therapist. Moreover, her ex-lover lived on the criminal fringe, and his life was a series of narrow escapes from the accidents into which his self-destructiveness constantly led him.

When she had been in treatment for several months, Liana brought in a terrifying dream about her lover. She saw him in a fire in which he had been seriously burned, except for his legs, which were protected by a pair of boots. Shortly afterward, Liana came in for another session in great agitation. She had heard from her ex-lover's family that he had actually been caught in a fire while asleep and had been badly burned, except for his legs, which had been protected by a pair of boots.

Shocked by the resemblance of this event to her dream, Liana was afraid that she had mysteriously caused the disaster. Dr. S. reassured her. We all have many dreams, said Dr. S., and it was only by coincidence that she had dreamed about the fire and the boots. Liana responded to this commonsense interpretation by withdrawing, and later told her therapist that she had been extremely angry, because she *knew* the dream was not just chance. However, she remained in therapy.

Sometime later she had another dream about her former lover. This time Liana dreamed that he had been shot, in his shoulder. Again, not long afterward, she reported that his family had informed her that he had been involved in a shoot-out in Chicago and had been wounded in the shoulder. Again, the dream's actualization made Liana fear that in some occult way she had been responsibile for the injury.

My colleague had integrity. At this point she realized that something was happening about which she needed more knowledge. She re-read Freud's thoughts on the occult,[4] discussed the situation with an older colleague, and told Liana honestly that she was now better informed about the possible occurrence of precognitive dreams. In a reassuringly matter-of-fact way, she explained that apparently some people do possess precognitive ability, which in Liana's case had no doubt been stimulated by her continued obsession with her former lover, but that there was no way at all in which Liana could have been responsibile for his misfortune, which he had clearly brought upon himself.

This time Liana was able to accept the reassurance of her therapist because the paranormal element in her dreams was taken seriously, and could thus be considered separately from her superstitious fear of responsibility for the disasters. The therapeutic relationship grew stronger—which was fortunate, because there was now a third dream in the series.

This time Liana dreamed that her ex-lover was in an automobile accident; he escaped alive, but a child was injured. As before, the accident occurred later, but this time Liana was able to accept her precognitive ability as something that was natural, although strange, and felt no guilt about the episode. Meanwhile, therapy had been progressing. Liana was gradually recovering from her obsession and finding other interests, and there were no more precognitive dreams. After two years, she terminated therapy.

Discussion of Liana's case must be speculative, but it seems to me that the therapeutic task was not to focus on the striking paranormal element in the dreams, but rather to relieve Liana of her fear that she possessed a mysterious, terrifying power to make them come true. In psychoanalytic terms, Liana had been frightened that her unconscious death wish toward her unloving former lover was now taking effect. The paranormal dreams must have evoked primitive, infantile fantasies of being able to destroy by thought alone. If her hostility could kill another person through her dreams, she must indeed be dangerous. Understandably, she could not believe that the impressive resemblance between her dreams and subsequent events was pure coincidence, but she could accept the explanation that she might occasionally demonstrate a precognitive ability that was unusual but not magical.

In considering why these dreams occurred, we must be even more speculative. They were not telepathic, but precognitive; the dreams preceded the catastrophes. If Liana had dreamed of the accidents at the actual time of their occurrence, we could assume that her ex-lover had been somehow reaching out to her for help or sympathy, and that she had received his message in her dreams. For most of us, this hypothesis would be easier to entertain than precognition, which raises disturbing questions as to the very nature of time.*

Of course, we can conjecture that Liana's senstivity to her ex-lover's future catastrophes was based in part on her obsessional longing for him and in part on the hostility evoked by her unhappiness about him. But Liana's story throws no real light on how and when precognition may occur. Many women, and many men, dream about ex-lovers, and there is no evidence of precognition. In my opinion, the only solid conclusion which can be drawn from this episode, as well as from similar episodes which are usually less impressive, is that the therapist does well not to reject the psi hypothesis.

Management of paranormal material that emerges during therapy must be determined by the same general guidelines the therapist follows in making other decisions. If discussion of the psi hypothesis would simply be an interesting topic, there is no reason for the therapist to bring it up. If the patient has paranoid tendencies, the therapist must be especially careful not to support a fear that others can read his thoughts, or that his suspicions—for instance, that someone is trying to poison him—may be supernatural messages. Often, however, as in the cases discussed in this chapter, material that strongly suggests the paranormal is related to feelings and conflicts of central importance, and in these instances the data that emerges from psi experiences can often be used constructively as part of the ongoing therapeutic process.

*Discussed at somewhat more length in Chapter I and in the Introduction.

*Chapter 3*

# AS IF THE PATIENT KNEW

"Jane," seeing an analyst for the first time, is naturally anxious. In a low voice, she explains why she wants therapeutic help. She is very shy and lonely, feels awkward in groups, and has difficulty in making friends.

Dr. Z., an experienced psychoanalyst, listens and nods encouragingly. She is conscientious and dedicated, and she has met many young women like Jane. It is, for the analyst, a routine first interview.

They discuss hours and fees, and set a time for the next meeting. As Jane leaves, the analyst casually notices that both of them are dressed in blue.

The first few appointments are uneventful. Jane continues to talk about her loneliness and shyness, begins to describe her childhood, offers no unusual material. There is only one noteworthy feature: On the day of their second appointment, both analyst and patient wear brown; on the third appointment, both again wear blue; on the fourth appointment, both wear red. The analyst notices these coincidences and thinks of mentioning them but says nothing. Nor does Jane say anything.

There are no more meetings. Jane leaves a message with Dr. Z.'s answering service, saying that she has decided not to continue therapy. Dr. Z. replies with a brief, friendly note expressing regret that Jane has terminated without discussing her reasons, and conveying her willingness to see Jane again. Jane never replies.

This story was told in an informal conversation with colleagues about the possibility of extrasensory communication between therapist and patient. The analyst who saw Jane firmly disbelieves in any such possibility, but tells the story as an odd experience that happened several years ago and still puzzles her. She is particularly puzzled, she admits, as to why she never mentioned to Jane the strange coincidence in their choice of identical colors for their four successive appointments.

If we do not invoke the psi hypothesis, we must assume that pure chance was responsible for these choices. This assumption is not difficult for their first appointment, but becomes increasingly difficult for each succeeding time. Coincidence does not seem impossible, but it does seem unlikely.

If, however, we apply the psi hypothesis, we can readily understand not only the "coincidences," but Jane's abrupt departure from treatment and Dr. Z.'s inappropriate silence regarding the identical choice of colors. It is relevant to understand the personality of Dr. Z. She is exceptionally self-sufficient. By choice, she has never married. She has friends and enjoys companionship, but spends much leisure time alone, and her friends have learned that she regards personal questions as an intrusion.

Jane, on the other hand, according to her self-description longs for companionship and contact. She does not understand why she lacks satisfying friendships. For this purpose she seeks treatment.

As every practicing clinician knows, the rational expectations with which most people seek psychotherapy are accompanied by a host of fantasies, often irrational. Consciously, most patients want help with work, marriage, anxiety, depression, and so on; unconsciously, they may seek magic. Perhaps on an unconscious level, Jane not only hoped that therapy would help her learn how to make friends, but that friendship and intimacy might perhaps be forthcoming from the analyst herself.

If we invoke the psi hypothesis, it was as if Jane had said, "I want to be like you, strong and successful, and then I won't be lonely any more," or possibly, "See, I am a very interesting person, I can even read your mind, please take a special interest in me!"

This latter possibility, involving the use of paranormally obtained information to win the therapist's particular interest and attention, has been described in the literature as far back as Freud.[1] A patient who knew of Freud's interest in the Galsworthy novels about the Forsyte family, picked up apparently by telepathy certain incidents in the analyst's life that led him to fear that their relationship was drawing to an end, and expressed through his dreams and associations the wistful plea "Come back to me, I am a Forsyte too." Similar incidents, in which the patient utilizes knowledge about the analyst that seems to have been obtained by extrasensory means in order to elicit a greater personal interest, are described by contemporary writers.[2,3] Indeed, a psychoanalyst who is especially interested in paranormal communication has reported that at a time when he was discussing the telepathic dreams of his patients at regular meetings of the Medical Section of the American Society for Psychical Research, his patients were particularly likely to offer him telepathic dreams. When these meetings ceased, the incidence of telepathic dreams decreased.[4] We may, of course, accept the possibility that the telepathic dreamers were motivated by an unconscious wish to please; however, it seems fair to conjecture as an alternative possibility that the analyst was more sensitive to possible telepathic dream elements when he was under an obligation to discuss this topic.

If we wish to accept the psi hypothesis as a basis for the similar color choices between Dr. Z. and her patient, it is entirely in keeping with what we know about apparent telepathic communication between therapist and patient that the first "coincidence" occurred in the first session. Several instances have been reported regarding seemingly paranormal communication before the first meeting, or even at a time when the choice of the therapist was still under consideration.[5, pp.173–175] This is exactly in line with the well-known fact that before a patient meets his therapist there is already a preliminary transference. If we accept the psi hypothesis, it is easy to see how the readiness to form a therapeutic relationship can set up conditions under which paranormal communication is possible, even before the initial interview. Indeed, one psychiatrist writes, "If . . . some telepathic events do not occur in the early stages of treatment, he (the writer) doubts the strength of the transference and the patient's unconscious motivation for help.[11, p.132]

Paranormal communication between therapist and patient, as in other situations, is frequently and perhaps typically based on feelings that are not clearly conscious, or are at least not verbalized. It would be not only absurd, but inconsistent with what we know about the operation of psi, to conjecture that Jane, getting dressed for the day, said to herself, "I have a hunch that Dr. Z. is going to wear brown today—I'll wear brown too." If Jane's longing for a special relationship with her therapist was strong enough to open channels for extrasensory communication, the whole process was presumably unconscious.

The analyst's failure to mention the color coincidence is also easier to understand if we invoke the psi hypothesis. Despite her strong personal need for autonomy and privacy, Dr. Z. was a sympathetic person, nor did she give allegiance to the doctrine that an analyst should always be strictly impersonal. Ordinarily, she would have acknowledged such a striking coincidence, especially with a shy new patient who needed personal contact. Nor would this acknowledgment necessarily have involved discussion of possible extrasensory communication. Dr. Z. might easily have said, "Well, I see we're wearing the same colors again today," and Jane would have felt a closer feminine kinship; perhaps, also, on a deeper unconscious level, she might have felt that her message was acknowledged.

Under these circumstances, it was clearly a technical error to ignore the coincidences—and, we remember, several years later Dr. Z. is still puzzled by her technical error. We cannot hypothesize that such an experienced therapist would have been so repelled by Jane's dependent needs as to be led into this error. But if we use the psi hypothesis, we can perhaps understand Dr. Z.'s behavior.

In her classical study,* Schmeidler found that individuals

*Discussed in Chapter I, *The Nature of Psi.*

who strongly reject the possibility of extrasensory perception ("goats") fall significantly *below* chance on a card-guessing experiment designed to test psi ability.[7] The inference, clearly, is that on an unconscious level, the goats had paranormal awareness of many of the correct cards, but (still unconsciously) chose the *wrong* cards to produce evidence in favor of their skepticism. Moreover, if the goats were further divided on the basis of psychological tests into well-adjusted and less well-adjusted individuals, the well-adjusted goats scored, with statistical significance, even lower.

As a well-adjusted goat able to recognize the occurrence of psi but unwilling to do so, Dr. Z. may well have known that at some level she and her patient were in paranormal communication about their color choices. Since her personal need for privacy was so intense, and her disbelief in the possibility of paranormal occurrences so strong, she had no recourse except to ignore the whole occurrence. She presumably experienced Jane's telepathic or precognitive awareness of her color choices not only as an indication of a paranormal occurrence, but as an invasion of her personal life, and therefore denied the whole thing by her silence.

This incident, in which the psi hypothesis not only can explain the initial series of coincidences but can also account for the subsequent behavior of both therapist and patient, provides a striking example of how this hypothesis sometimes seems the most logical way of looking at events. In this incident, as with others that follow, the only alternative to applying the psi hypothesis is to accept a belief in meaningless coincidence, events without a cause, a universe of accidents.

With Jane and Dr. Z., the motivation seems clear: Jane's wish was for intimacy and attention, Dr. Z.'s wish was for autonomy and for the preservation of her non-paranormal view of reality. Presumably, it was Jane's motivation that established a channel for psi communication. Nevertheless, analyst and patient had strong emotional needs in the same area; Jane's unfulfilled dependent needs, in a sense, parallelled her analyst's strong need for independence. Pederson-Krag;[8] Fodor,[5] Eisenbud,[3] and others have suggested that telepathic communication between analyst and patient "is a function not only of the repression of emotionally charged material by the patient, but of the repression of similar or related emotionally charged material by the analyst, as well."[5, p.185]

My own observations from my practice and from conversations with colleagues also suggest that when the patient obtains information about the analyst that presumably could not have been obtained through the usual sensory channels, there may be emotional tension in the therapist as well as in the patient. It is my impression, however, that the feelings on either side are not necessarily *repressed,* although frequently the patient's seemingly paranormal information about the therapist has to do with material that either therapist or patient is unwilling to discuss.

Eisenbud[3, pp. 241–242] tells of an analytic patient, a physician, who got onto the couch as if he were disabled, swinging his right leg up with both his hands. The patient had no idea why he did this, but remembered that as a boy, when he had suffered a fracture, he had to manage his leg in this same way. However, the broken leg, long since healed, had been the *left* leg, and it was the *right* leg which he now treated as if it were disabled.

This action, Eisenbud was convinced, was an unconscious message for the analyst. On the preceeding day, Eisenbud's son had broken his *right* leg, and had been given the attention of his father all night long. It is difficult to quarrel with Eisenbud's interpretation, which was that the patient was conveying the plea, "Stop thinking about your son and pay attention to me! I, too, broke my leg." Here, as in Freud's famous Forsyte story and the story of Jane, was the clear message "Care about *me!*" It is probably not unfair to Eisenbud to assume that, after his difficult night with his injured son, he had said to himself, "I hope that I'll be up to doing good work today with my patients," a feeling that may have contributed to the opening of the telepathic channel.

In these episodes, information about the therapist's personal life possibly obtained through extrasensory perception emerged as *behavior* for which there was no conscious motivation. More frequently, such information emerges in dreams. Since dreaming is an altered state of consciousness in which the usual barriers to stimuli arising from the unconscious are in part suspended, it is understandable that sleep in itself may create a condition favorable to paranormal experiences. Such dreams, as Freud first pointed out,[1] are subject to the same distortions as other dream material such as symbolism, condensation, reversal, denial, and other complex processes familiar to students of psychodynamics. In particular, they are shaped by the patient's feelings toward the therapist, both realistic and transferential, which may either be unconscious or which have not been adequately dealt with in the course of therapy. And in my own practice, when paranormal communication seems to appear, I have usually found some anxiety within myself, or some failure to deal with an important aspect of the therapeutic relationship.

"Susan" had been working with me for several months. She spoke rather freely of her feelings and experiences, but had difficulty in looking at me and rarely called me by name. When I called her attention to this difficulty, she withdrew, and I deemed it wise not to press her, as therapy in general seemed to be going well.

Because of scheduling difficulties, we had been discussing the possibility that she might see me in my suburban home rather than in my New York office. Soon after this discussion, she dreamed that she was in my living room, and described it with some strikingly accurate details, including the well-worn Oriental rugs and a rather awkward placement of the piano, although there were other details which in no way resembled my actual living room.

Because I am increasingly convinced that, in most cases, the therapist should not discuss the possibility of paranormal communication until other elements of the dream have been dealt with, I first questioned her about these unfamiliar details—a bust of Beethoven and a framed wall tapestry. They were, she told me, almost exact representations of ornaments that she had almost forgotten, but that she now remembered from the living room of her parents when she was a little girl.

Next, still restraining my surprise at the apparently telepathic elements of the dream, I asked the routine question, "How would you feel about really seeing me in my house?"

With slight embarrassment, she answered, "I would like it—I liked the house in my dream, although it wasn't—well, it wasn't elegant." Looking around my office openly for the first time, she added, "I like your office too, although it isn't tidy."

Gradually it now came out that in the transference she had

developed an irrational admiration for me, understandable in view of my age, which was close to her mother's, and in view of the fact that her mother had been a depressed woman who had developed few tastes and interests of her own. Susan did not wish to resemble her mother, had idealized me, and naturally wished for personal closeness. Her distant behavior had been a defense against this wish, which had been gratified in part by the telepathic dream. By fusing the living room of her childhood with my living room, she had expressed the wish "If only you had been my mother!" At the same time, I suspect, she had resented the professional reality of our relationship, and in an innocent revenge had dreamed about the "not elegant" aspects of my home.

Susan had no way of knowing what my living room was like; we had no mutual acquaintances and she did not recall ever having conversed with any other patient who might have seen me at home. Since the dream spoke for itself, its analysis could have proceeded in much the same way even if I had not regarded it as an instance of psi communication. However, after we had discussed the dream along the lines described above, I did say to Susan rather lightly, "I think we must be in tune—you really dreamed about my living room pretty much as it is." I did this partly to acknowledge our rapport, and partly because I did not wish her to be frightened or astonished when she actually saw the room. As with most non-psychotic patients who are capable of extrasensory perception, she seemed amused and pleased, but not especially surprised. Also, as is generally the case with a dream that suggests paranormal elements, this dream work proved especially worthwhile, helping to bring about a warmer and more spontaneous relationship.

The dream of another young woman, "Laurine," in which the telepathic element was even more striking, had a less gratifying outcome. At that time I was just beginning my practice. This was my first experience with a telepathic dream, and I made the mistake of focusing on the paranormal element instead of treating the dream primarily as therapeutic data.

Laurine had been seeing me under clinic auspices for only five or six weeks when she reported a dream in which she had seen me wearing a silver filigree necklace. Just recently a friend had given me such a necklace, which I had never worn. Startled and delighted, I told Laurine about my necklace, probably in the naïve belief that she would regard the dream as an indication of a meaningful rapport between us.

My mistake was twofold. First, some people who do not trust their own powers of reality testing are frightened by the notion of telepathic communication and should not be introduced to this possibility without careful consideration. Second, I did not then realize that a telepathic dream is most likely to occur when there are special difficulties in verbal communication that should take priority in a discussion of the dream.

With Laurine, my excited exclamation about her telepathic dreams did not seem to arouse anxiety, but she did react with a rather bored and dissatisfied air. In what seemed to be a change of subject, she began to speak of her unhappiness that she could not afford pretty clothes, hence did not have as many dates as she would like. Soon afterward, she terminated treatment in a letter that expressed great dissatisfaction with her therapy, and also stated that because of the great distance between us, socially and financially, I could not be really interested in her and would not be able to help her.

Only then, reviewing what had gone wrong, did I realize that Laurine had resented my title of "Doctor" at the clinic, my carefully chosen professional clothing, and her general feeling of inferiority at being seen in a clinic rather than privately. Her telepathic dream, it would appear, said something like, "And now she's got a new silver necklace, too!"

As expressed in the dream, it seems to me that her wish was not for closeness, but for further justification for her resentment. Telepathic dreams, like other dreams, are sparked in part by the wishes of the dreamer. Even in the impressive number of spontaneous telepathic dreams or apparitions in which someone is informed of the death of a beloved person, there is a wish. This wish is not necessarily that the beloved should die, but that the dreamer should *know* about it, and thus not be totally cut off from the beloved at the moment of death.

My naiveté about Laurine's dream was in ignoring the wish, or rather in assuming that the wish was for paranormal closeness. If I had followed the basic therapeutic rule of asking for further information and had simply inquired, "How did you feel about seeing me with a silver necklace?" Laurine might have begun to express her resentment directly, and our therapeutic relationship might have been salvaged.

Laurine's dream, incidentally, once more demonstrates a basic point about psi: It is unreliable. Not only was the silver necklace of little intrinsic value, but at that time my family and I had been under considerable realistic anxiety about money.

The dreams thus far described are relatively simple. Far more frequently, a dream that suggests the possibility of telepathic communication between patient and therapist presents a mixture of disguises and distortions. If there are paranormal elements, they are usually disguised, and sometimes come to light only after the dream has been dealt with therapeutically.

"Paula," a sensitive and talented woman in her forties, had been in psychoanalysis with me for about three years as part of her own psychoanalytic training. She was beginning to see patients under supervision and had impressed me with her extreme intuitiveness about what her patients were thinking and feeling. Indeed, I had warned her that her very intuitiveness might become a problem if she did not give sufficient attention to the overt statements and behavior of her patients; she might create anxiety by leaping too quickly from conscious to unconscious material.

Our work together had been gratifying to us both, and I expected Paula to be moving soon toward termination, although we had not yet discussed a date. Then one day she reported a dream in which she saw me standing on the platform of an old-fashioned train, waving good-bye as the train receded. At once I felt a chill, and thought, "She is foreseeing my death."

I immediately recalled that within the next few days I had an appointment with my physician to explore a condition he feared might be serious, and recognized that I had considerably more anxiety about this threat to my health than I had permitted myself to admit. Since it seemed unwise to discuss the possibility that Paula had sensed my personal anxiety, I handled the dream in the conventional analytic manner, asking for associations. It did not surprise me when she said, with hesitation, that the image of someone waving good-bye from a departing train reminded her of death. There the association stopped, and she turned to other matters that seemed more urgent; I went along with her in dealing with the other material, accepting her resistance to the thought of death and knowing that since this theme was important it would emerge again.

Two weeks later, my physician reported that a new set of laboratory tests had been clearly negative. Perhaps it was not a coincidence that during her very next session Paula told me that she planned to terminate treatment at the beginning of summer vacation. Her dream, in which she saw me as leaving her instead of seeing herself as leaving me, was a clear example of reversal. She was unconsciously seeking to place the responsibility of termination with me rather than accepting it herself. When I offered this interpretation she accepted it with amusement and relief.

The dream now led into analytic work which was valuable in dissolving the transference and in enabling Paula to terminate comfortably. During her late teens, Paula's father had been in frail health. He was devoted to Paula, an only child, and she had feared that her departure to attend an out-of-state college might worsen his condition and perhaps even cause his death. The father, probably without conscious purpose, had encouraged his daughter's anxiety in the hope that she would choose to live at home while attending a local college.

We had of course dealt with these memories and their significance in the course of Paula's analysis. But neither of us was consciously aware of Paula's fear that if she left me by terminating treatment it would cause my death. It was a completely unconscious, transferential fear.*

It is my impression that in all three of these dreams, the channels for extrasensory communication were opened not only by the difficulties of the three women in relating to me, but by difficulties of my own. Paula had probably picked up my personal anxiety about my health, although I had never discussed this with her and showed no sign of illness. With Laurine, my contribution to the telepathic dream was even clearer. I really did not like her materialistic sense of values, but my youthful ideal of what a

---

*It is well known that in certain phases of treatment a female therapist may evoke a father transference, and vice versa.

psychotherapist should be prevented me from acknowledging within myself any negative feelings toward my patient.

With Susan, who saw me as the perfect mother, there was a strong countertransferential element. At that time I was greatly concerned about one of my children and was dissatisfied with my handling of the family situation. I believe that I unconsciously sensed Susan's idealization of me, but failed to become consciously aware of it because I felt that I did not deserve it. Otherwise, I would almost certainly have recognized and discussed the idealization and she would not have needed to produce a telepathic dream.

Risky as it is to generalize about conditions under which psi phenomena may occur, it does seem that personal knowledge about the therapist is most likely to be obtained by seemingly paranormal means when some unverbalized wish, need, or anxiety of the patient is present. Corresponding wishes or anxieties on the part of the therapist appear sometimes to be present, as indicated by several of the above cited episodes, but in other episodes appear to be absent or at least unidentifiable.

A charming story in which motivation on the part of both therapist and patient appeared to be simply the wish for a warm, helpful relationship has been told me by Dr. Betty Phillips,* a therapist who has a special interest in working with underprivileged children. One of her patients was a ten-year-old Black, "Lorraine," referred by her school for withdrawal and depression, which were easily understandable in view of her seriously deprived background. Dr. Phillips was able to develop a friendly relationship with the child, a relationship that had to be based primarily on nonverbal communication such as Lorraine's use of a blackboard and chalk.

One day Dr. Phillips, who was usually interested in anything Lorraine did, found herself bored. The child was drawing sports pictures—a man kicking a football, a basketball and basket—that seemed to be leading nowhere. Partly from her own boredom and partly to help Lorraine develop verbal skills, the therapist suggested, "You can sometimes tell me such nice stories. How about a story today instead of drawing?"

*The therapist has given permission for use of her name; the patient's name is, of course, fictitious.

Lorraine seemed pleased, and told her story with slight hesitation. "Once upon a time there was a nice lady named Betty. She lived near a volcano. One day the volcano exploded.* It was very dangerous but Betty didn't get hurt. She escaped safely and she got married and had two nice children. They were named Mark and Janet and they all lived happily ever after."

Now this story was beyond coincidence. As a young girl, Dr. Phillips had lived in Hawaii and had actually experienced the eruption of a nearby volcano from which she had safely escaped. And, indeed, she did later get married. One of her daughters was named Janet, and another one grew up to marry a man named Mark. There was no possible way for Lorraine to know any of this. Dr. Phillips had never thought it appropriate to discuss her personal life, nor did Lorraine know anyone who could have known the names of her therapist's family.

No hypothesis seems available to explain this episode except that in a wish to be closer to her therapist, Lorraine had picked up the data, and as is typical of psi occurrences, not quite accurately, from Dr. Phillips's memories. Lorraine's motivation was thus clear: She chose the story telling, on an unconscious basis, because she was unable to say outright to her therapist, "I like you and I'd like to be closer." Dr. Phillips's motivation appears to be the simple, straightforward wish for good rapport with her little patient rather than the "repression of emotionally charged material."

It is of special technical interest that Dr. Phillips chose to say only "That's one of the nicest stories I ever heard! Thank you so much for telling it to me." Perhaps a less experienced therapist might have responded with something like, "How interesting! I did have an experience with a volcano once, and I do have a daughter and a son-in-law named Janet and Mark."

Such a response, as Dr. Phillips recognized, might easily have led the little girl to confuse fantasy with reality and perhaps have even made her afraid of her own extrasensory gifts or have caused her to place unrealistic reliance upon them. As to the circumstances under which this communication occurred, it is

---

*This episode occurred before the eruption of Mount St. Helens in 1980, an event which naturally would have increased the statistical probability of Lorraine's thinking of a volcanic explosion.

perhaps not too far-fetched to speculate that Dr. Phillips's boredom while Lorraine was drawing sports pictures may have represented an unconscious recognition that Lorraine actually had something else she wished to communicate, and gave the child a chance to do so by suggesting a story.

In sharp contrast to this almost idyllic episode, there are episodes in which a patient seems to obtain data by paranormal means in order to discredit the therapist and to express ambivalence. This happened, apparently, with the patient who dreamed about my silver necklace. An even more striking example that has become well-known in the annals of parapsychology, is the incident that Montague Ullman ironically calls the "Chromium Soap Dish Caper."[4, pp.50-51]

Ullman, a psychoanalyst interested in parapsychology, was having difficulties with the construction of a suburban home, which was costing more than he had expected. A chromium soap dish had accidentally been shipped to him, and Ullman, in a mood he describes as "belligerent dishonesty," did not return the dish. One of the workmen noticed the dish lying unused and made a teasing remark, to which Ullman responded with a "sheepish smirk." This episode had come to Ullman's mind during a conversation with a neighbor on the same day that one of Ullman's patients had the following dream:

> . . . Someone gave me, or I took, a chromium soap dish. I held
> it in my hand and I offered it to him. He took it. . . . Then I
> sort of smirked and said knowingly, well, you're building a
> house. He blushed. He smirked . . . .

This dream, as evidence for the psi hypothesis, is certainly impressive. It is also of great interest clinically. Ullman describes his patient as a profoundly distrustful person who naturally included therapist and therapy in his mistrustfulness. The message of the dream seems to be, "Good, I've got something on you! Now I know that I'm right not to trust you." At the same time, Ullman sees the dream not only as an expression of mistrust, but also as the patient's effort to maintain some relatedness while passing through a period of profound withdrawal bordering on schizophrenia.

This particular dream also raises a question of general interest to students of parapsychology that perhaps has something to do with the bitterness and intensity of the skepticism sometimes elicited by the psi hypothesis: If telepathy can indeed occur, can someone "read our thoughts" against our wills? There is no final answer to this question, but LeShan, who has examined the literature thoroughly, states that he has found "not one case of telepathic information being 'transmitted' that the original holder of this information really wished to keep secret."[9, p.190] Ullman was obviously embarrassed only slightly over his peccadillo about the chromium soap dish, although it would have been easy to conceal the episode; his interest in parapsychological phenomena is evidently greater than his need to maintain a snow-white record in relation to chromium soap dishes.

If we now reexamine all the above episodes in which a patient reveals knowledge about the therapist that seems to have been paranormally obtained, it seems fairly clear that in each instance there is an implicit message:

> Dr. Z.'s patient, Jane, seems to have conveyed, "I want to be like you—see, I'm already like you, we wear the same colors, take a special interest in me!"
> Eisenbud's patient: "I broke my leg, too, just like your son. Take care of *me*."
> Susan: "I wish that you had been my mother."
> Laurine: "You bitch—you've got everything, now a new necklace. You can't be interested in *me*."
> Paula: "I'm afraid you'll die if I terminate and leave you."
> Lorraine: "I like you and I want to be close to you."
> Ullman's patient: "I'm right not to trust you—but I'd still like you to know that I'm interested in our relationship."

This perspective on apparently-paranormal episodes between therapist and patient suggests several principles appropriate for their therapeutic management.

First, the therapist should not be seduced or distracted into emphasizing possibly-paranormal elements in a therapeutic situation at the expense of adequate attention to other possibly more important aspects of the situation. There is sometimes no need to discuss the information that seems to have been obtained through paranormal processes, but rather a need to accept it on an emotional level, as Dr. Phillips did with Lorraine. With some patients, it would be difficult to help them integrate the psi hypothesis into their current picture of reality, and there is no need to place such a strain upon a patient unless he is having troublesome psychic experiences.

Next, the therapist should consider the strong possibility that data about himself that seems to have been paranormally obtained may be of special importance to the therapeutic situation (as it was with Susan and Paula) and should not be ignored (as Dr. Z. did with her patient Jane).

And finally, since there is considerable evidence that paranormal communication may be a two-way process, and hence may involve the needs of the therapist as well as of the patient, any indication of its occurrence should impel the therapist to take a closer look at his own feelings. Here, again, is a special application of a fundamental principle; the therapist should make every effort toward self-understanding, especially in relation to his practice. And here, again, even though acceptance of the psi hypothesis involves radical changes in our conventional concepts of space and time, it does not seem to require basic changes in our general approach to psychotherapy.

## Chapter 4

# IN THE THERAPIST'S CHAIR

## Telepathy or Intuition?

*Everyone possesses in his own unconscious an instrument with which*
*he can interpret the utterances of the unconcious in other people.*

—Sigmund Freud

Any experienced therapist who pays close attention to his patients sometimes finds himself in possession of information that has not been verbally communicated. We say to ourselves, "This person is frightened . . . or angry . . . or guilt ridden," even though the patient has not expressed such feelings and may not even be aware of them. We use theoretical knowledge and professional experience and also our observation of such nonverbal signals as posture, gestures, skin color, voice intonations, changes in breathing, perhaps even eye movements, which enable us to piece together data the patient has already offered. These observations may occur on a subliminal level of perception. We integrate all this data, frequently on an unconscious or preconscious level, and there emerges a therapeutic "hunch" usually described as intuition. No need, here, to invoke the psi hypothesis.

Yet at other times even the most finely honed power of observation and the richest clinical background do not seem to account for these hunches. It is my personal conviction, based on my own experience and on discussions with various colleagues, that the hunches are sometimes based upon, or facilitated by, paranormal communication. Occasionally the hunch presents highly specific information that the patient has never discussed or that may even be unconscious. And these hunches come to the therapist in various forms: sometimes a visual image, sometimes a bodily sensation, sometimes an idea, and—most uncannily of all—sometimes as an impulse toward a therapeutic intervention that has not been deliberately thought out but which frequently proves to be highly effective.

It is not always essential for us, as clinicians, to discriminate between hunches based on observation and experience, and those which may be based in part on paranormal communication. Our task is to use the hunches constructively to avoid or minimize the risks entailed.

For me, a therapeutic hunch occasionally appears in the form of physical sensation. In an interview with "George," a robust middle-aged man seeking help with a marital problem, I kept experiencing a sharp pain in my stomach, which I had never felt before and which in some indescribable way did not seem to *belong* to me.

Since George and I had already ascertained that our respective schedules would make it impossible for us to work together, the purpose of this interview was only for me to make an appropriate referral, and there was therefore no reason for me to inquire about George's physical health. Nevertheless, playing a hunch related to my stomach pain I asked George casually, "Tell me, do you have any special medical problems?"

"No, I'm a lucky one." But George hesitated, then went on. "Well, lately I've been getting indigestion. But I think it's about things at home . . ." And he went on about his wife.

Having made a referral for marital counseling, I played my hunch. When was George's last medical examination? Two years back, nothing wrong. Would he consider another examination? He could see his own physician, or I would give him a name.

George agreed with surprising readiness, perhaps because

he knew intuitively that he might not be well. A few weeks later, calling me to thank me for a satisfactory referral, he also thanked me for suggesting medical examination. A stomach ulcer had been found at a stage early enough that it could be treated by diet.

In my opinion, the pang in my own stomach (which has never occurred since) was based on a telepathic sensitivity to George's condition; it is perhaps relevant that I had taken a liking to George, and regretted that we could not work out a therapy schedule. In any case, it seems most unlikely that my own background, psychological not medical, would have enabled me to pick up indications of a stomach ulcer even on the basis of subliminal cues.

Rather often, I have had a somewhat similar experience while conducting a marathon group, in which ten to sixteen people remain together for two to five days. We take our meals together, and if the group meets at a woodland inn or a seaside resort, we also swim and walk together during rest breaks. A strong sense of mutual warmth and trust develops, which is especially conducive to extrasensory communication, both among the participants and between the participants and myself.* Among the latter is a special phenomenon I have come to think of as "my marathon headache."

By some stroke of physiological good fortune, I am literally never subject to headaches. Eyestrain, smoke-filled rooms, fatigue, nervous tension—none give me headaches. While conducting a marathon, however, I sometimes have a feeling which can perhaps be called the *shadow* of a headache, and which—like the stomach pang I experienced with George—somehow does not seem to belong to me. Invariably, when this happens someone asks, "Elizabeth, have you an aspirin?" I never have any idea which of the group participants will ask this question, therefore

---

*Chapters 7 and 8 describe apparently paranormal communication and transpersonal experiences in these groups. Readers are also referred to my book, *Marathon Groups: Reality and Symbol.*[1] Over a period of almost twenty years, I have conducted perhaps 400 of these groups, which I regard as a uniquely valuable therapeutic experience for many people, especially in conjuction with more conventional one-to-one therapy.

my marathon shadow headache cannot be explained on the basis of subliminal clinical observation.* Nor is the request for aspirin by any means a common occurrence; it occurs in perhaps one out of five marathons.

These are not isolated examples; many occurrences indicate that psychic resonance to the physical discomfort of another person may take the form of an analogous discomfort, as reported by other clinicians. [2, Ch.5] It is tempting to hypothesize that such phenomena occur when the therapeutic process can be furthered by their occurrence. But here, again, we find that psi is capricious. My shadowy stomachache was useful to George, but I can see no particular therapeutic purpose served by my shadowy marathon headaches. Other episodes, however, do suggest the possiblility that the therapist's intention of being useful may be served by paranormal communication, and also the possiblility that a personal quality or experience of the therapist may facilitate paranormal communication.† Here are two examples that sustain these hypotheses; both of them also illustrate the apparently paranormal spontaneous acquisition of information through visual imagery.

A colleague describes an initial interview with "Cynthia," whose five-year-old marriage was in serious trouble. Her husband was engaged in a homosexual affair. He had not proposed a divorce, but he showed less and less interest in Cynthia.

As Cynthia went on, the therapist suddenly envisioned a cello. They had not spoken of music, certainly not of cellos, but

---

*My therapeutic policy is to withhold the aspirin and ask instead, "When did you first notice the headache?" Usually it turns out that the participant has a strong emotion that he does not express. Most frequently, the emotion is anger. The headache victim may have been irritated by another participant, or something has evoked anger toward an important person in his life. The headache disappears when the anger is fully expressed verbally, or through the familiar bioenergetic technique of pillow pounding. As for my shadow headache, it immediately disappears.

†The Dutch psychic Croiset is said to have nearly drowned in a canal as a child, and to be especially useful in locating the bodies of children who have drowned in the canals of Holland. [3, p. 49]

the therapist was so sure of this hunch that he inquired, "Tell me, did you ever play the cello?"*

The cello, it turned out, was all-important. Cynthia had indeed been a cellist, and music had been an intensely meaningful part of her life. But now her cello was unused and stored in a closet. She had considered becoming a professional performer, but feared that this ambition would conflict with her marriage. Masochistically, she put away the cello.

Therapy went well. My colleague helped Cynthia work through the unconscious masochism that had been a factor in driving her husband (who, apparently, was bisexual) toward homosexuality, and which had also made her a far less interesting person than the vibrant, music-loving woman he had married. Gradually the marriage regained its vitality. Apparently, my colleague's telepathic image of the cello helped therapist and patient to identify Cynthia's basic conflict.

Another element in this story may be significant if we wish to explore conditions under which psi phenomena may occur. The therapist himself is homosexual, although he had also had significant relationships with women. And when he was telling me about his image of the cello, his actual words were, "I saw a cello between her legs." Although this is certainly the position in which a cello is played, one need not be a classical Freudian to speculate whether the cello was not only a musical instrument, but also a phallic symbol. Indeed, it was by the attempt to reject and repress the healthy masculinity in her nature, which Jung would call the *animus*, that Cynthia had endangered her marriage. Returning to her music, she reclaimed this aspect of herself and once more became interesting to her husband, who concurrently undertook individual psychotherapy.†

*For reasons to be discussed later in this chapter, it would seem to me, in general, a wiser course to have introduced the cello theme indirectly or gradually; at any rate, my colleague's choice of a therapeutic intervention was evidently effective.

†It seems appropriate to apologize once more, to clinicians who may read these accounts, that case histories are necessarily very much shortened and oversimplified, since the primary focus of attention is on the psychic and transpersonal dimensions of psychotherapy.

Can we justifiably speculate that bisexual conflicts within the therapist himself made him especially sensitive to his patient's unexpressed conflicts? There is no way to demonstrate this possibility, but in my own therapeutic practice I have sometimes been able to relate apparently paranormal perceptions about my patients to my own conflicts and life experiences. One such episode occurred in a marathon conducted in Germany.

For me, paranormal communication seems to occur more often in groups with some built-in difficulty with the spoken language. Over the years I have conducted perhaps 50 marathon workshops in Germany and Holland. They are attended voluntarily by teachers and therapists interested both in personal growth and in learning more about Gestalt and encounter techniques. These participants understand my English and their English is very adequate for communication on an intellectual level. However, if early life experiences are being relived, the participant is asked to speak his childhood language. With some help from an informal interpreter, and with close attention to body language, I can usually empathize with the participant. Communication in this way appears to work; indeed the language difficulty actually seems to facilitate empathic or telepathic communication.

Heinrich, a participant in a five-day therapeutic workshop in Germany, came with the presenting complaint of tachycardia. Several specialists, unable to find any physical basis, had recommended psychotherapy, a suggestion Heinrich greatly resented. He was a research chemist who saw psychotherapy as appropriate only for the treatment of grave mental illness and who prided himself on being scientifically minded. However, Henrich decided to try the workshop as a way of exploring the possibility that emotional problems might underlie his symptom.

It required several days before Heinrich developed enough confidence to speak about his problem. When he finally did so, he approached the situation to the best of his conscious ability. He listened carefully to every comment made by myself or my cotherapist,* spoke with great sincerity, and followed our suggestions to the letter.

Henrich could not recall at what point in his life he had

*John Brinley, M. S. W.

begun to experience tachycardia, nor could he connect it in any way with conscious anxiety. For example, he had easily gone through a crucial professional situation on one occasion, but on another occasion had been forced by the mysterious symptom to cut short a pleasant evening with his wife at the skating rink. Physical exertion seemed to bring on the palpitations occasionally, but not always; for example, a steep mountain climb had caused no difficulty. Sexual activity caused no problem.

None of these preliminary explorations seemed to be getting anywhere. I asked Heinrich to embark upon the fantasy trip called "a journey through the body."*

With meticulous care, Heinrich made sure he understood the directions and then complied to his utmost ability. He chose to enter his body by way of his mouth, moved upward, and thoroughly explored the regions of his brain, offering a survey in which a neurologist might well have taken pride. He moved downward through the larynx and esophagus, went through his right and left arms, and finally arrived at his lungs. The group was half asleep. By now we liked and respected Heinrich, but were bored by his pedantry. Luckily, however, I became aware that I was bored, and asked myself to wake up. As I became more alert, a visual image came to me from out of nowhere, the image of an elderly lady, holding in her lap some sort of handiwork.

Henrich was droning on. I listened to him, and inwardly I looked at the old lady. She seemed to be a nice old lady, and I had the vague feeling that she had to do with Heinrich, not with me.

By now Heinrich had arrived at his heart, and was describing its right and left ventricles. Then came the moment of drama. Suddenly he stopped, and with the inimitable surprise of a literally minded person who, for the first time, consciously faces an "irrational" aspect of himself, he lost his perfect English and said, "Mein Gott, was ist das?"

"What, Heinrich?"

He returned conscientiously to English. "Around my heart I see a twist of woolen yarn. A thread of knitting wool. But what can it be doing there?"

Automatically, I said, "Stay with the woolen yarn, Heinrich.

*Developed by William Schutz.[4]

Just stay with the picture in your mind and see what you think of next." In another part of my mind, very vaguely, the word "grandmother" seemed to be heard.

Heinrich frowned, eyes shut, concentrating deeply. "It's gone now—I just see my heart. I cannot think of anything." Opening his eyes, he shook his head in frustration and I decided to take a chance.

"Heinrich, I've just gotten this idea from nowhere at all. Let's try it out. I wonder if you had a grandmother?"

"Ach, ja, I haven't thought of her in years. She died when I was—oh, a little boy, six maybe seven . . ."

The memories came slowly, then more easily. When Heinrich was a little boy, his grandmother had completely dominated the household, a sweet and loving tyrant. She was especially fond of Heinrich, her only grandson. Then, gradually, the grandmother's health began to fail. . . .

The rest of the story can probably be anticipated, although several hours of work were required for the group (now wide awake and interested) and myself to draw it forth, since Heinrich had forgotten or repressed these childhood events. As she grew weaker, the grandmother doted upon Heinrich more and more, and was particularly solicitous about his health. Was he too hot? Too cold? Hungry? Had he eaten the right foods? Most of all, he mustn't run and play too hard—he might injure his heart. Now, in his thirties, the taboo of his grandmother—all the stronger because he had loved her—was still in force.

Psychotherapy, like psi and like the human personality itself, is far from easy to understand. We never did find out, for instance, why Heinrich was able to climb a mountain, but developed tachycardia on a skating rink, nor did the tachycardia miraculously disappear after the memories of the grandmother had been recovered. However, Heinrich did recognize finally that there indeed were major emotional problems bound up in his heart symptoms, and made a firm decision to enter individual psychotherapy.

Like most examples of patient-therapist telepathy, the episode of Heinrich offers no objective evidence about the occurrence of telepathy, since no data exists except for my subjective conviction that the picture of the grandmother occurred to me *before* Heinrich visualized the strand of knitting wool. I took a shot in the dark in questioning him about his grandmother, a skeptic would say, and proved correct by chance, despite the fact that I had met Heinrich for the first time in that workshop and knew nothing about his background.

But if we do consider this episode in light of the psi hypothesis, we may note that telepathically I was not in touch with Heinrich's conscious thoughts, but with memories and feelings that were unconscious to him until our work in the marathon. The psi experience represented a breakthrough of Heinrich's unconscious memories not into his conscious mind, but into *mine*.

What aspects of this particular situation made *Heinrich's* repressed memories come into *my* awareness? My conscious motivation was clear enough: I wanted to be therapeutically useful. Heinrich's motivation was equally clear, although conflicted; he wanted to be rid of the distressing heart symptoms, but was reluctant to recover painful childhood memories.

Empathy, a key factor in psychic communication, may well have been facilitated by a similarity between Heinrich's childhood and my own. Like Heinrich, I went through a childhood in which well-meaning but unnecessary attention was paid to trivial matters of personal health and safety; I never developed psychosomatic symptoms, but had to struggle to achieve a normal enjoyment of outdoor sports and activities, and this may well have sensitized me to Heinrich's problem.*

The examples cited thus far deal with experiences of which the therapist is conscious: I was aware of my stomach pangs and my marathon headaches; my colleague was aware of his cello image; I was aware of the word "grandmother" and my image of the woolen strand. At other times, the paranormal hunch is not

*Why had Heinrich repressed the memories of his grandmother? This question was presumably explored in the subsequent course of his individual psychotherapy, but we may conjecture that the memories were painful partly because he loved her and grieved for her death; partly because, as children do, he may have felt that he killed her by being a "bad boy" and not taking care of his health; and partly because during her lifetime he had resented her well-intentioned overprotectiveness.

experienced consciously, but emerges in the form of spontaneous remarks.*

Among famous examples of this type of episode is Theodor Reik's classical story about a young woman, a psychoanalytic patient, who had never recovered from the tragic ending of a long past love affair. Her analytic work with Reik was at a standstill. In the session described, after a long silence she mentioned a visit to her dentist, who had pulled a tooth. Another silence. She then glanced across the room at Reik's bookcase and remarked, "There's a book standing on its head."†

Reik continues:[5, p. 260]

> Without the slightest hesitation and in a reproachful voice I said, "But why did you never tell me that you had had an abortion?" *I had said it without an inkling of what I would say. It felt as if not I, but something in my head had said it.* [Italics mine.]

It then came out that the abortion, in those years regarded as a serious moral crime, had actually been performed by her physician lover, and that she had resolved upon silence to protect him, a resolution which had inevitably blocked the progress of her analysis.

Naturally, it is not impossible that Reik, as he himself speculates, had reached his conclusion by means of an unconscious chain of logical inferences, and certainly his experience and sensitivity would have made this possible. Yet he insists *(ibid):*

> I did not think of any psychoanalytic theory. I just said what had spoken in me and against all logic, and I was correct.

*The dangers of yielding uncritically to spontaneous impulses will be discussed later; this type of spontaneity by no means negates the importance of a solid theoretical background but rather points up its inestimable value. Reik's *Listening with the Third Ear,* from which the above anecdote is taken, still seems to be by far the best account in the literature of the union of psychodynamic theory and extraordinary empathic ability, which in my opinion goes beyond intuition, although Reik does not specifically invoke the psi hypothesis.

†It must be remembered that the fetus is normally born head first.

Perhaps the most dramatic of my own experiences in this area, in which it is sometimes difficult to discriminate among the intuitive, the paranormal, and the transpersonal aspects of the therapist's experience, occurred during a marathon when I was working with "Maria,"[6]a capable and attractive woman in her mid-thirties, who was in individual therapy with another psychologist. She had been depressed, but after two years of hard therapeutic work she had progressed greatly in her ability to enjoy life and was functioning well.

A hard-core problem remained. Maria's mother, whose own life had been unhappy, seemed out to destroy Maria's growing happiness. When things went well, Maria's mother warned against misfortune. If Maria enjoyed her work, she would be fired, or else would overwork and have a breakdown. If Maria was interested in remarriage, the man would prove a scoundrel and desert Maria.

> "It's like a curse," Maria said.
> "Why don't you just not see her any more, not talk to her?" suggested a group member.
> "Because—well, she's my mother, after all. I'm all she has. Besides—well, I don't think that it would really help."

Of course, Maria was entirely right. Cutting herself off from her mother would not help. She would feel guilty, and the introjected mother would remain, still wishing ill. If she broke relations, could she ever come to terms with her mother as an actual human being?

It seemed to me that Maria needed a chance to let out her rage and resentment. Accordingly, using the familiar role-playing technique, I sat down opposite her on the floor and asked her to pretend I was her mother.

Accepting me as a surrogate, Maria poured out her anger. She wept, cursed, pounded on a pillow, and cried out "I hate you, Mother!" As usual after catharsis, she felt relieved. She reached out to me with affection and said warmly, "Oh, I do wish you *were* my mother!"

On a rational level, this therapeutic episode seemed satisfactorily complete. Maria had vented her rage, returned to reality, and now hopefully could better handle her mother's destructiveness.

Then came an experience which at that time was altogether different from my past experience as a working therapist, though since then I have had it often. I simply did not plan my words or know what I was going to say next. There was an actual physical chill, as is frequently described by people during a paranormal episode. Words spoke themselves:

> "I *am* your mother. Through me there is speaking the
> part of your mother who wishes you well. Be happy
> and accept your happiness."

Maria began to cry again, more quietly. We were all silent. After a while, again able to think logically, I pointed out that Maria's mother must have given her many positive messages. During a difficult childhood in a war-torn country, Maria's mother had been the most important person in her life. And Maria, despite her emotional difficulties, had grown up strong enough to handle her own life, strong enough to enter therapy and profit by it, and now strong enough to reach toward greater happiness.

Maria agreed. Months later, she telephoned to let me know that her mother's predictions of doom now seemed easier to bear; she could even receive them with light-hearted, affectionate teasing. A few years later, when her mother died, Maria let me know that their relationship and final parting had been loving. She had gone through normal mourning, and regarded the marathon episode as a turning point in their relationship.

What happened? My clinical experience was certainly sufficient to carry out this rather theatrical therapeutic intervention, but I did *not* plan it. Like Reik, I felt that I was acting altogether without my own volition. Had I utilized my clinical knowledge unconsciously to carry out rather an unusual therapeutic strategem? Was I telepathically in touch with Maria's deep awareness that her mother had indeed possessed a benevolent aspect? Or, as Jung might have speculated, was I in touch on a transpersonal level with the loving, healing archetype of the Good Mother?

In Reik's abortion story, and in my story of Maria, it was apparent that the therapeutic interventions were of great significance, but sometimes these intuitive remarks seem casual and even trivial. A colleague tells me of a first interview with a retiring young woman who found it difficult to talk about herself. At a loss for words, my colleague found herself noticing the girl's white blouse, immaculately clean and beautifully ironed. Without thinking, or with some vague idea of putting the new patient more at ease, she asked spontaneously, "Who ironed your blouse?"

The patient, startled, blurted out, "How did you know about my mother?" Out came the patient's problem—her dependency on an overprotective mother who insisted upon doing things the girl would really have liked to do for himself. And with this statement, therapy could begin.

Although in general I do not regard myself as psychic, and indeed cannot recall in my own life a single precognitive dream, I have in my practice had several experiences which suggest the possibility of precognition; one such experience is especially impressive because it may have helped prevent a serious traffic accident.

I was working with a woman who is not self-destructive, and who is an excellent driver. As she left my office, after a session which had not been distressing to either of us, I said, "Drive carefully," a phrase which to me seems over solicitous and which I never use routinely.

My patient, on her way home, was driving at her usual sensible speed along a four-lane highway, and had just decided to pass a truck and cut into the faster lane on her left—a maneuver which, as she later reported, would not ordinarily have been unsafe. Just then my warning came back to her, and she decided to drive ultra conservatively. A moment later, one of her tires blew out. If she had gone into the left lane at that moment, she would have been in real trouble.

Here I had not the slightest conscious feeling that my patient was in danger. My remark was not only unprepared, but inappropriate. We might conjecture that my patient knew she needed a car checkup and that I picked up her concern, yet on a conscious level she believed her car was in good order.

Here is another episode in which I behaved involuntarily, unthinkingly, in the therapeutic situation: My patient, "Lee," enjoyed fantasy trips that often brought up meaningful and useful data from the deep unconscious. I was listening closely while, in a semi-trance, she was swimming downward in an unknown ocean (a common symbol for the exploration of unconscious depths).

Without thinking, I rose from my chair with a vague idea of glancing out the window, which was near the telephone. At that moment the phone rang unexpectedly; I picked it up and said in a low voice, "Please call back later."

I went back to my chair and Lee went on with her fantasy. After we had discussed it, she said, "But how did you know the phone was going to ring and interrupt me?"

"I didn't know. I thought I was just going to look out the window."

"But you've never looked out the window before in my sessions."

She was correct, nor was there any reason for me to look out the window. It was exactly *as if* I had precognitive knowledge that the phone would ring. But with Lee, as with the woman who avoided a possible traffic accident, I had absolutely no sense that anything unusual might be going on.

If I do sometimes have telepathic knowledge of my patient's background, it seems to appear most frequently when I am role-playing the patient's mother, a favorite technique of mine. If I role-play the "bad mother"—who may be punitive, arrogant, whining, demanding, seductive, or indifferent—it is to help the patient to release his pent-up rage, never released directly against me, but often expressed in physical catharsis through pillow-pounding. Less frequently I role-play the "good mother," with the purpose of helping the patient get in touch with the benevolent aspects of his mother, as did Maria.*

*Of course, the type of dramatic episodes related in this chapter and in subsequent chapters do not constitute a "cure." Like every other therapeutic strategem—a useful psychoanalytic interpretation, a physical release of tension through bioenergetic methods, a well-chosen behavioral desensitization, an accurately selected Gestalt dialogue—it is at best only one of many small steps toward the therapeutic goal.

When I undertake this type of role-playing, I usually begin with getting some basic information about the "bad mother." "What was she like when she was bad? Was she cold, brutal, martyred? What did you call her, and what did she call you? What kind of voice did she have—loud, soft, cajoling, harsh, complaining?" I don't ask for detailed information, but nearly always the patient gives me a clear feeling about the most painful moments in his childhood. We sit opposite on the floor, cross-legged in the middle of the group, and reenact what happened years ago.*

Over and over, men and women have said to me, "You were *exactly* like my mother! That was just how she sounded, that was just what she said!" With a background of classical psychoanalytic training, I am of course entirely aware that transference must play an enormous part in these episodes, and that my patient wishes to see me as his mother so that he may express and work out the conflicts he could not overcome in childhood. Nevertheless, what happens in some of these episodes suggests that I pick up by paranormal means some information not conveyed in words. There was, for example, the episode which I recall as the Pig Mother.

"Jack" had been brought into the marathon by my co-therapist, with whom he was in individual therapy. Jack was deeply depressed, but able to function adequately in an impersonal business situation. He had occasional physical affairs with women, but never a love relationship. He had been placed in a succession of foster homes from the age of seven, and could remember little of what had happened before then. In short, his background was so deprived and his pathology so severe that it was something of a miracle that he could function at all and was able to seek therapy.

This was a three-day marathon, and for the first two days Jack said little, although he listened attentively. Hoping to help Jack talk about himself, I began to ask him about his early child-

*In a marathon group, it is not always myself who takes the role of the bad mother or the longed-for good mother. Frequently another marathon participant will take the mother role. The father role, similarly, may be enacted by a male co-therapist or by another male participant. A later chapter describes this procedure further.

hood, before he had been placed in foster homes. He replied courteously, but could remember very little.

As I spoke with Jack, I began to notice an odd speech impediment in myself which I had experienced before only when I had a bad cold coupled with fatigue. My voice caught in my throat and became at once shrill and guttural, almost like a grunt.

"You sound funny," said someone in the marathon.
"Elizabeth, you don't sound like yourself."

My co-therapist came over and whispered, "Are you okay?' I felt okay, but my voice kept sounding more and more strange. And I had an odd knowledge of what I felt like saying, in this strange, high, guttural voice. I wanted to say, "I'm going to send you off. I don't want you. I'll kill you!"

Since Jack had almost no conscious memory of his mother, except that she had placed him in a foster home and had never seen him again, I did not dare offer to role-play her with him. If his mother had really wished to kill him, the knowledge of this would be there somewhere, unconsciously, and he was probably not yet ready to face it.

Jack solved the problem for me. He was therapeutically naive, but he said, "Elizabeth, will you pretend to be my mother?"

I had no choice. I said, "Of course," and sat down on the floor with him in the center of the group. To my total astonishment, he said, "Mom, did you ever want to kill me?"

I literally could not answer. My voice was blocked. Only odd noises came forth, pig grunts. In the clinical, rational part of my mind, I thought, "His mother put him in a foster home because she was afraid she'd kill him." I was in no physical discomfort, but when I tried to speak, I choked and could say nothing.

Jack glared at me. He said distinctly, "Mom, you are a pig. You make me sick. I'm going to vomit you out." He left the group, went out into the bathroom, and came back looking relieved. As soon as he came back, I again had control of my voice.

Now we could talk. The group was babbling excitedly. "Elizabeth, you really sounded like a pig!" "Jack, did you really vomit? You look a whole lot better." "Jack, why did your mother put you in a foster home?"

Jack, looking more relaxed then he had looked since the beginning of the group, said slowly, "I don't want to talk about it now. But I remember something. Mom used to get real mad and beat me up, and when she got that mad she couldn't talk. She grunted like a pig."

Very softly, I said, "Perhaps your mother put you in a foster home because she didn't really want to kill you." This suggestion was not a sentimental placebo; I have known parents who were afraid, perhaps quite rightly, that they could not control their murderous rage, and who sent children away in order to save them.

But at the time Jack could not take this in. Curtly, he said, "I've done enough for today." He was quite right. During the rest of the marathon weekend he was quiet but not withdrawn, attentive, and relaxed. As for me, I was rather more tired than usual, but had no further difficulties with my voice.

What happened? I have some data, because my co-therapist continued working with Jack for some years.* Apparently his mother was psychotic, and in uncontrollable rages threatened the life of her little boy. This was confirmed by the records of the social agency that had placed Jack. She had committed suicide a few years after turning Jack over to the agency. We know that memories of childhood remain alive in the repressed unconscious. On a deep level, therefore, Jack had remembered the attacks of murderous rage in which his mother lost her voice and only grunted like a pig.

But what happened to me? I do not believe that in any way I was possessed, or even influenced, by the "spirit" of Jack's mother. However, I do think that telepathically I picked up Jack's repressed memories in a way that affected my voice *before* I knew anything about the rages of Jack's mother.

Jack's mother, we can assume, went through a dreadful conflict in which her fury toward her son was pitted against an instinctual wish to save him. We may assume this because, in fact, she neither destroyed nor abandoned him, but (as the social

---

*Since my co-therapist in that marathon is still working with Jack, he does not wish his name to be cited, even in the preliminary acknowledgements.

agency's records showed) took an active part in arranging his placement. It is my hypothesis that Jack unconsciously retained a memory of how this pitiable and destructive mother lost her power to speak, a memory which I picked up telepathically.

The question remains as to why I *behaved* like the Pig Mother instead of helping Jack reconstruct his memory in verbal terms, which as a therapeutic strategem would have been less effective. My conjecture is that when I role-played the Pig Mother, I was unconsciously in touch with the two great archetypes of motherhood, the Evil Mother (which I acted out) and the good Great Mother (providing empathy for this tragically deprived man). With Maria, also, I was perhaps in touch not only with her deep awareness of her mother's benevolent aspects, but also with the archetype of the Great Mother in myself. Indeed, my belief is that these good and evil archetypes exist in every woman, just as their parallels exist deep in the collective unconscious of every man.

Great mediums, such as Leonora Piper and Eileen Garrett, may possess remarkable telepathic and clairvoyant powers in trance. Since I am personally unable to accept the concept of "spirit guides," which impart psychic knowledge to the entranced medium, I must hypothesize that I role-played Jack's Pig Mother and Maria's good mother in a semi-trance that brought me into touch with them telepathically and also into touch with my own deep unconscious mother-wisdom. This hypothesis is supported by other anecdotal evidence suggesting that a therapist may, under certain circumstances, function in trance, perhaps even without a conscious procedure of self-hypnosis.

The late psychiatrist, Milton Erickson, a master of hypnosis,[7] told one of his seminar groups that he had once seen a psychoanalytic colleague with a vexatious symptom for which he had vainly sought treatment from several other colleagues. Awaiting his distinguished patient, Erickson reported that he had told himself, "This man is more intelligent than I am. If I am to help him, I must rely on my unconscious." Accordingly, Erickson placed himself in trance . . . and, two hours later, awakened with the knowledge that he had greeted the patient and had worked with him, but otherwise could not recall what had occurred. The story of course, had the anticipated ending: The patient's symptom disappeared.*

At least once I have had a similar experience. My patient, "Sylvia," was expecting her first baby. She loved her husband, was in good health, was delighted, and expected no problems. Yet she experienced considerable fatigue and nausea. She was told that this was normal in the first trimester, but when the discomfort persisted into the fifth month, both of us began to suspect an emotional component.

Sure that Sylvia really wanted the baby, I looked for problems in her relationship with her own parents. Her father had died when Sylvia was very young, and she had an unusually warm relationship with her mother, who appeared enraptured by the prospect of becoming a grandmother.

Nevertheless, Sylvia told me, her mother was fond of contrasting Sylvia's discomfort with her own easy pregnancy. Why should Sylvia be suffering from nausea? "*I* never did," boasted Sylvia's mother. Clearly, the implied message was that Sylvia was not quite her mother's equal as a woman. In order to put this implicit message into words, I suggested that I would play Sylvia's mother. She agreed, I took a chair other than my usual seat, and we began.

The session was over. I saw Sylvia to the door. The remainder of my day was busy, and it was not until Sylvia's next session that I thought about my role-playing.

Back for her next appointment, Sylvia was elated. She felt wonderful. All the symptoms disappeared shortly after she had left my office. She bubbled, "I just don't know how you did it! When you played my mother, you had her very words, her tone of voice." Only then did I realize that I could recall nothing of that session after the moment when I had decided to play Sylvia's mother.

Sylvia told me what had happened. Faced with her mother as role-played by me, in a situation where she could not actually hurt her absent mother's feelings, Sylvia had suddenly realized that

*Personal communication, Dr. Rea Rabinowitch, who attended this seminar.

the older woman was envious. She loved Sylvia and wanted the grandchild, but she also envied the excitement of pregnancy, childbirth, and caring for a first baby. Sylvia, an alert and sensitive woman, recognized now that she had intuitively sensed this envy but had been unwilling to acknowledge it, and had unconsciously apologized by developing physical symptoms. In our role-playing, she had expressed resentment at her mother's attitude and I could suddenly remember one phrase that Sylvia had uttered: "You jealous bitch, you just wish it was you having this baby!"

My mimicry of Sylvia's mother may not have been as remarkable as she believed; nevertheless, since in general I am not subject to memory lapses, I may well have been working in a semi-trance in which I not only could pick up Sylvia's unconscious resentment of her mother's envy but also Sylvia's mental picture of her mother's voice and mannerisms.

Like the great mediums, Erickson could induce a trance condition in himself. This I cannot do. But there seem to be similarities between a light trance condition and the "evenly hovering attention" of Freud's famous recommendation to psychoanalysts. When I am paying full attention to my patient, I do not think about theory or speculate consciously about the patient's feelings. Under these conditions there is sometimes a special sensitivity to the patient that may be termed empathy, intuition, or sometimes perhaps telepathy. Nor is my experience exceptional; many colleagues have acknowledged an identical experience, which they sometimes hesitate to share from fear it may be thought unscientific.

Psychic intuitions carry specific risks. So indeed, do theoretical formulations attained entirely through the intellect (if, indeed, it is possible to use intellect alone, uncolored by emotion). Every therapist, no matter what his theoretical framework, must constantly choose among a variety of interventions. A bioenergeticist must decide upon which pattern of muscular tension he will work with at a given moment; a psychoanalyst must choose among several interpretations, all of which may be correct; even a Rogerian, who views his task as involving simple acceptance and reflection, must discriminate among shades of feeling.

And not only is the therapist faced with continuous choice on an intellectual level, but he is also faced with the immense reality of countertransference, which today is seen as including not only the therapist's conscious and unconscious response to the patient's transferential attitudes, but as a global response to the patient's entire personality. He must, moreover, insofar as possible, set aside personal needs and wishes during the therapeutic session. With all these requirements to meet, are we not further muddying the waters by suggesting that the therapist also pay attention to psychic messages from sources we do not understand, in accordance with laws we have barely begun to explore?

But the waters are already muddy and cannot be cleaned up by ignoring the murk. It seems impossible for any therapist, however he may try for total rationality, to remain completely unaffected by paranormal factors.* The psi phenomenon, capricious as it is, exists whether or not we like it; the practical implication is that the practicing therapist does well to consider his hunches as possibly valid even if they seem irrelevant.

Yet it is also dangerous to accept the psi hypothesis so uncritically that any random thought may be accepted as valid information, telepathically obtained, about the patient. Some hunches do seem based on paranormal processes, and others spring from the therapist's personal needs. If we accept the psi hypothesis, what are our guidelines toward therapeutic responsibility?

Let us suppose that a competent therapist suspects that a patient's self-punitiveness and periodic depressions are related to the death of a younger brother of whom the patient, as a child, was very jealous. The therapist does not say, "You wanted to kill your brother and feel responsible for his death," or even, "You really hated your kid brother." He might say, "Tell me more about how you felt when your brother died," or "Everybody gets sore at kid brothers sometimes. You probably did too, unless you were some kind of angel." It could take a long time before the

---

*The reader is reminded again of the classical sheep-goat experiment [8] and of the episode recounted in Chapter III, in which a highly skillful therapist blundered by not acknowledging behavior that seemed paranormally determined.

patient is able to recognize that her hostile feelings did not cause the brother's death.

Now let us suppose that in an early interview, even before they discuss the relationship, the therapist has a sudden, vivid image of the patient strangling her younger brother. This image may originate in the therapist's personal background, a recent television show, or even a tentative theoretical conjecture appearing as imagery. It may also be a telepathic perception. And if it is indeed a telepathic perception, the same therapeutic caution is still needed.

Not every therapist who accepts the psi hypothesis would agree. A colleague who accepts telepathic communication as a matter of course believes that it occurs only when the patient really wants to discuss whatever topic is involved but is blocked. Certainly, good therapeutic results were obtained by Reik in speaking of his patient's abortion and by my colleague who saw the image of his patient holding a cello. Here we can think of LeShan's opinion that information does not become telepathically available if the sender really wishes to keep it secret. Nevertheless, it seems to me that possibly-telepathic information about a patient that appears as a hunch should be treated not with ordinary but with extraordinary caution, and for these reasons:

First, as already suggested, the apparent hunch may originate not in telepathic communication but in the therapist's own unconscious mind.

Next, the telepathically obtained information may present itself in a distorted form. Like everything with its roots in the unconscious, telepathic material reaches consciousness in a disguised form, subject to the various defenses and distortions we know about from dreams and fantasies. If the therapist takes his hunch too seriously, he may present it to the patient in a way that seems wildly inappropriate and may result in loss of confidence.

Another risk is that if the hunch is correct, the patient may see the therapist as having quasi-magical powers. *Perhaps he can read my mind!* This can be dangerous if the patient tends to be paranoid. Fear and suspicion may follow if the patient thinks the therapist can read his *thoughts,* although nearly every patient feels immense relief if the therapist can understand his *feelings.*

Finally, there is danger that a patient who perceives his

therapist as shaman or magician may become dependent. The magician has the answers, and there is no need for effort.

Most dangerous of all is the possibility that the therapist himself may, perhaps unconsciously, begin to regard himself as a guru, a magician, placing less and less reliance upon his solid knowledge of psychodynamics and technique. He may forget that any hunch may be the product of his own needs and feelings, and not a psychic communication from the patient. It is easy to imagine a self-indulgent therapist drifting into a relationship in which he and an appealing patient forget external reality and enjoy a telepathic mother-baby symbiosis. The ancient metaphor of Scylla and Charybdis well expresses the need to steer between blind rejection of the psi hypothesis and uncritical acceptance of any event that appears paranormal.

## Chapter 5

# PATIENTS WHO MAY BE PSYCHIC

*We must follow up all clues to the existence of untapped possibilities like extra-sensory perception. They may prove to be as important and extraordinary as the once untapped possibilities of matter.*

—Sir Julian Huxley

If we accept the psi hypothesis, we face an entire new range of decisions regarding diagnosis and therapeutic management. Absolute rejection of the psi hypothesis is quite unrealistic, but it is simpler. If the patient reports a psychic experience, the therapist need only decide whether his patient is ignorant, superstitious, or actually delusional, and may accordingly either enlighten him or treat him as psychotic.*

Acceptance of the psi hypothesis involves more complex decisions. Is the patient's report of a telepathic or precognitive experience credible enough to be taken seriously? Or is the patient simply delusional? Perhaps he is seeking psychic experi-

*This chapter deals primarily with the therapeutic approach to people who report psychic experiences. Chapter 8 discusses mysticism and transpersonal experience.

ences to avoid a realistic examination of his emotional problems? Even if the reported psychic experiences appear genuinely paranormal, are they used as an escape from life problems or as a grandiose enhancement of the self-image?

There is also the vital question of how the patient regards his psychic experience. Some individuals, coming from an ethnic background in which psychic phenomena are seen as spirit manifestations, are surprisingly matter-of-fact about paranormal events. Others are deeply disturbed by apparent ESP experiences; they fear the supernatural, or madness. Still others are less alarmed by psychic experience, but are reluctant to share them with a therapist lest they be suspected of psychosis.

Therapists themselves differ sharply as to the possibility of extrasensory perception. As shown by questionnaires sent out to random samples of psychiatrists,[1,2] a sizable percentage of clinicians accept the psi hypothesis, others regard belief in psychic phenomena as a sign of confusion or even delusion, others see the experimental data as untrustworthy or even fraudulent.[4] Most of the therapeutic episodes reported in this book come from my own practice or from colleagues who either accept the psi hypothesis or at least regard it as logically tenable. However, one psychiatrist has told me in all seriousness that he would automatically regard any patient who reported psychic experiences as a candidate for pharmacological treatment.

An overview of people who report psychic experiences or show high ESP ability on laboratory tests reveals a wide range of psychological traits and emotional health. In laboratory experiments with Zener cards used to test for telepathy, clairvoyance, and precognition,* it was found that as a group people who were outgoing and creative were psychically more "gifted" than rigid and withdrawn people.[3] People who have demonstrated exceptional psychic gifts, such as the famous medium Eileen Garret, are often exceptionally intelligent and practical. At the other end of the spectrum, some serious students of parapsychology believe that there is sometimes a dynamic relationship between paranormal experiences and extreme pathology, even schizophrenia. Eisenbud writes "It is not at all rare to see people who have been

---

*Described in Chapter 1.

on the ragged edge to begin with pushed into their private hells by attempting through immersion in the psychic world to come to grips with their real inner problems."[5, p.65] Ullman, also a psychiatrist, believes that psi experiences may sometimes represent "a last desperate foothold of relatedness"[6, p.51] as an attempt by a decompensating schizophrenic to maintain some kind of contact with reality. Spotnitz has pointed out that schizophrenics show an "extreme sensitivity to the unverbalized and *even the unconscious pre-feelings* of others" (italics mine).[7, p.6] None of these practitioners imply that psychic experiences call for a diagnosis of schizophrenia, but only that with some individuals they may be clinically associated. Here we may consider alternative hypotheses, which await further accumulation and evaluation of clinical data.

Our first theory is that certain individuals are endowed from childhood with unusual paranormal ability, may even have telepathic or precognitive experiences in the early years. Such childhood experiences are described in the autobiographies of Eileen Garrett, Rosalind Heywood, and other psychics who were able to function excellently and use their gift in socially useful ways.

However, such children may find it difficult to discriminate between ordinary perceptions and those mediated by psi. Moreover, their psychic perceptions may have been constantly derided or rebuked by adults. Such a child might be diagnosed as schizophrenic and subjected to restraint, drugs, and electroshock, and might eventually end up with actual mental illness.* Thus, paranormal gifts might well contribute to the confusion and withdrawal characteristic of schizophrenia.

Another viewpoint is that psychosis is caused by biochemical anomalies, usually constitutional but sometimes exacerbated by stress and anxiety. If we assume, as do many parapsychologists,

---

*The late Itzak Benthov, a physicist interested in paranormal phenomena, in several lectures to professional audiences expressed his belief that many people are hospitalized as schizophrenics because they are psychically gifted and are indiscreet in recounting their paranormal experiences to others; he thought these people were discharged when they learned to conceal their psychic abilities. It is to be hoped that his viewpoint was exaggerated.

that everyone possesses some degree of psi ability but that our waking consciousness normally serves as a barrier or filter to prevent the breakthrough of psi perceptions, we can further conjecture that in the schizophrenic this barrier does not function adequately because its biochemical base is defective. Thus we would regard the biochemically based psychosis as primary, and the psi experiences would be a by-product of the psychosis rather than a partial cause.

In general, the psi experiences associated with schizophrenia seem to occur in an unpredictable manner. In contrast, great mediums such as Mrs. Garrett are typically able to enter and leave the trance state, in which psychic knowledge seems to be obtained, by their own choice. Controlled experimental tests with mental patients show no special evidence of telepathic ability, which is not surprising in view of their characteristic difficulties in attention span and voluntary cooperation.[8]

It is certainly clear that psychic experiences do not necessarily imply delusional pathology. This important point is made by Eisenbud[5, pp.47ff] in discussing the classic *Phantasms of the Living*,[9] in which three respected nineteenth-century scholars report carefully documented accounts of apparitions of persons on the verge of death, or in a dangerous crisis, seen by a friend or relative. Eisenbud states:

> Of the 702 cases reported . . . none of the people . . . gave a history of ever having had a frank psychotic episode. Most of them claimed to have had only one such waking hallucination in their lifetime . . . Many of the respondents claimed to have been skeptical about psychic occurrences before their experience and some admitted frankly to just as great a skepticism afterward, preferring to regard the strange event as an inexplicable break in the continuity of everyday reality.

The following anecdotes involve patients whose diagnoses represent a wide range of pathology, and whose reported psychic experiences call for an equally wide range of therapeutic approaches, dependent not so much on diagnostic considerations as on the meaning of the psychic experience to the individual.

A former patient of mine occasionally had strong but incorrect premonitions that something terrible had happened to her husband when he was late in coming home for work. Several times these premonitions became so powerful that she telephoned his office, called various friends, and even called the local police. Only in prolonged psychotherapy did she recognize that her invalid "premonitions" were based partly on dependency, partly on a wish to control her husband, and even to some extent (in line with the famous Freudian "death wish") on her hostility toward him for not gratifying her dependent needs.

Another former patient, a professional woman whose reality testing was, in general, excellent, became obsessed by the belief that her former lover, who had decisively rejected her, was telepathically "calling" her. The conviction became so intense that, in a transitory psychotic episode, she went to his home in another city, found him absent, and sat down on the doorstep; when she refused to go away, he called the police.*

Episodes such as these have led some clinicians to discard the psi hypothesis altogether. It is obviously unwise to accept uncritically a subjective conviction, however strong, that a bonafide premonitory or telepathic experience is taking place.

Often, it is of slight importance for the therapist to decide whether or not a particular set of clinical data suggests extrasensory ability. A colleague tells me the case history of "Miriam," in her middle twenties, who sought therapy because of intense shyness and social isolation. Miriam handled her business life without difficulty, probably because her job as manager of a small department store required only impersonal business contacts. But she had only two or three women friends, whom she saw occasionally, and she was so stiff and uncomfortable around men that she was almost never asked for dates.

The telephone in Miriam's apartment was a symbol of great emotional meaning. She lived alone, and spent most of her evenings hoping that the phone would ring. When it did ring,

---

*In an article on the obsessional quality of certain instances of unrequited love, I have called attention to the fact that a lover who has been rejected by the beloved often entertains a strong delusional belief that there is still a telepathic bond between them.[10]

Miriam said, she always *knew* who it would be: Jane, suggesting lunch; Phyllis, suggesting shopping; once she had *known* that it would be a man, seeking a date. This last premonition proved correct, but the date was a failure because of Miriam's self-conscious shyness.

Some evenings she focused all her thought on the telephone, willing it to ring. When she could do this, Miriam insisted, the telephone *invariably* rang, even though it might be a wrong number.

Miriam also told a dream that indeed seemed precognitive, since she recounted it in therapy *before* the dream events occurred. She dreamed that an old school friend she had not seen in years dropped in unexpectedly at her office and invited her for lunch; she was wearing a rather unusual blue and green scarf. In her next therapeutic session, Miriam reported that these events had actually taken place three days after the dream, down to the appearance of the blue and green scarf.

My colleague, who had never before encountered psi phenomena, at first thought it was his responsibility to gently dissuade Miriam from accepting these incidents as paranormal. He asked her to keep a record of calls from her women friends and tally them against the occasions when she "knew" who would be there when she picked up the phone. He asked her to tabulate times when she concentrated and it did not ring, and times when it rang without her concentration. He regarded this approach as a way to strengthen her ability to handle reality, since he suspected that she was putting her energy into magical thinking rather than into improving her social situation. In this he was certainly correct, but since Miriam saw him for only one session each week, most of her therapeutic time was spent in debating the validity of her possibly psychic experiences.

However, after the precognitive dream about the blue and green scarf, my colleague began to consider the psi hypothesis, read Eisenbud and Ehrenwald, and came to the conclusion that Miriam's intense longing for companionship might actually be producing paranormal occurrences. He told her to forget about the telephone tabulations, and instead focused on her paralyzing shyness, which had to do with a childhood in which she was treated as almost worthless and was also required to suppress every show of feeling.*

Slowly, Miriam became able to initiate calls to her women friends, instead of longing for them to call her. Next she became able to suggest occasional lunches to her co-workers. Her therapist decided she was ready for group therapy, and to her amazement Miriam found herself accepted warmly by the group. After two years of treatment, Miriam was still quite shy, but had a fairly satisfying social life and could seek out situations in which she might meet men. There were no further precognitive dreams, and she no longer "knew" who was calling when the telephone rang.

Were Miriam's telephone hunches pure fantasy? Or did her intense loneliness and her concentration on the telephone really enable her to "know" who was calling, perhaps even to impel her friends to phone through an unconscious telepathic response to her great longing? Certainly, her precognitive dream is the only convincing example of psi at work. What is of importance to the practicing therapist is that experiences that might have been paranormal were set off by her intense need; that there was no therapeutic value in focusing on the paranormal possibility; and that therapeutic results were obtained by exploring the needs that presumably facilitated the occurrences.

Here are further cases in which the patients believed that paranormal events were occurring and in which the therapists were able to use the "occult" experiences constructively.

"Martha," in her thirties, had been seeing a therapist for several years. She had been hospitalized briefly when younger, and was described as close to schizophrenia, but able to function. She held a routine job, lived alone in a furnished room, and in the course of therapy was beginning to be slightly less afraid of other people.

But as Martha improved, a terrible new symptom appeared, so frightening that she trembled when she talked about it. There was a clothes closet in her room, and when she opened the

*The description of Miriam's psychodynamics is inevitably oversimplified here, since we are interested primarily in its relationship to her possible psychic experiences.

door—there was her mother, seated in a wheelchair, glaring at her.

Martha's relationship with her mother had been frightful. The older woman, frankly schizophrenic, had spend most of her life in mental hospitals. She and Martha had a pathological relationship, at once hostile and symbiotic, until the little girl was nine, when her father's relatives legally took her away and sent her to a reasonably kind aunt who fortunately lived in another part of the country. However, Martha's mother always kept in touch, although at erratic intervals. There were letters, photographs, requests to visit. When she was grown up, Martha did visit her mother two or three times, but the visits always ended in disastrous scenes in which the mother reproached Martha for neglecting her, and accused her of "whoring."

And now here was Martha's mother, in her wheelchair, behind the door of Martha's closet. When Martha opened the door, she never knew whether her mother would be there. She would close the door quickly, and when she reopened it in the morning, the mother would be gone. She slept with a chair barricading the closet door.

On an intellectual level Martha recognized that the woman in the wheelchair was probably a hallucination. It could not be her mother's spirit, because her mother was alive. But it was visually real, and Martha was frightened.

Inquiring more closely, my colleague discovered that every apparition occurred when Martha had gone out in the evening with acquaintances, as she had been able to do recently. There was no apparition in the mornings when Martha opened the closet door to get her clothes for work, nor when Martha came straight home to cook dinner on her hot plate and spend the evening alone. Oddly enough, Martha realized she *knew* that in the mornings the mother would not appear.

"It seems," my colleague suggested, "that your mother doesn't mind your going to work, but she does mind your going out and having fun."

"But it isn't really my mother—I mean, it can't be—or is it?" Martha's intelligence told her that the appearance was a hallucination, but she felt it as malevolent and real.

"Let's not bother about that yet," my colleague said. And, in a brilliant therapeutic approach, she suggested that Martha "talk to her mother," using the Gestalt empty chair technique, and imagine that her mother was seated opposite her. She would then assert herself, tell the mother to go away, say that she had a right to her own life, and so on.

This was difficult, but Martha finally managed it, and the confrontation was repeated many times. The same procedure was repeated again in the next session, and the next. After half a dozen sessions, Martha came in triumphant. Her mother had not appeared again since her first confrontation . . . until last night.

"What happened last night?"

The story was dramatic. Martha had deliberately opened the closet door and *willed* herself to see her mother. Sure enough, the hallucination gradually appeared. And Martha ordered her "mother" to go away, shut the closet door firmly and not in panic, reopened it—and the woman in the wheelchair was gone.

Martha was laughing gleefully. "I bet she never comes again!"

The therapist was cautious. "Probably not—but if she does, now you know what to do."

According to my colleague, who told me Martha's story about six months after the wheelchair episode, the mother did not reappear. As for Martha, she continued to get better very slowly. Eventually, she admitted to her therapist that although she knew the woman in the wheelchair had been a hallucination, she had also been totally convinced that her mother was actually visiting her "on an astral plane."* If my colleague had focused on persuading Martha that the apparition was unreal, I do not believe she could possibly have helped her patient as she did by giving her support in confronting the toxic introject, which she had projected as a hallucination.

A special problem in therapeutic technique is posed by patients who believe in what they call "presentiments" or "hunches." Spontaneous cases of precognition, many well-documented, in-

---

*The possibility that Martha's possessive, malevolent mother actually managed to achieve a psychically perceived appearance would not be altogether ruled out by those parapsychologists who believe in the possibility of out-of-body travel.

deed occur.* However, even a therapist who accepts the psi hypothesis must recognize that many people use a belief in hunches to avoid thinking through their decisions realistically, or use it to disguise unconscious neurotic fears.

Among such cases in my own practice is the case of "Dirk," a jovial Irishman† in his early thirties who had consulted me for intermittent depression and for a drinking problem replaced by compulsive teetotalling when a friend died from cirrhosis of the liver. He was a construction engineer, head of an independent consulting firm, married with three children.

Dirk seemed to have an intuitive business sense. When he played "hunches" related to his business or to investments, he came out ahead. Knowing that this way of thinking is fairly common among successful businessmen,[11] I accepted Dirk's beliefs in the validity of his hunches—until the episode of the Big Contract.

This was a long-term contract as consultant for a huge national construction firm which would have pushed Dirk's personal income close to six figures. For years, he had wanted the Big Contract, but Dirk was now anxious. Finally he blurted out that he had a hunch—"strongest I've ever had—" that if he took the offer something terrible would happen.

"What kind of terrible?"

"Well, I might get sick, or something might happen to Betty or one of the kids. Last night I had a really hairy dream—"

The dream was textbook clear. Dirk was seated behind an immense desk in a sumptuous office, surrounded by beautiful secretaries, one of whom brought in a message that the President wished Dirk's advice on an important decision. Just at that mo-

---

*See discussion and references in Chapter 1.

†Although it would be difficult to document this possibility statistically, there is perhaps some truth in the popular notion that certain ethnic groups, such as the Welsh and the Irish, have an especially high incidence of psi-gifted people. Psi, like other variable human traits, may depend in part on genetic factors. Or perhaps there is less anxiety and more receptiveness to psychic experiences among these groups because of cultural tradition; hence, children would be less likely to conceal or repress any natural paranormal ability.

ment King Kong, whom Dirk had seen recently in a television rerun of the old movie, climbed up outside the building and demolished the office, the staff, and Dirk himself with one sweep of his paw. Dirk woke up sweating, with a strong conviction that catastrophe would follow his acceptance of the contract.

Any psychoanalyst, and probably most well-read laymen, could guess the meaning of the dream. With Dirk, who had a classical Oedipus complex, it was unmistakable. Success meant outstripping his father. He had never exceeded his father's maximum income; with the Big Contract, he would draw ahead. And outstripping his father, on an unconscious level, meant annihilation. King Kong, of course, did not represent the aging father of the present day, nor even the actual father of his childhood, but rather the archaic, primitive father of the deep unconscious, perhaps rooted in the Jungian archetype of racial memory.

It was not difficult to help Dirk understand the meaning of the dream, also the meaning of the hunch. They carried the same message: "You are afraid of success." We also discussed the possibility that Dirk actually, on an unconscious level, *intended* to fail in handling the Big Contract, out of his self-destructive fear of becoming too successful, and that the "hunch" expressed this intention. As Dirk began to assimilate these insights, the anxiety dwindled and the Big Contract seemed manageable. If from the beginning I had treated Dirk's hunches as irrational, Dirk would almost certainly have felt that I was condemning him for superstition and credulity. It would then have been far more difficult to help him realize that the King Kong dream and the presentiment of disaster were merely products of unconscious anxiety.

With "Kathy," a dream she believed supernatural proved a turning point. She had sought help primarily for anxieties about her first pregnancy and impending childbirth. As a small girl she had watched her mother undergo a difficult and painful pregnancy, ending with the birth of a handicapped sibling, and she herself was naturally afraid that something might go wrong. With the help of a medical geneticist, who reassured her that neither her mother's difficulties nor her sibling's handicap were hereditary, she went through pregnancy without undue anxiety.

Kathy was especially eager for her mother, who had been ill for some years, to see the baby, her first grandchild. When the prospective grandmother died, a month or so before the baby's birth, Kathy was devastated and went into a moderate post-partum depression, partly because of an unconscious sense of guilt that her own pregnancy and delivery had been so much easier than what she had watched her mother undergo. Kathy and I tried to work this through, but her depression continued for some weeks.

When the baby was nearly two months old, Kathy came into my office looking happy. Last night, she told me, she had dreamed that her mother was standing by the baby's crib, looking down at him and smiling fondly. It was a pleasant dream, and easy to understand as wish-fulfillment. But at breakfast, her husband told her that when he had gone into the baby's room to say good morning, he had distinctly smelled lavender, the grand-mother's perfume.

As Kathy did not wear lavender scent, she leaped to the conclusion that, in spirit, her mother had indeed come to visit the baby, a comforting thought. I did not wish to disturb her with my skepticism, and instead told her truthfully that I was sure her mother would indeed have been proud and fond of her grand-child. In clinical terms, Kathy had been able to arrive at a recon-ciliation with her introjected mother, despite the fact that her pregnancy and childbirth had been more successful than her mother's. As Kathy saw it, the dream was a visit from her mother's spirit, as proved by her husband's perceiving the lavender odor, and certainly it seemed to me both unkind and unnecessary to question her belief.

A psychic element does, however, remain. If Kathy's story is correct—and I had never found her confused about daily events—her husband smelled the lavender, and told her about it, *before* he knew about her dream. This seems to be an instance of telepathic communication between husband and wife. Kathy's dream, perhaps, was meaningful enough to reach her husband telepathically. But my therapeutic task was to reinforce her sense of warm emotional contact with her remembered mother and had nothing to do either with the possibility of spirit visitations or with the psi hypothesis.

In the cases recounted above, the existence of a paranormal element is at best dubious; fear or wishful thinking brought about experiences the patients interpreted as psychic. In comparison, here is an episode in which motivation again seems important, but in which the paranormal component is far more impressive, and which once again exemplifies the irritatingly unpredictable way in which paranormal events seem to take place.

I recently conducted a small workshop of practicing psychotherapists* in which we shared stories about the occurrence of paranormal phenomena in our work. Among the participants were three younger therapists, "Tom," "Alicia," and another young woman, all of whom worked in a nearby psychiatric hospital and who were close friends. Alicia, who impressed me as a realistic person not inclined to flights of fancy, told us a story corroborated by the other two therapists, who had heard of the event on the day of its occurrence.

It was Christmas day. The three young people, with another unmarried man who shared Tom's apartment, had decided to celebrate together. Unfortunately, Alicia had to be on duty in the hospital that morning while the other three prepared dinner in the apartment. Partly as an experiment, and partly to take Alicia's mind off the dreariness of a hospital Christmas, they decided in advance that at ten o'clock Alicia would try to send Tom a telepathic message.

Playfully, Alicia hit upon the phrase "Drink Jack Daniels." She knew that Tom rarely drank anything but wine, but knew also that a bottle of Jack Daniels would be available because his roommate preferred this whiskey.

The ward was quiet. Alicia was in the nurses' station, concentrating on her message. Abruptly, one of the ward patients, a young man, ran out of the day room looking agitated and screamed at her, "Stop calling me Jack Daniels! That isn't my name! Why are you calling me Jack Daniels?" Alicia was perfectly sure that she had not muttered the words aloud, and in any case the day room was down the hall, well out of hearing.

We all wanted more information. The patient, Alicia told us, was overtly psychotic, out of contact, with hallucinations and delusions. Regretfully, she also told us that she had been too surprised to respond therapeutically, but had concentrated on

*At a meeting of the Eastern Regional Chapter of the American Academy of Psychotherapists, June 1980.

calming the patient and getting him back to the day room. As for Tom, he had received no message, either in words or in a sudden impulse to have a Christmas drink of whiskey.

The patient's actual name had no resemblance to Jack Daniels. What had happened seemed beyond coincidence. Telepathically, he had picked up Alicia's attempted telepathic communication to her friend Tom.

Our professional group now had some interesting questions. Each therapist contributed his opinion of what would have been Alicia's wisest therapeutic reaction. All agreed that she should have begun by affirming the patient's real identity, with a statement such as, "Of course your name isn't Jack Daniels. I know who you are. Your name is Joe Smith."

Thereafter came a difference of opinion as to whether or not Alicia should have told the patient that she had actually been thinking of the name Jack Daniels. Some participants thought that this would be unwise since the patient's contact with external reality was already shaky. Wouldn't this procedure, argued the conservatives, actually strengthen his delusional belief that his various fantasies were real?

Others, including myself, thought it might be helpful if Alicia told the patient the true story. Alicia might have asked such questions as "How did you hear me calling you Jack Daniels? If you remember how it sounded, did it seem to come from me in the nurses' station, or was it like a voice inside your head?" Perhaps such a conversation might have strengthened the patient's ability to discriminate between overt, spoken messages and those received by paranormal means.

We also speculated as to why the patient was telepathically sensitive to this particular message. My guess is that the young man was resentful about spending Christmas in a hospital ward, hence was tuned in to a message that was part of the comradeship among the attractive young staff members. Perhaps he had even heard them planning their Christmas party. Unluckily, there was no chance for Alicia to explore the situation; the patient was transferred to another hospital within a few days. The impending transfer, of which he had been informed although he had not appeared to understand the information, may have further sensitized him to a social situation from which he was excluded. If we indulge ourselves in planning an ideal therapeutic approach to the "Jack Daniels" patient, it seems clear that the best focus would be upon his loneliness and his confused sense of identity, rather than on the paranormal aspect of his experience.

Thus far, the patients who have been discussed brought into therapy experiences they regarded as possibly psychic, but which were either isolated episodes (Kathy and the "Jack Daniels" patient) or episodes that centered around a life problem (Miriam, Martha, Dirk). A somewhat different problem in therapeutic management is presented by the patient who believes that he has psychic powers in general, and who may either wish to develop them further or may be afraid of them. This group includes patients for whom the cultivation of paranormal experiences should, for one reason or another, be discouraged.* With Linda, for example, I was actually dictatorial.

Strikingly beautiful, high-strung, energetic Linda handled a difficult job well, while constantly getting into scrapes that often involved marijuana and excessive drinking. Two divorces, two children in custody of former husbands, a succession of boy friends—Linda liked excitement. It was alarming when, early in therapy, Linda announced excitedly that she had heard of a New York witches' coven and intended to join.

Knowing little of covens, I could see them as an outright fraud, a hysterical quest for dubious adventure, or a dangerous flirtation with evil psychic forces. Since Linda herself firmly believed in her own psychic powers, with some impressive precognitive dreams to back her up, I decided to work with the last of these alternatives.

Firmly and indeed truthfully, I told Linda that I was uncertain about the efficacy of black magic but definitely believed in the existence of human evil, and believed also that a deliberate attempt to make use of evil forces could be disastrous.

"If you call up the Devil," I said theatrically, using a metaphor in which I have no literal belief, "The Devil comes. What will he want you to do? And what will happen to *you*?"

---

*The noted medium, Eileen Garret, is quoted as saying to hopeful neophytes who wished to consult her for development of psychic powers, "My dear, until you have more personal stability and emotional maturity, psychic development is not for you."[12, p.12]

Linda had not really thought it through. The adventure had attracted her; there were no conscious fantasies for using the coven for revenge. My challenge frightened her, and she gave up her plan, although reluctantly.*

In a very different context, "Deane" was also faced with a conscious decision of whether or not to try to develop paranormal powers. Deane was an unusually sensitive and gifted fourteen year old, with the appearance and demeanor of nineteen. There was no sign of emotional disturbance. He was lonely and wished he could be closer to his peers, but the loneliness seemed to arise from a superior intelligence that placed a gulf between him and his classmates; I was confident that he would find love and companionship when he grew older.

Deane was not my patient; I knew him only through my intensive weekend marathon groups.† During a coffee break, he told me that he had undergone several out-of-body experiences. They were not dreams, but they occurred at night before he fell asleep. He felt that he was rising from his body, looking down at himself on the bed, then floating out the window and observing the street outside as if from the air. With a mixture of anxiety and pleasure, he permitted himself several such experiences, until he "met" an older man who said to him in a friendly way, "Yunge maan, gai ahaion," which is Yiddish for "Young man, go home!" Deane did not understand the Yiddish expression, but could reproduce it phonetically for his parents, who told him the meaning. Deane perceived the man as wise and benevolent, and decided against any further out-of-body experiences.

I told Deane that little was known about out-of-body experiences; that some intellectually respectable people believed they occurred; and that he might possess psychic gifts, which in time he might decide to develop. But despite his intelligence and maturity, at fourteen he was probably not ready to handle what-

*In three years of treatment, Linda became more oriented toward external reality, and was able to channel her need for excitement into less questionable activities; for instance, she took up karate.

†Ordinarily, I would not have placed a teenage youngster in an adult group, but Deane's parents (both psychotherapists) thought that an adult group would be appropriate, and after meeting Deane I agreed. It worked out well.

ever psychic gifts he might possess. Moreover, his greatest wish was for peer relationships, and psychic experiences might set him even further apart.

Was Deane the victim of a schizophrenic delusion? Had he perhaps invented the experience for the adventure and attention? Neither conjecture fitted with my impression of Deane. Was it the fantasy of an imaginative youngster? Or a true out-of-body experience? With no corroborative evidence, there can be no verdict.

In any case, Deane's encounter with the man who told him to "go home" is of special interest. The accurate use of Yiddish, which Dean did not know consciously, is understandable, since as a child he had heard Yiddish spoken by relatives and might in trance have remembered enough to fantasize the accurately worded message. It is the message's wisdom, not its language, which is striking. Those who hold that our personalities survive as discarnate spirits may think it possible that Deane encountered a friendly spirit, perhaps a relative, who offered good advice. For me, whether Deane's experience be regarded as an out-of-body trip or a vivid fantasy, it is easier to think that he encountered a symbol of his own unconscious wisdom, personified as a friendly older man.

People who believe that they have psychic powers and are interested in developing them typically do not consult psychotherapists. Some of them do not realize that they might profit by psychotherapy, although a certain proportion would probably be seen as disturbed by most clinicians. Others fear, with considerable justification, that they might not be treated with respect. They are more likely to turn toward one of the Eastern religions, to seek training at a "mind control" institute, or to become a disciple of a psychic in private practice. If they are wise or fortunate, they may end up working with a non-sensational, non-commercial group such as the Consciousness Research and Training Project in New York; if less wise and fortunate, they may find themselves with a fraudulent or dangerous cult such as the group that perished at Jonestown.*

---

*Such alternatives are discussed more fully in chapter 9, along with suggestions on separating wheat from chaff.

It does occasionally happen, however, that a therapist is faced with a patient who requires help in handling paranormal experiences or experiences interpreted as paranormal. The case of "Cecilia" is in no way spectacular, but it exemplifies an interesting problem in psychotherapeutic management.

Cecilia began a five-year analysis with me when she was in her middle thirties. Despite her charming social manner and her ability to function, most clinicians might have hesitated between a diagnosis of hysteria and a diagnosis of borderline schizophrenia. A few years before, in a panic reaction to the breakup of her marriage with a domineering, successful older man, she had made several suicide attempts and had spent several months in an excellent mental hospital where she had been spared electroconvulsive treatment and had instead received intensive psychotherapy. She had given up three young children to the custody of her husband in another state, and was now in New York living on alimony and entertaining rather vague plans of becoming a therapist.

One striking symptom was a hypersensitivity to the unexpressed feelings of other people. Attending a party, she seemed to *know* that a woman who seemed poised was actually in utter panic, a man who seemed cheerful was inwardly in deep depression, a married couple who seemed happy were full of mutual hatred.

Surprisingly often, these perceptions were verified. The cheerful woman tried suicide, the happy couple filed for divorce. More important, the feelings Cecilia picked up from other people made her feel so overwhelmed that she tended to avoid many social situations. This was a major problem; it was essential to Cecilia's well-being to develop adequate personal relationships.

Because Cecilia's intuition was so frequently verified by subsequent events among her acquaintances, I did not try to persuade her that she was simply projecting her own inner feelings, an interpretation that might have been true in some instances but would have injured her already shaky self-esteem. Instead, I suggested that she might be sensitive to subliminal cues ignored or missed by most people. Moreover, I explicitly recognized the possibility that she might indeed possess telepathic ability, and informed her of the Duke University card experiments. This information, offered in a matter-of-fact way, helped relieve Cecilia's anxiety since she was wavering between a belief that she was psychic and a fear that she was on the verge of psychosis.

Regardless of the source of Cecilia's perceptions, we agreed that she must find a way to handle them. Resorting to symbolism, I suggested that when she was with other people, to keep their feelings from disturbing her, Cecilia might imagine herself protected by a shield.

Quite correctly, Cecilia rejected this symbol. She wanted to learn how to enjoy companionship more fully, and felt that the symbolic shield would make her feel separated. Therefore, I invented a more mundane symbol, suggesting that Cecilia visualize an ordinary window shade somewhere near the top of her forehead, which could be pulled down at will to shut off disturbing perceptions. Her ears and eyes would still be open so that she could deal with people on the surface, accepting whatever social role they chose to play. Cecilia was amused by this symbol, accepted it, and reported gleefully that it seemed to work and that she was becoming more at ease in conventional social situations. She was eventually able to discard the symbol of the window shade, which had merely been a means of changing her attitude toward her environment, and could allow her hypersensitivity to function only when she chose.

Cecilia succeeded in obtaining professionally acceptable training as a psychoanalyst and was highly successful, especially with very withdrawn or schizophrenic patients whose feelings she seemed to sense intuitively. But she experienced a major personal tragedy from which her gift did not protect her. She had a long, intense love affair with a man considerably younger than herself. He finally left her for a woman young enough to raise a family. Her heartbreak, from which she recovered very slowly, was intensified by the fact that she never had the slightest suspicion that her lover was involved with someone else. Her sensitivity did not work; she did not *want* to know.

If we now consider as a group this small sample of patients who underwent experiences they believed to be paranormal, there seems to be no common denominator in terms of diagnosis, degree of pathology or health, or life circumstances. However, it does seem possible to formulate broad, general principles that may be useful in dealing with reported psi phenomena.

1. *Focus should be upon the patient's feelings* and not upon the validity or invalidity of the psi experience. The therapist should not be primarily interested in testing or disproving the possible paranormal element in whatever is reported by the patient.

A colleague of mine, now a highly respected psychoanalyst, tells me that during her personal analysis, she had told about a dream dealing with a series of bizarre events in her family; it was conventionally handled by the classic method of free association and interpretation. But a week later the bizarre events occurred almost exactly as she had dreamed them, and the therapist spent several sessions trying to persuade her that it was pure coincidence, or that she had actually made unconscious observations enabling her to predict the unlikely occurrences. My friend, untroubled by the possible occult factor in her dream, finally acquiesced. She said, "He seemed so upset that I finally pretended to agree with him." Nobody, I am sure, would consider this a sound therapeutic relationship. The therapist had focused upon convincing his patient that precognition was impossible, rather than upon why the strange events were so important that she had foreseen them in her dream. It seems obvious that this therapeutic approach was motivated by the therapist's own anxiety.

Even when the patient's experience seems clearly delusional or hallucinatory, as in the example of Martha, nothing is to be gained by argument or reassurance. Common sense ("But you *know* that's impossible!") cannot shake a delusion, nor can reassurance ("Don't worry, you're just imagining this!") quell anxiety. If the therapist deals with the emotional meaning of the reported psi experience, it simply becomes a part of the ongoing therapeutic process.

2. *Placing the reported psychic experience in a rational context* is especially important for people who are either afraid of events that seem psychic, or who enjoy the idea that they may possess "supernatural" powers. It is helpful for the therapist to explain, in a matter-of-fact way, that there is considerable scientific evidence supporting the belief in such phenomena as telepathy, which need not be regarded as occult or frightening, although we do not understand the laws which govern the phenomena. My own favorite example is the classical card experiments at Duke because of their scientific precision and because they are without

emotional significance. With this technique, anxiety is usually relieved.

3. *Emphasizing the unreliability of dreams, hunches, and premonitions* is especially important for patients who attach great importance to their possible psychic abilities and are in danger of becoming slaves to their own fantasies. With such people, in addition to pointing out that even confirmed believers in the psi hypothesis do not regard psychic phenomena as always reliable, I may tell a personal anecdote, in retrospect amusing.

One that I have told is of taking a plane for a routine professional engagement and finding myself increasingly anxious as I approached the airport. Seated in the plane, I felt sharp foreboding. Would there be a crash? Would I have a coronary with no physician available? My panic mounted to such heights that I actually picked up my flight bag and headed for the exit just as the doors closed; I was shepherded back to my seat by a solicitous stewardess who assumed this was my maiden flight.

Nothing happened. The flight and the professional meeting were uneventful; nothing that would have needed my attention occurred back home. I am not generally subject to anxiety attacks, and I have flown all over the world without a twinge. Like a conscientious therapist, I tried to scrutinize my feelings for signs of unconscious conflict, but found no clue.* The only meaning of this episode appears to be a confirmation of what we already know about psi—that, despite episodes in which there is good reason to believe that lives were saved and disasters averted by someone's hunch, these hunches cannot wisely be used as a daily guide.

---

*Supportive friends have suggested that perhaps the plane was actually in some mechanical danger that I sensed clairvoyantly and that did not develop; that someone else on the plane was very anxious and I picked it up telepathically; and so on. None of these reassuring conjectures keeps me from feeling rather ridiculous, but the story is at least clinically useful.

*Chapter 6*

# THE CIRCLE OF THE GROUP

## Paranormal Communication?

A distinction has already been made between extrasensory perception, in which we may obtain information by means of telepathy, precognition, or clairvoyance, and transpersonal experience, in which we feel in touch with an aspect of reality that is higher, deeper, and more luminous than the familiar sensory reality around us.

In my own personal and professional life, I have most often seen and experienced both paranormal and transpersonal phenomena in the time-extended therapy groups known colloquially as marathons.* Possibly-paranormal phenomena will be discussed in this chapter, and transpersonal experiences in the next.

In these groups, there is no intention of exploring the possibilities of paranormal communication or of deliberately evoking transpersonal experiences. Individuals attend voluntarily to deal with personal problems or to facilitate personal growth. Since I am in private practice and charge private fees, my marathons generally attract people who can communicate with others and who function adequately in society. There are usually equal numbers of men and women, with a typical age range of 20 to 60.

*Described in Chapter 4 and in my book, reference 2.

Every marathon therapist uses his own variations. I like to meet with ten to sixteen people over a period of three to five days, preferably in a woodland setting, often working with a male co-therapist. The group works for several hours each morning, afternoon, and evening, with a two-hour break during the day for rest and exercise, and ample time for sleep. We remain together all during our work sessions and share our meals. The setting is informal, most people preferring to sit on floor cushions.

There is no preselected program of group exercises. Every marathon takes a different course. Whoever wishes to deal with his present feelings, his past traumas, or his current problems says something like "I want to work," and whatever happens next depends upon the situation. I may use techniques adapted from Gestalt therapy, encounter, bioenergetics or psychodrama, or may simply invite the group to join me in discussion. There is often a release of emotion that has been bound up in unconscious conflict, typically between the healthy (ego-syntonic) part of the personality and a toxic introject. Also, therapeutic episodes frequently offer the participant an opportunity to relive a traumatic episode from his past and give it a happier outcome, as described in the classic phrase "corrective emotional experience."

The marathon group can be seen as a situation of prolonged pressure, in which participants are virtually forced to give up their defenses.[3] This is not my philosophy. I believe that the time-extended format offers group members an opportunity to express and explore their deepest feelings *voluntarily*, and that consequently an atmosphere of deep trust and mutual warmth can emerge. Hostility is expressed and accepted, but is typically worked through in terms of the participant's life experiences, rather than by encouraging hostile interaction within the group. Under these circumstances, participants often relate to one another in ways which seem to go beyond ordinary empathy and intuition, although it is difficult to distinguish between communication that strongly suggests a paranormal element* and communication based on sensitivity and caring that does not necessarily require invocation of the psi hypothesis.

*As in the episode of the "Pig-Mother," described in an earlier chapter.

In successful marathons, the atmosphere is seldom consistently solemn. Sometimes the group experiences the mystical intensity of the transpersonal experience; sometimes it relives with an individual the terrible pain of a childhood trauma; sometimes we are playful and lighthearted. This playfulness is not a defense against intimacy, but an outbreak of joy. The episode of "Joe" is an example of this kind of useful playfulness, and also of the way in which group messages can be conveyed without words, although covert signals certainly cannot be ruled out in this particular incident.

Joe arrived late for a country marathon and explained that he had been delayed by a long argument with his wife over a possible separation and divorce, an argument that had been going on for years.

"Have you tried marriage counseling?"
"Yes, but all we did was argue while the counselor listened. He didn't tell us what to do."
Another group member tried to provide insight.
"Maybe you enjoy the arguments."
Joe felt misunderstood,
"I'm miserable. I can't go on like this and I don't see how she can either."
"So why don't you leave her?"

Joe went on with his compulsively repetitious theme. He'd asked advice everywhere. His parents didn't think they ought to tell him what to do. His friends did not agree; some thought the couple should remain together, others disagreed. One of their grown children wished the marriage to endure, the other advised separation.

It was the characterological defense familiarly described as the "Yes-but syndrome," in which every attempt to help is met with argument.

In desperation, I proposed that the group itself should make the decision as to whether or not Joe should leave his wife. At once they accepted my idea, and we voted.

"In favor of Joe leaving his wife, please raise your hands."

Seven hands went up.

"In favor of Joe's staying, raise your hands."

Seven hands went up. The group numbered fourteen members, in addition to Joe.

"It's a tie," I said seriously. "Joe, you must cast the deciding vote."

The group was breaking into laughter. After a while Joe laughed outright, and spoke up solemnly. "I vote—I vote for continued indecision!"

Now the real issue emerged. Joe did indeed like the indecision.* He (and probably his wife) had been maneuvering for years to get opposite advice from everyone, to go on reaping the dubious benefits of their half-declared warfare. Now we could discuss Joe's marriage on a more realistic basis. We were careful not to take sides in his decision, but Joe left the group determined to work hard for three months to improve his marriage, then end it if his efforts did not work.

Noteworthy is the group's even division on the vote. It was not intended as a bona fide expression of opinion, but as a way to help Joe understand his feelings. Yet I had given no signal, and the group divided evenly without a sign of covert communication. Did they intuitively sense my therapeutic maneuver and join in it? Was the even split pure chance? Was there, possibly, telepathic communication among the members, based on a mutual wish to help Joe? This minor episode, not especially dramatic, is typical of the subtle group network of communication.

The most clear-cut examples of interaction which seem to support the psi hypothesis do not usually come from interaction of the entire group, but from role-playing.

In every type of therapy that aims toward basic personality change, effort is made to understand the influence of key childhood figures, particularly parents, and hopefully to undo the toxic aspects of this influence. Toward this end, psychoanalysts make use principally of transference interpretations; transaction-

---

*As described above, a group member had offered this very insight earlier. Insight, however accurate, is rarely valuable except when fleshed out by an emotional experience.

al analysts attempt to identify and dissolve negative childhood messages or "scripts;" psychodramatists try to reproduce traumatic episodes as precisely as possible; and so on. Well applied, all these techniques can bring about good clinical results, but in my opinion the technique most likely to be effective is the Gestalt empty-chair approach,* used when the patient is trying to work out a conflict, past or present, with a significant person. Seated across from the empty chair, he visualizes the significant Other— usually a parent—and addresses him as if the Other were actually present. The patient then changes chairs, assumes the role of the Other, and the dialogue may continue for some time.

This superb technique enables the patient to ventilate rage, resentment, fear—and sometimes love—that has been repressed and may even have been partly unconscious. Moreover, by externalizing the negative aspects of the parent, the patient loosens the influence of the toxic introject,† and is able to see that some of the negative messages he gives himself come from experiences of the past and are no longer relevant to his life. Best of all, as the patient continues to play the role of the malevolent Other, he may see life-supporting implications in messages earlier perceived as wholly negative, and begin to accept and forgive the Other. This can be done only after fear, hurt, or rage have been fully ventilated, but to the extent that it does happen, the toxic introject loses some of its poison and may even become nourishing.

Usually in marathon groups, I ask the protagonist to choose someone in the group to represent father, mother, or sibling. The protagonist is instructed not to choose on the basis of age, personality, or appearance, but entirely as a "hunch."‡ The

*Another detailed example of this technique is offered in Chapter 2. For further examples, see Perls' *Gestalt Therapy Verbatim.*[5]

†Introject, of course, is rather a Freudian than a Gestalt term, but seems the clearest and most succinct expression.

‡Quite often, although by no means always, I am chosen to role-play the mother, as described in preceeding chapters. At other times, age and appearance are disregarded entirely, but gender nearly always remains constant. For instance, a man might choose a younger man, or someone of a different ethnic background, to role-play his father, but would almost never ask a woman to do so.

chosen role-player, similarly, is given only minimal information about the actual personality of his model, and is told simply
to use an intuitive sense of how the model might have felt and
spoken.

What follows is often breathtaking, not only in its dramatic
intensity, but in its therapeutic consequences for *both* participants, the protagonist and the partner whom he has selected for
role-playing. The protagonist seems to have an uncanny awareness, possibly telepathic, of who is most appropriate as a partner.

Here are three brief anecdotes typical of the empathic or
telepathic interplay that can take place between members of a
marathon:

> At the beginning of a marathon my usual procedure is to go
> around the room and ask each participant to share some-
> thing they want the group to know about them. This breaks
> the psychological ice, since the sharing is entirely voluntary,
> and usually brings to attention someone who is ready to work
> on a personal conflict. In the initial round "Lucie," a woman
> in her mid-thirties, tells us that her problem is an alcoholic
> husband. After some preliminary discussion, she is asked to
> pick a man in the group who can symbolize her husband.
> Unerringly she selects "Rog," who has told the group almost
> nothing about himself; but I know that Rog has a history of
> severe alcoholism although he has been dry for two years. He
> shows none of the physical signs of an alcoholic background,
> and Lucie herself told us later that she "had no idea why I
> picked Rog—it just came to me that he would be right." The
> ensuing dialogue sharpened Lucie's understanding of her
> husband's problem and strengthened Rog's determination
> to remain sober.

> "Samuel" wants someone to role-play his father, and selects
> "Barry." During the role-playing Barry suddenly tells us that
> he has been having acute abdominal pains, which he has
> never suffered before and for which he knows no physical
> reason. Samuel then tells us, for the first time, that his father
> frequently suffered from acute gastroenteritis. Neither Bar-
> ry nor anyone else in the group had any way of knowing this.

"Al" tells the group that he would like to work with a recent nightmare in which he dreamed of being attacked by a vampire. He is requested to role-play the vampire and to select a victim. He selects "Susan," who rather hesitantly accepts the victim role, and they go through a pantomine in which he pretends to attack her, vampire fashion. Only afterward does it emerge that Susan also, alone among the group members, has suffered from vampire nightmares. The upshot is a serious discussion of nightmares and unreasonable fears, in which all group members participate.*

Even more impressive are incidents in which one or both of the protagonists, through their role-playing, become conscious of aspects of an important childhood relationship, or a current relationship, which have hitherto been denied or repressed.

"Derek," a dark, burly man in his mid-thirties, who gives rather an aggressive impression, tells the group that he never seems to live up to his own expectations. He does well in business; why can't he do better? He was runner-up for his club racquetball championship; why didn't he win? It is not that Derek is unduly ambitious, but rather that he feels worthless unless he is on top.

Derek has been working with my co-therapist for about six months, and knows that his problems have to do with his father, a domineering, powerful person who was always critical. Derek was angry and hurt, nor could he ever confront his father, who had died about the time Derek entered college.

"I'd like to give him hell," said Derek gloomily. "The way he always put me down!"

The group was already familiar with the procedure of asking someone to role-play the significant other, and Derek under-

*The technique of asking a group participant to role-play whatever creature he fears in his dreams has a double advantage; if the creature represents an unconsciously feared toxic introject, its origin may be identified as a frightening childhood figure; if the creature represents an unacknowledged hostile part of the self, the projection may be reclaimed and assimilated by the role-playing. One is reminded of Anna Freud's charming story[6] of the child who advised his sister, "If your're afraid of a ghost in the hall, just pretend you're the ghost who's frightening you."

stood that he could make this choice. "You be him," he said, and picked the man who seemed the most unlikely, "Scott," at twenty-five probably the youngest participant, a quiet blonde youth who taught literature in high school. My first suspicion was that perhaps Derek had selected someone whom he could bully as his father once had bullied him, rather than someone who could symbolize his father. However, since I trust the process, I asked the two men to sit in the center of the circle, facing one another.* Having ascertained that Derek called his father Pop and that his father called him Dere, I waited for them to begin as they chose.

To my surprise, Scott went first. His voice was almost thunderous, quite different from his usual mild tone. Even the lineaments of his face seemed different.†

"You little prick!" he yelled. "I looked at your school paper, and guess what. You lost again. Ran for class president and couldn't make it."

Derek was so astonished by Scott's lucky guess, or telepathic hunch, that he broke role. "Jesus, you really got it right," he said. "Only difference, it wasn't class president, it was basketball captain where I lost out."

Scott paid no attention. "What will become of you?" he roared. "A loser, that's what you'll be. A second-rater. Once a loser always a loser."

From notes made after the group, I can reconstruct the dialogue only approximately, though in substance it was confirmed by other participants. It was intensely hostile and dramatic. As Derek's father, Scott continued to rage and taunt him. Finally, Derek got in touch with his own primitive rage and began shouting back. Both men got to their feet, loudly exchanging

---

*Groups tend to arrange themselves in a circle. Whoever is the center of therapeutic attention, an individual or a couple, naturally takes the middle. At first I saw this as simply a way of allowing everyone to watch what went on, but now I suspect that this arrangement facilitates a flow of psychic energy around the group and from the group members toward the central participants.

†Skilled actors, of course, can change their appearance surprisingly by changing the set of their facial muscles. In therapeutic role-playing, this same kind of alteration is unconscious and involuntary.

threats. At moments I had to remind myself that, at some level, both men knew that they were playing roles, for it was hard not to be afraid of an outbreak of physical violence.*

Suddenly the tension broke. Scott burst into tears. "Damn it," he sobbed, "I wanted you to be the best! I was never—never good enough myself, I wanted *you* to be first-rate." He choked, his speech was almost incomprehensible. The anger vanished. In a few moments the men were in each other's arms, hugging each other awkwardly, pounding each other's shoulders in the traditional male gesture of affection.

There was no further reason for role-playing; we talked it out. Scott's father, in fact, had much resembled Derek's. Nothing was good enough, no achievement was sufficient, although the emphasis had been upon scholarly achievement rather than on sports and leadership, and why had he not been class valedictorian, instead of just salutatorian? The men exchanged reminiscences. Derek had reacted by becoming assertive, Scott by becoming rather withdrawn, but their backgrounds were essentially the same.

Here is an excerpt from the letter I received from Derek some months later:

> I always hated my old man. Spent my whole life hating him and wished I had the guts to tell him so before he died. I still think he was a bastard and a stupid bastard but now I can see that in his way he cared. Tell you something crazy, Elizabeth. My wife wants a kid and I've been holding off because I was afraid I'd treat the kid like my old man treated me. Now it's different. I can see things to like about my father, the old

---

*When I began conducting marathons in 1963, release of rage through role-playing or bioenergetics was unfamiliar to many therapists, and primal therapy had not appeared upon the scene. Colleagues voiced anxiety lest group participants be carried away by an opportunity to express rage through shouts and pillow-pounding; they feared there might actually be dangerous fights. Never, in my hundreds of marathons, has this occurred, although it sometimes seemed close. Of course, participants are screened, and I would rely upon clinical considerations in encouraging expressions of rage.

bastard, not many but some, more things to like about myself, and if I have a son I guess I'll like him too. . . .

Scott's letter was different:

> Until the role-playing with Derek, I never knew how much I hated my father. Apparently I put the whole thing underground. I never had men friends, and I've always been detached with my students, especially the fellows. When the hate broke through, a lot of other feelings broke through too. It will take time, maybe a long time, but I feel warmer and much more alive since I faced how much I hated my father. Even now I can't believe I'll ever love him or forgive him. But maybe, maybe, maybe. . . .

How had Derek "known" that mild-mannered Scott was precisely the right person to role-play his father? We might conjecture that Scott, recognizing the similarity between his childhood experience and the experience of Derek, had responded to Derek's description in some subtle way, perhaps through changes in breathing or posture, and that Derek had picked this up subliminally and therefore selected Scott. We might conjecture also that, through intuition, empathy, or telepathy, Derek picked up their similarity. If so, the knowledge was not necessarily conscious. Accumulated data on paranormal processes, both anecdotal and experimental, indicates that paranormal knowledge originates in the unconscious mind and breaks through into consciousness under circumstances as yet not understood, and often disguised by the familiar defense mechanisms of psychoanalytic theory.

None of these possibilities accounts for the accuracy with which Scott hit upon the unexpressed feelings of Derek's father. My personal conjecture, knowing how remarkably rich is our repository of unconscious knowledge, is that Derek was aware on some deep level that despite his father's bullying there was some goodwill far below the surface, and that this awareness had been picked up by Scott telepathically.

Scott's experience seems different. His hatred and resentment of his father had been deeply repressed, probably since early boyhood, and—as does occur when massive repression takes place—many positive feelings had been repressed along with the hatred. Role-playing Derek's father, he came into contact with his hatred of his own father, and as a result, the feeling of being "warmer and much more alive" broke through also.

Occurrences in which two or more participants seem to have an uncanny awareness of one another's deepest needs and feelings are common in marathons, although the possibility of paranormal communication does not always seem so strong as in the episode of Scott and Derek. However, role-playing episodes almost invariably bring out important feelings that could not have been predicted, and that are usually related to the protagonist's choice of someone to play the Other, or, less often, to a suggested choice by another group member.

"Jane" and "Ellen" were participants in a marathon nearing the end of its second day; group members already had a good deal of information about one another. Jane, a college senior, had told us about her deep hurt over her mother's lack of affection. As a child, Jane told us, she could remember few hugs, no bedtime stories, no unexpected treats.

"Food, clothes, and dentist," said Jane bitterly. "That's about all."

At the college dormitory, Jane envied girls whose mothers called every Sunday. She would have liked to spend the summer holiday with her mother (a well-to-do widow) who instead had sent Jane a generous check for a trip to Europe and then gone off elsewhere on her own. Jane was not altogether miserable; she got fair grades and enjoyed dates and friendships, but she felt deprived.

Ellen, also, had told us a good deal about herself. She was a quiet, buxom housewife whose marriage was unsatisfactory. Her husband travelled a great deal, and she believed that he had mistresses. Her life centered around her children, two grade-schoolers and one teenager.

Ellen had a slight, chronic depression for which she was seeing a therapist who referred her to the marathon. Worse, there was constant gnawing anxiety about her life, when, in the natural course of events, her children would leave home. There would be nothing left for her. Worst of all, what if something happened to one of the children?

"Even when they're at school," said Ellen, "I don't feel quite safe. I only feel good when we're all together at home at night and I'm sure they're all right. Thank God, they've got good health— but if one of them got sick—"

Jane broke in. "Oh, Christ, I wish I had a mother like you! When I had flu at school last year, Mom called, told me to get the best doctor possible, and would I call her back when I felt better."

"How about playing it out? Jane, she's your ideal mother. Act it out, how it would happen if you were mother and daughter."*

Eagerly, the women complied. They moved into the center of the circle, reached out, and clasped hands.

> Jane:   Oh, Mom, I love you so much.
> Ellen:  I love you too, Jane.
> Jane:   Mom, do you really care about me?
> Ellen:  You're my whole life.
> Jane:   Can we spend my summer holiday together?
> Ellen:  Of course, my darling. You come home and be with me. We can have lunch together every day. I'll take you shopping. I'll take you to the movies. We'll just be together all the time.

There was now a slight break in this maple sugar dialogue. Jane hesitated, then went on.

> Jane:   Yes, Mom, but sometimes I'd like to do some other thing. Like, I might want to date sometimes, or have lunch with a girl friend.
> Ellen:  Why do you need anyone but me?
> Jane:   Oh, I do need you, but I could need other people too. What will you do when I'm away, Mom? I'd like to play tennis. Maybe I'd even like to get a summer job. We couldn't be together all the time.

*This appropriate suggestion came from a group member. One of the most valuable features of a marathon group is the creativity members develop in dealing with one another's problems, not by interpretation, but by suggesting active procedures.

Ellen's voice now sounded different. It was unsure, yet it was more authentic and less sweet.

Ellen:     Well—maybe I might like some time to myself too.

Jane:     What would you do, Mom?

Ellen:     Well, I guess I never told you this. But actually I'm not so awfully old. I got good grades in school. Sometimes I think maybe I could go back and take a course or two, they call it Adult Education. I always wanted to know more about painting. But you kids— you take up all my time—

Jane (breaking role):     Ellen, how old are your kids, actually?

Ellen (also breaking role):     Nine, ten, and thirteen. Would you believe it, I still tuck them into bed at night? Make sure they're safe, turn out the lights—

Jane (still being herself):     How absolutely disgusting!

Ellen (now angry and glaring, and identifying Jane with her real daughter):     You brat, you don't appreciate me! I've given my whole life up for you—

Jane (also angry):     Who the hell wanted your whole life? You're a blackmailer, that's what you are. You give up everything for your children and so you'd like to have them give up everything for you. Thank God, *my* mother's got some independence!

Ellen (almost screaming):     Your mother's a cold-hearted, selfish bitch! She doesn't give a damn for anybody but herself!

Jane:     At least she had the guts to go off on a trip! Maybe she's looking for a man. I hope she finds one. She's kept her looks up. That's more than I could say of you. You ought to lose ten pounds and get a hairdo. You husband's married to a cow. No wonder he plays around!*

---

*This dialogue, as reported, was seen as substantially accurate when I later showed it to my co-therapist, but this version is condensed; the actual shifts in emotion probably took longer.

The role-playing dialogue broke off at this point. Jane and Ellen stared at one another, astounded at their mutual anger.

Any psychotherapist will understand the mother-daughter dynamics that emerged from the role-playing. Ellen felt that she had no identity except as the mother of her children; if anything went wrong with them, or if they became independent, she would no longer exist as a person. She was unconsciously resentful of her sacrifice, and the resentment, along with suppressed rage at her husband's neglect, was an underlying factor in her slight chronic depression.

Jane, also, had justification for resenting her mother's self-centered detachment, but with Ellen, she was able to realize that there was something positive about her mother's independence. Jane was deprived, but she had been given an implied permission to be autonomous.

This particular episode did not end in a warm, symbolic mother-daughter embrace. The women treated one another with gingerly courtesy during the remaining hours of the marathon. Nevertheless, I believe that the Ellen-Jane encounter allowed Ellen to begin to see that she needed to keep her children dependent for her own personal reasons, and that this need was blocking her growth as a separate human being. As for Jane, although there was no healing of the deep hurt inflicted by her mother's coolness, she could to some extent see the value of having been allowed to make her own choices.* Her letter, received several months after the marathon, makes this clearer:

> Yes, my mother is selfish. Her husband, my father, died when I was about thirteen. She wasn't a very warm mother up to that point, either. She wasn't mean, she always saw about the right clothes and the right dancing school and all that stuff. She was kind of cold, she didn't hug me, but she was way ahead of her time on things like vitamins. But she did take care of herself. She was selfish enough to go off and have fun. As a matter of fact, I had a great time on that trip to

*However dramatic a therapeutic episode may be in a marathon or elsewhere, insight and catharsis need to be followed by cognitive integration for genuine personal growth to occur.

Europe that she gave me the money for. I went to youth
hostels and found that I could walk a long way without
getting tired. . . .

Was there a paranormal element in the way Jane and Ellen
each expressed exactly the underlying feelings that could be most
helpful to the other, without the slightest conscious intention of
*trying* to be helpful? On a conscious level, Jane was seeking from
Ellen the kind of devotion for which she yearned from her
mother. Ellen was seeking for an equally unrealistic adoration
from Jane as representing her children. If they had acted out
these conscious wishes in their role-playing, it would have been
useless to both of them, just as it would have been quite useless to
both Scott and Derek if they had simply gone on expressing
mutual rage instead of allowing a breakthrough of underlying
feelings. Such episodes occur in marathon groups often enough
to warrant the conclusion that, under certain circumstances, people can be sensitive to dimensions of interpersonal experience in
a way that seems to transcend information obtained by ordinary
means. In these two episodes, as in most others here related, we
may hypothesize telepathy or we may prefer the more accepted
but almost equally mysterious terms of intuition and empathy.

Similar incidents have occurred in my small supervisory
groups. These groups consist of younger therapists currently
seeing their first patients; they are self-selected in that all of them
have chosen me as supervisor rather than having been assigned to
me, and they are conducted informally, on a first-name basis,
with coffee. Although we discuss diagnosis and technique, strong
emphasis is placed on unconscious transferential and countertransferential elements. Under these circumstances, especially
when I ask the young therapist to role-play the patient, it frequently emerges that the therapist possesses knowledge of the
patient, or of factors in the therapeutic relationship, which may
be of paramount importance but of which the therapist was not
consciously aware. There often appears to be a paranormal element in the way this information emerges.* For example:

*This method is fully described elsewhere.[7] Nelson has also dealt
with paranormal elements in supervision.[8, 9]

It is a new group, consisting of eight people; since we have met for only three sessions, we as yet know little about one another. "Theresa," who has hardly spoken, wishes to discuss a young woman whom she feels "she simply doesn't understand."

According to custom, we obtain basic information—"How long have you been seeing this patient? How often? What were her reasons for seeking help? What is her background and life situation?"

Somehow or other, Theresa answers these questions without giving us the patient's name.* Now I ask Theresa to role-play her patient, and as I have been requested to role-play the therapist, my first task is to find out what they call one another.

"She doesn't use my name at all," Theresa says, "and come to think of it, I don't use her name either."

"Well, I believe in using names. What is her name?"

"Sarah," replies Theresa—at least, I *hear* the name of Sarah. In accordance with the supervisory group's custom, Theresa leaves the room and reenters as her patient, and since I pick up an impression of shyness, I begin the therapeutic dialogue with a neutral greeting.

"Hello, Sarah, how's it going?"

Theresa starts. At once she breaks from role. She actually drops her handbag in surprise. She says, *"How did you know my daughter's name is Sarah?"*

"I didn't know you *had* a daughter. I heard you say Sarah."

"Sarah's my daughter's name. The patient's name is Laura. I said Laura—I thought I said Laura—what *did* I say?" Understandably confused, Theresa looks around the room for help.

It was, of course, quite possible that Theresa made "a Freudian slip." But everybody in that room, except for myself and one other member, had heard the patient's actual name, "Laura." One other supervisee, a young man who had already given me the impression of being exceptionally intuitive, heard the name

---

*This omission is not unusual among younger therapists, but is nearly always significant. Most often it denotes a wish to remain at a safe therapeutic distance; as will be seen, there were other reasons with Theresa.

"Sarah." None of us, as I quickly ascertained, had known either name previously.

The names, of course, are phonetically similar. But it seemed far beyond coincidence that both the other supervisee and myself had heard the daughter's name and not the patient's. First asking Theresa if she would object to revealing personal material, I requested her to discuss any similarity between her daughter and the patient, any parallels between mother-daughter relationships in the two families, and any way in which her patient evoked her own motherly feelings, whether critical or loving.

What came out was that Theresa identified her patient with her daughter, because as children both had suffered an almost identical minor physical handicap which had been a social disadvantage. She also was identifying herself with Laura's mother, who had tried genuinely but rather ineffectually to help the handicapped little girl. Her feelings, truly unconscious to her, had confused her in the therapeutic relationship. She yearned over her patient's unhappiness instead of dealing with it realistically and constructively. Of all this she had been quite unaware— but it was known to her unconsciously, and my young colleague and myself had apparently picked up *her* knowledge not through a "Freudian slip" in her speech, but through a possibly telepathic Freudian slip in *our hearing.*

Another supervisory procedure suggests the possibility that, by extrasensory or intuitive means, the members of the supervisory group may become aware of information about the patient of which the therapist is not yet conscious, but which has been subliminally perceived. This procedure, group fantasy, is appropriate only after the members of the supervisory group have developed an atmosphere of trust.

The therapist, "Marya," had worked for several years with "Angela," who on the whole has made gratifying progress. Angela functions well in a congenial profession and has a satisfactory marriage.

A major problem remains. At 34, Angela is obsessing painfully over her conflict about having a baby. The family is financially stable, and both partners believe that they are ready for parenthood. But Angela is frightened, and her therapist cannot seem to reach the root of her fears.

As we discuss the case, there seem all too many possibilities for Angela's anxiety. Her mother, although she gave birth to four children, complained endlessly about the appalling sufferings of childbirth; could Angela fear similar suffering on an unconscious level, although consciously she now dismisses her mother's complaints as martyrdom? Her father had been a rejecting parent; was Angela afraid that her husband would change toward her if he became a father? Was it possible that Angela did not really want a baby at all, but simply regarded motherhood as the right thing? And, finally, as the eldest child, Angela had borne responsibility for three younger brothers; could she be shrinking, understandably enough, from the responsibilities of child rearing? All of these possibilities, said Marya, had been explored, yet none of them seemed to resolve the dilemma.

We decided to try a group fantasy. This method, which most supervisory groups enjoy, requires each of us to close our eyes and be receptive to any thoughts or images about the patient. Here is what we fantasied about Angela:

Frank saw a young girl standing in a kitchen, stamping her foot in frustration.

Elinor saw Angela as a child, chained to a tree in her backyard.

Gary saw Angela, again as a child, taking a sailboat out into blue water, then turning back.

I saw a large and very unattractive plastic doll.

Most important, the therapist herself saw Angela thrusting a knife into the neck of the eldest of her young brothers, whom she had experienced as unbearably difficult.

All these images seemed clearly related to Angela's resentment when, only a child herself, she had been required to serve as babysitter. The therapist had explored this resentment. But a key element had been overlooked, probably because Angela had repressed it so deeply. Almost at once, after we had shared our fantasies, Marya exclaimed, "I think that Angela actually wanted to *kill* that kid!"

In our next supervisory meeting, Marya reported that she had tactfully raised this possibility with Angela, who had been able to discuss her murderous feelings, of which she had been only dimly aware. If she had a baby boy, might she not hate him as she had hated the obnoxious brother? Might she not even want to kill the baby? The deadlock was broken; Angela could now make her decision about motherhood without being haunted by murderous feelings from the past.

The telepathic element here is dubious,* but the episode does point up the power of group intuition. Every one of us focused on Angela's sense of frustration as a child. Clearly enough, Marya had suspected all along that her patient feared her own murderous thoughts toward boy babies, but this suspicion had not been available to her until the group fantasy. These group fantasies, of which the Marya-Angela incident is a typical example, very often prove to have a common denominator that offers a clue to the therapist's difficulty, even though the difficulty may not have been specifically identified in the preliminary discussion.

Phenomena which occur in marathons and in supervisory groups suggest a communication within the group on an extrasensory level; the possibility of an extrasensory group network has also been explored in a nonetherapeutic situation.

Research recounted in the book *Conjuring Up Philip*[4, op. cit.] has not received much attention either from scientists or from the press, but it is exceptionally well-documented and raises extraordinary possibilities not only about human communication but about psychokinesis, the direct effect of mind upon inanimate matter.

In 1973, eight members of the Toronto Society of Psychical Research set out to discover whether they could collectively produce a psychic phenomenon. None of them were mediums or professional parapsychologists; they included an industrial engineer, an accountant, and various other well-educated people, none of whom were particularly inclined to believe in ghosts or spirits.

Their procedure was ingenious. They *invented* a ghost, an entirely imaginary English knight of the seventeenth century, a Royalist living in the time of Cromwell, for whom they also

---

*Because of Gary's sailboat fantasy the therapist remembered that Angela had spoken several times of how much she would love to sail, but Marya had not reported this to the supervisory group.

invented an unhappy marriage and a romance with a gypsy girl. They met weekly, sitting in full light around a table, and attempted to induce "Philip" to manifest himself by using meditation and concentration.

Philip, however, gave slight indication of his presence until the group changed its tactics and decided they were trying too hard, or perhaps began to feel that the whole experiment might be absurd. At any rate, they began to relax, enjoyed their evenings together, laughed, and told jokes. They also, as is clear from the book, began to enjoy one another's companionship. Philip, who had been instructed to produce one rap upon the tabletop for yes, two raps for no, began to converse with the group. Through the rapping he answered many questions about his personal life, although he never produced historical information not already known to at least one member of the group, and indeed occasionally produced inaccurate information which corresponded to historical misinformation held by one of the members. He liked jokes, in response to which he sometimes produced a loud, rolling series of raps. The table itself seemed to take on a personality, and would move about in a way that impressed the group not only as lively, but as humorous. And all of this would certainly have been dismissed as science-fantasy, except for the fact that these occurrences were witnessed by many socially respectable and scientifically accredited guests who could detect no trickery; tapes were taken of the rappings; and the Canadian Broadcasting System brought in video equipment which showed that the table would sometimes make startlingly perceptible movements when only two or three pairs of hands were touching it, exerting no observable pressure. (However, the possibility of subtle, unconscious, and nonobservable pressure cannot be entirely excluded, since the table was never seen to move when no one touched it.)

None of the group members believed that they had evoked an actual ghost or disembodied entity. They believed that the Philip phenomena were "a composite manifestation of our own subconscious wishes, feelings, and thoughts." (*Ibid,* p. 85) For anyone who has been willing to examine seriously the evidence for the existence of psychokinesis, however disconcertingly it undermines the centuries-old belief in the complete dichotomy between mind and matter, the Philip manifestations in themselves are significant. They also imply that extrasensory communication not only can take place among group members but may* also be associated with positive therapeutic results.

My strong impression that a therapy group works better if the participants are able to laugh together is supported by the finding of the Philip group that the extrasensory manifestations were definitely associated with an atmosphere of gaiety and friendly camaraderie. Let me stress that the spontaneous gaiety often associated with therapeutic progress is neither defensive facetiousness nor an unwillingness to face the tragic aspects of human existence; it is simply an expression of the ability to share and enjoy life's pleasant aspects.

There was a strong and increasing affection among the group members, which parallels the feelings that develop in a successful marathon, and which seemed to be associated with the strongest of the Philip manifestations. For example, the Philip experimenters report that when a man who was a general favorite would enter the room, the table (under several pairs of hands which were exerting no observable pressure) would not only jiggle but would sometimes actually move a foot or more toward the door as he came in. Group participants perceived this as a psychokinetic expression of their welcoming feelings toward their favorite member.

Although the Philip group was set up as a psychic experiment and there was no intention to use it as therapy, the authors report that during the year of weekly meetings the members experienced an improvement in their social relationships outside the group as well as within it and an increase in a general sense of

*At the annual meeting of the Eastern Regional Association for Humanistic Psychology in April 1979, in collaboration with Dr. Richard Cohen, I conducted with 30 volunteer subjects a workshop in which a simple test of telepathic communication between group members and Dr. Cohen, with adequate experimental precautions, was given at the beginning and again after a two-hour session of encounter games designed to establish a sense of trust and intimacy. Telepathic communication appeared to be facilitated in the predicted direction; the results approached, but did not reach, statistical significance.

well-being. The group, presumably, did serve in several ways as a therapeutic situation, although inadvertently. One may speculate that its therapeutic aspects included a strong mutual interest in a project that was voluntarily undertaken; an enjoyable once-a-week group situation; and a sense of group trust and intimacy. On an even more speculative level, we may wonder whether the development of extrasensory powers, provided that the individual possesses a sufficient degree of ego-strength to keep in touch with commonsense realities, is in itself a stimulant toward personal development.

*Chapter 7*

# TRANSPERSONAL EXPERIENCES IN GROUPS

## Myth, Ritual, and Symbol

*Myth embodies the nearest approach to absolute truth that can be stated in words.*

—A. K. Coomaraswamy

The term "transpersonal" is subjective. It may denote a sense of unity with nature, with the cosmos, or with God.* The simplest understanding of this area of human experience involves a literal interpretation of the words "beyond the personal," that is, beyond the limitations of the individual ego, which may imply mysticism or spirituality, but may also consist simply of a deep awareness of oneself as part of humanity.

In groups, particularly marathon groups, transpersonal experiences are frequent, but seldom include religious overtones. Rather, they consist of a sense of deep communion with other

---

*See the Introduction for the "statement of purpose" from the *Journal of Transpersonal Psychology*. Attempts at formal definitions include feeling "close to a powerful spiritual force that seemed to lift you out of yourself"[1] and "opening up a sense of wider horizons of meaning."[2, p.176]

human beings in terms of the great events we all share—birth, childhood, life struggles, bereavement, and the expectation of death. Here, in the words of marathon participants who sent me letters after the marathon\* are descriptions of feelings that resemble Maslow's peak experiences and can justifiably be called transpersonal:

> "I felt reborn." This particular expression, typical of people who have undergone transpersonal experiences, has been repeated literally dozens of times by marathon participants.

> "It's a year A. M., that means After Marathon, and I still feel that I am living in a better world with nicer people."

> "Life is so beautiful and people are beautiful and I'm beautiful!"

> "All the colors looked brighter. The trees looked greener. I had a glass of beer and nothing ever tasted so good."

> "I looked at all the people on the street and they smiled at me, I guess because I looked so happy and we were all friends."

> "At the end of the group everybody sat in a circle and we all held hands. It was the first time in my life I had ever really felt close to other people. I've always been isolated, inside me, though I'm regarded as a good mixer, and by the way I've never felt completely iso-

\*It is by no means implied that all marathon participants undergo transpersonal experiences, nor is the marathon experience itself always positive. During the five-year period I expressed an interest in written feedback, about half the participants responded. Some of those who failed to reply may have been less enthusiastic about their group experience.

lated since. Anyhow, I suddenly noticed that I was sitting between two certain people, holding their hands, and then I realized that in the beginning these were the two people in the whole group that I didn't like, and now it was really as if I loved them. . . . "

"The principal effect that . . . lasted well into the next day was the overwhelming feeling of inner peace, completeness, and total serenity. I was filled with the fullness of myself. . . . It was enough for me just to sit and just to breathe. Such an experience of pure being may come, I believe, once or twice in a lifetime."

As noted in the preceding chapter, I make no attempt to foster transpersonal experiences. I play no mood music, do not request the group to meditate, and do not discuss transpersonal values, as do some leaders whose stated purpose is to help members achieve a higher level of spiritual consciousness.

When I use group fantasy, the purpose is to help individual members explore personal feelings, and after my initial suggestions about beginning a fantasy,* each participant is free to continue the fantasy wherever his own feelings lead him. This is in contrast to leaders who try to elicit feelings about fundamental human experiences by directing the group in *specific* fantasy explorations of their own birth, or expectations of what death might be like. My belief is that not all group participants are at the point where birth or death fantasies would be useful to them, and

---

*For example, if a group seems stuck on a superficial plane, I may invite everyone to imagine themselves descending a long dark flight of steps into a cave (a common symbol for descent into the unconscious) and then share with the group whatever it is they find. Another example of this kind of free fantasy is described in *Look in the Box,*[3] in which participants are asked to visualize a covered box, then remove the cover and see what is inside. Each participant, of course, sees something different. The contents of the box may then be treated as dreams and often provide excellent therapeutic material.

that a fantasy symbol offered by the leader might be meaningful to some participants, but not to others.*

The group situation in itself is admirably suited to use of the great universal human symbols, myths, and rituals. It is not unusual for a member of the group, or indeed the group as a whole, to select a symbol for the expression of an emotional conflict with little or no guidance. Indeed, the entire marathon may center around a common theme for which an appropriate symbol is chosen by the group itself.

For instance, in one marathon the theme (arising spontaneously in a group of mature people, all of whom functioned well in society) was the difficulty in achieving emotional independence from parents and from early feelings of neediness, fear, or anger. Participants began to share very early memories. It happened to be near Easter time, and on the coffee table was a bowl of alabaster eggs, one of them especially beautiful. The beautiful egg was passed from hand to hand; whoever was working held the egg. This symbolism, I believe, was wholly unconscious, nor did I call attention to it until the closing phase of the group, when it is important to return to nonsymbolic reality.

A symbol bridges the gap between individual feelings and wider realities. Frequently, a group member will use a universal symbol to represent highly personal feelings. This was done by "Lenore," a lovely, mature woman who spoke of her difficulty in parting with a ring set with two diamonds, an engagement ring from her first marriage, which had ended in divorce. Both Lenore and her former husband were now happily remarried; their two teenage daughters were lovely and happy; all was well. Why, then, could Lenore not take the engagement ring from her hand? She did not care for it as an adornment, and her present husband, understandably, rather objected to her wearing it.

*An example is Assagioli's directed fantasy in which group members are asked to slowly visualize the opening of a rose from a green bud to a full-blown flower. There is no discussion; the fantasy in itself is seen as a means toward self-fulfillment.[4] However, several people who participated in groups in which this fantasy was used have told me regretfully that they were unable to commit themselves to the experience, perhaps because they found the fantasy too directive.

Using the familiar Gestalt technique, I asked Lenore to talk to the ring and see what came to mind. Could she keep it on meanwhile? Lenore inquired. Yes, of course.

Gazing at the ring, Lenore spoke about the happier moments of her former marriage, its growing difficulties, her genuine pleasure that her former husband had found another woman. She spoke slowly and dreamily. At last she began to talk about her two daughters—"my flowers, my jewels—" and slowly drew the ring from her finger and put it down.

"You are what's left—you are my daughters. If I take you off, if I give you away or sell you, it will mean leaving them. Letting them go. They're growing up, it's hard to know that soon they'll go away and leave me—"

To Lenore, the ring symbolized the good fruit of her first marriage, her two girls. It would have been an insult to Lenore's intelligence and feeling if we had pointed out that, after all, the ring was just a piece of jewelry.

Finally Lenore's face lit up. She would go to a jeweller, and have each diamond set into a separate ring—one for each daughter! She put the ring into her handbag and did not wear it again.

In groups, the deep emotional experience of one participant usually triggers another. Soon after Lenore's experience with the ring, "Elena" began to speak of her own mother, who had been conscientious and usually kind, but Elena always felt that her mother had been reluctant for her to grow into full womanhood.

In her individual psychotherapy, Elena had been exploring the possibility that she was unconsciously complying with her mother's taboo. At thirty-two, exceptionally attractive, with a history of several serious love affairs, she still had never married. Elena's mother had never liked the men she dated; the only approved suitor had been physically unappealing. And then Elena remembered the lipstick.

When she was eleven, Elena had explored her mother's dressing table. There was a lipstick! Like any normal eleven-year-old, Elena tried it on, admired herself in the mirror, then put it back.

Later, there was a family scene. Elena's mother stormed downstairs furiously. "You stole my lipstick!" The lipstick had rolled off the dressing table and was gone.

The rest of the episode was blurred in Elena's memory. The lipstick finally was found where it had rolled under the dressing table. But how did Elena's mother know that Elena was guilty, and why was Elena's mother so furious? The little girl felt like a criminal.

There was a chorus of support from the group. "Your mother didn't want you to be pretty." "Your mother didn't want you to grow up." "I wish *my* daughter would wear lipstick—she's got that awful scrubbed-face look." "Your mother didn't want another woman in the family."

The support comforted Elena, but the interpretations meant little. It was Lenore who found the perfect symbolism. She rummaged in her handbag and drew out three lipsticks linked together by an ingenious manufacturer who was marketing them as a unit, different colors for different costumes.

"Which color do you want?" asked Lenore. Seriously Elena tried each color, made her choice, and accepted the preferred lipstick as a gift. No interpretation was necessary for Lenore, after the deeply symbolic decision in which she had found a way to express love for her daughters while at the same time accepting them as independent people. Her inner conflict was healed, and as Elena's mother surrogate she was able to support the younger woman in her enjoyment of independent sexuality through the symbolic lipstick.*

Another deeply moving episode in which, as with Lenore and Elena, the protagonists developed their own symbolic scenario with almost no direction from the leader involved "Lisa." She was a stately Black woman in middle years, a successful educator, who for the first day of the marathon said almost nothing.

Lisa had been persuaded to enter the marathon by her friend "Elaine," who had attended previous groups. Only with Elaine's help was Lisa able to begin talking; she was clearly not a timid woman, but she was reserved and found it difficult to ask for help.

---

*The symbol of the lipstick could justifiably be criticized by feminists to whom it might represent submissive sexual enticement. But a symbol is personal. To Lenore and Elena, it meant sexual independence and maturity.

Her problem, Lisa told us, was that she must complete work on her doctoral degree within six months. There was little to do, only the oral defense of her thesis. Three years ago she had been almost at her goal, then she had been unable to meet with her advisory committee, and now the administration was insisting that she complete her work or lose her credits, credits that represented an enormous investment of time, energy, and money.

With the group, I assumed that Lisa might suffer from the familiar fear-of-success syndrome, and suggested that we form a "committee" before which Lisa might appear and act out her fears. But there was no vitality in the scenario. This was clearly not the right approach.

Again Elaine supported her friend. "Tell them what happened just before the hearing." And then we heard of Lisa's tragedy. Just a week before her dissertation hearing, her son had died. She had cancelled the hearing, and had never been able to request another.

Richie, sixteen years old. He'd been away for his first year at college (he was precocious and a fine athlete) when he had been attacked by a rare neurological virus, which had taken his life within four days. Lisa told us about it in a level voice: the unexpected phone call from the college, her trip to see him in the hospital, his death four days later.

"That's all," said Lisa.

After six years, Lisa was still frozen in her grief. She had not said farewell, therefore the mourning was not over.

The group asked gentle questions. Did Lisa regret that it had taken her a day to recognize the seriousness of Richie's illness and make the trip to visit him? No, she had trusted medical information that his condition (this was the first day of the infection) was not dangerous. Did she feel that better medical care might have saved him? No, he'd had the best.

But there was one thing she regretted. She was certain that her son had realized she loved him. But she had not *told* him so often enough. She was not talkative, not demonstrative. She wished that she had more often told Richie how she cared for him.

"Is there anyone in the room, Lisa, who might represent Richie for you?"

"Yes. Him." Lisa nodded toward "Jon," the youngest man in the room. These choices are sometimes made in terms of an externally appropriate factor, such as age, but (as was shown in the preceeding chapter) the choice is also nearly always appropriate on a deeper level, as it proved with Jon.

The young man and the stately older woman sat on the floor together, facing one another in the center of the circle. It was apparent what depth of feeling lay behind Lisa's self-control. They spoke in simple terms.

"I love you, Richie."
"I know that, Mom."
"I wish I'd told you so more often."
"Oh, Mom, I knew it."

After a moment they embraced. But there was something incomplete. Lisa seemed to be clinging to her "son," reluctant to let go although she was still restrained. She had neither relinquished him nor expressed her deep sorrow. It was my hope that Jon, role-playing Richie, would say something like, "Well, good-bye, Mom, I've got to go now," and express the finality of their parting by leaving the room. But Jon's intuition was better. He remained.

"Richie, I just don't want to let you go." Somehow or other— without suggestions from myself, my co-therapist, or any group members—they were on their feet together. She stood behind him, arms clasped loosely around his neck and chest, and they began to walk around the room, a solemn procession of two, she clinging to him and yet somehow distant. They paced together in unison. They went outside (it was an outdoor setting, with doors and picture windows looking out on greenery) and through the windows we could see them, gravely and silently pacing the lawn.

"There's something spooky," said a member of the group. The scene could have been comical or sentimental. It was neither. It was archaic, archetypal, almost fearsome. It was every bereaved mother clinging to every lost son. They paced slowly for an endless time—perhaps ten minutes by the clock—and finally came back into the room.

"I can let go of him now," said Lisa. She let go. She sat down. She was crying quietly. Her friend Elaine sat down close to her.

Jon, with the extraordinary tact I have again and again marvelled at in marathon participants, made no attempt to sit near her, but took his place silently in the circle. The group was quiet for a long time, then sensed that Lisa did not wish to discuss what had happened, and moved on to business with other members.

Lisa, although she was attentive, said little that day. In the evening, she did not join in wine and conversation, but went to her room. A day later, she told us that she had not finished.

"I said good-bye to Richie, but I haven't buried him."

Again there was no need for guidance. Jon came over and lay down in the center of the circle.

"Cover his face," she said. Never have I heard such intense, controlled grief in a voice.

Someone found a scarf and, seriously and gently, offered it to Lisa. She placed it over Jon's face. He lay motionless. Then Lisa cried at last. Tempestuous weeping was not in her nature, but at last she was releasing her grief.

Conscientiously, Jon remained with the scarf over his face until we signalled him to rise. He looked shaken. Nobody can role-play such a scene with sincerity and not feel shaken afterward. He did not wish to discuss what the episode had meant to him, but affirmed his aliveness indirectly, discussing whether to change some of his professional plans and whether to become committed to the girl whom he was dating.

In the closing phase of the marathon, when we came up from the depths and down from the heights and back to the levels of common sense reality, my co-therapist* reminded me that the spell had never been undone. In the simplest way that I could, I attempted to undo it. I asked Jon and Lisa to sit once more facing each other on the floor and gave them lines.

"I'm not your mother and I never was." Lisa repeated it after me.
"I'm not your son and I never was." Jon repeated it.

They repeated their lines several times, gazing steadily at one another. Then someone in the group suggested a final, closing line.

*Dr. Stanley Meyers

"But we can like each other anyway." They said it simultaneously, then embraced. Jon, whose relationship with his actual mother had been somewhat disturbed, said "How I would have liked you for a mother!"

Still embracing him, Lisa looked up and laughed—a clear, spontaneous giggle, in which there emerged a natural joyousness that had been buried underneath her grief.

"Wouldn't everybody be surprised!" she said. It was the first time anyone had remembered their difference in color, so completely had they represented the archetypal mother and son.*

> "I got a lot out of this marathon," said Jon, toward the end. "A lot of new things."
> "And a lovely new Black mother."
> "That's a first too," said Jon. As far as I know, neither Jon nor Lisa had the faintest interest in seeing one another again.
> "I got what I came for," Lisa said. "I said good-bye to Richie."

The Lisa-Richie episode may be called transpersonal because their love for one another, although it involved role-playing, transcended the limits of their individual egos, and also because Lisa seemed to become the incarnation of every bereaved mother. This, I think, is why we all watched in such intense, awed silence as they solemnly paced together, she clasping him, along the lawn outside the picture window.

Although every therapeutic procedure is unique, this episode is among many examples of an approach I have found to be

*A few of my humanistic friends have sometimes wondered why, in a marathon attended by some Black participants, I do not begin by focusing on possible racial tensions, to "clear the air" before the therapeutic work begins. Of course, I would do so if I felt tension in the group about this issue, but often, as in this marathon, color is quite irrelevant. Perhaps there was a special poignancy in the way Jon and Lisa transcended color.

extraordinarily effective—the fantasized acting out of communication with the dead.*

To some Western minds this fantasy, even as a therapeutic procedure, may seem bizarre. Yet in innumerable cultures, ranging from pre-Westernized Japan to the various tribes of American Indians, not only have ancestors been worshipped, but it has been believed that communication with the dead occurs in dreams, visions, and trances. Ancestor worship is seen not only as a way of honoring the dead, but as a way of avoiding their ill will, thus expressing the ambivalence parents and children seem to feel toward one another, in varying degrees, in all cultures. If we accept the Jungian concept of the collective unconscious, a repository of the entire history of the human race, we can understand the readiness with which even a tough-minded and sophisticated group member may enter into this fantasy.

My procedure is simple, although it varies according to the needs of the individual participant.† I simply ask the protagonist to suspend whatever religious or scientific beliefs he possesses, or does not possess, about the possibility of survival after death, and imagine that the person for whom he is still mourning can listen and answer "either from heaven, if you happen to believe in heaven, or in some kind of science fiction sixth dimension, if it's easier for you to think that way." As yet, no one has found it difficult to accept this suggestion, nor has it ever led to sterile arguments about the possibility of survival.

---

*Since describing this procedure in a publication,[5] I have received several letters from colleagues telling me that they have also found it dramatically effective. For instance, an experienced psychiatrist wrote, that she had struggled vainly for a year to bring a patient out of a depression that followed the death of her husband; it was finally resolved only after several imaginary dialogues with him.

†When a patient must deal with the memory of a deceased person, the therapist can choose his technique on the basis of individual need. My general feeling is that the empty-chair dialogue technique, described in the preceding chapter, is preferable if the patient is attacking himself via a critical or angry introject. Communication with the dead is preferable if the patient wishes to express love, seek forgiveness, or find reconciliation.

There are several methods by which the fantasy may be carried out. As with Lisa, someone in the group may be chosen to represent the deceased person. Further examples indicate various other procedures.

"Joanna," a successful business woman with a good marriage, tells the group about a telephone talk with her mother many years ago. The quarrel had been sharp, since both women were hot-tempered, although their relationship was generally good. Before a reconciliation could occur, Joanna's mother had

---

Clinical questions are also important; if the patient's sense of reality is at all fragile, I would choose the empty-chair dialogue technique in preference to communication with the dead, because the former approach allows the patient to externalize his internal conflicts and gain distance from them, while the latter approach might indeed foster delusional tendencies if they are already present.

Occasionally, I have been asked whether, in working with outright delusional psychotics, who are usually hospitalized, I would use the empty-chair approach. Consider, for example, a hospitalized patient diagnosed as schizophrenic who conducts continual silent dialogues with the spirit of a dead grandfather. The question is, "But if my patient is already delusional, won't it intensify his delusions if I ask him to imagine the 'grandfather' is actually sitting in the empty chair?"

My own experience with hospitalized psychotics is more limited than my experience with socially-functioning patients, but many Gestalt therapists have found the empty-chair technique useful with seriously disturbed patients. This is justifiable theoretically. We all know that it is simply not possible to convince a delusional patient that his hallucinations are unreal by confronting him with common sense arguments.

The "grandfather" already is all too real to the patient, who hears his voice internally and projects it as an auditory hallucination. If he is asked to imagine the grandfather actually sitting in the empty chair, instead of residing just within his mind, some distance is obtained and the grasp of the introject may be slightly loosened. If, then, he sits in the chair and speaks for his grandfather aloud, instead of projecting his internal voice silently, he is in a somewhat better position to evaluate the grandfather's statements. He may even gradually gain the insight that he has not really been speaking to his grandfather's spirit, but to an aspect of himself.

died unexpectedly. Joanna did not often think about this tragic episode, but experienced great pain whenever she did recall it.

Joanna was asked if she ever visited her mother's grave, and replied that for a time she had visited it each year, and had always gone away feeling bad. After a while she stopped visiting.

"Let's do it differently, here and now." Joanna agreed, and in the center of the room I set up a mock grave, consisting simply of pillows arranged in a line to suggest a coffin.* I asked Joanna to pretend that she was visiting her mother's grave and speak to her as she had done before.

Very seriously, Joanna took a few flowers from a nearby vase, approached the grave and knelt, placing the flowers gently on the floor. "Mother," she said, "I'm sorry. I'm so sorry you died when we were mad!"

Now came what I had planned as the whole point of the enactment. Very softly I suggested, "Now you be your mother, Joanna. Be her spirit. Lie down in the grave and answer the way she would answer Joanna."

Joanna lay down on the pillows, closing her eyes. After a while she said, without the slightest theatrical quality in her voice, "Is that my daughter? Hello, Joanna. My goodness, are you still remembering that old fight? That's silly of you, hon. Forget it."

Joanna remained rapt for a few minutes longer. Then she sat up and began to laugh. "And then she'd say, How are the kids? Are you still feeding them those crazy vitamins? She thought I was nuts, the way I gave them vitamins. Alphabet soup, she called it. A, B, C, D . . ."

The group, which had shared Joanna's tense, rapt quality, now began to laugh with her. Joanna got up and gave the pillow a kiss. "Good-bye, Mom," she said. During the remainder of the marathon Joanna spoke several times, in amazement, about her feeling of delight and relief. Later, she wrote:

*I am aware that this use of improvised stage props may seem absurd on the printed page, as may several of the episodes in this chapter. However, they are received by the group with a deep seriousness I have seldom seen other than in a religious ceremony. One marathon correspondent actually described it as "the sacred hush."

I guess you know, Elizabeth, I don't believe in mysticism, and frankly, sometimes I think you're pretty far out. I don't think I communicated with my mother's spirit or any of that you-know-what. But actually, I realized for the first time that she wouldn't have held our fight against me. We had lots of fights and we always made up. In another day she'd have called me or else I'd have called her. I've completely stopped feeling bad about the whole thing and now I don't think about her much, but when I think about her I feel good.

Why did Joanna succeed in making contact with the loving, healthy aspects of her relationship with her mother in the group, when she had failed in the visits to her mother's actual grave? Perhaps this was partly because the atmosphere of a cemetery carries a sense of gloom, while the warmth and goodwill of the group made it easier for Joanna to remember what her mother really had been like—obviously a good-hearted, humorous, hot-tempered woman, much like Joanna herself. Certainly, I do not believe that the spirit of Joanna's mother actually "possessed" her when Joanna assumed her mother's role, although the identification in role-playing was useful in helping Joanna understand that, beyond question, her mother would have easily gotten over their quarrel.

Another example, where a different technique was used:

"Tom," in his early thirties, had lost his young wife under tragic circumstances when they had been married for only a year. Now he wished to remarry, but (although he knew consciously that this was unrealistic) he had an uneasy feeling that this would somehow be unfair to his first wife. It was suggested that he select a woman from the group to represent his first wife; he chose "Felicia," and held a conversation with her in which she told him that she would be delighted if he could remarry and be happy. After their conversation, Tom told us that although he could be imagining it, it seemed to him that Felicia's tone and mannerisms were uncannily like those of his first wife, and he could now believe that she would really have wished him to marry again.

Having seen many similar instances in which roles of unknown persons are played with startling accuracy, I think it possible that Felicia picked up telepathically from Tom some of the mannerisms and phrases of his first wife. Moreover, from Tom's description she did seem the type of person who would have wanted him to be happy despite her death. We must, of course, also consider the possibility that Tom's wishes made him imagine a resemblance between Felicia and his late wife. At any rate, Felicia was able to put Tom in touch with the well-wishing aspect of his wife and thereby to diminish his guilt feelings.

The dissolution of guilt over the death of a beloved is one of the most useful functions of fantasy communication with the dead. "Arlene," in her middle twenties, was haunted by guilt over the death of her sister "Jean," who had been killed in an automobile accident while she was attending school away from home. Jean had been uncertain as to whether she wished to remain at home and attend the local university, or go away to college, and Arlene, who had greatly enjoyed her own college life, persuaded her sister to go away. Arlene's self-reproaches, on a conscious level, were based on the feeling that if she had not convinced her sister to attend college out of town, the accident would never have occurred and Jean would still be alive.*

Since her sister had been cremated, I could not ask Arlene to make an imaginary visit to the grave, and instead asked whether she could imagine that her sister's spirit might visit her in a dream. She answered yes, she could imagine it quite easily.

My setup for this scenario was that I myself (with Arlene's permission) pretended to be Arlene, asleep, and that the real Arlene was to play the role of her sister's spirit. Here is the ensuing dialogue:

> Myself (as Arlene):    Jean, Jean, is that you? Have you come to see me in a dream?
> Arlene (as Jean):    Yes, Leenie, I've come to see you. How are you?
> Myself (as Arlene):    Oh, Jean, I'm so unhappy.
> Arlene (as Jean):    Why, what's the matter?
> Myself (as Arlene):    I'm unhappy about your death. I miss you, and besides, I feel I killed you. It was my fault you were in that accident.

*This material is adapted from one of my previous publications.[5]

Arlene (as Jean):    Oh, that's ridiculous. How could it have been your fault?

Myself (as Arlene):    I talked you into going away to college.

Arlene (as Jean):    You thought I'd have more fun that way than staying home with Mom and Dad.

Myself (as Arlene):    But maybe if you hadn't gone away you'd still be alive. I feel as if I killed you. Can you forgive me?

Arlene (as Jean, beginning to cry):    Oh, Leenie, you didn't kill me. It was just an accident. There isn't anything to forgive. There was this other crazy driver, you know that.

Myself (as Arlene):    Do you want me to be happy, Jean? When we were kids, we were always nice to each other, even if we did have fights sometimes. You were such a cute kid, I was so proud of you! You were such a nice kid. I guess you'd want me to be happy, huh?

Arlene (as Jean, crying):    Oh, please be happy. Leenie! Don't brood about me any more. Go on, go out and have fun.

Arlene cried for a while and then went back to her place in the circle, looking radiant despite her weeping. Weeks later came her feedback letter saying she was "feeling fine."

In this particular episode, I had volunteered to play the role of Arlene because I had a clear idea of how I hoped the dialogue would go and wished to steer it that way. My strategem was selected only after I had acquired some knowledge of the sisterly relationship, which had been essentially positive, with Arlene taking a proud and protective attitude toward the younger girl. It was also essential to acknowledge in the dialogue that there had been some sisterly fights, the memory of which presumably intensified Arlene's guilt.

It would also have been possible, obviously, to ask Arlene to pick out another group member to impersonate Jean, and to play herself. It is quite certain that whoever Arlene selected would have played Jean as loving and forgiving. But by asking Arlene herself to identify with her sister, it seemed to me that she would become more deeply convinced that Jean could not possibly hold Arlene responsible for her death.

We have considered four episodes* in which the process of mourning was completed, or at least accelerated, through fantasy communication with the dead. Why is this approach so effective? What happened in these episodes?

In each case, a sense of guilt prolonged the feelings of bereavement. Psychoanalytically, we may think in terms of Freud's classical concept in *Mourning and Melancholia*. The bereaved person attempts to retain the lost love object through introjection, then reproaches himself as he has unconsciously been reproaching the beloved for deserting him by dying. With Lisa, Joanna, and Arlene there were additional reasons (although the reasons were not rationally justifiable) for a sense of guilt preventing them from completing the mourning process. When the introject was once again projected outward through role-playing, it became possible for the bereaved individuals to see the lost love object more realistically; thus Lisa could believe that Richie knew she loved him, Joanna could see that her mother would not hold the telephone quarrel against her, Arlene could recognize that her sister would not consider her responsible for the car accident, and Tom could realize that his deceased wife would be happy if he remarried.

This Freudian conceptualization, however, does not explain the intense feelings evoked by these scenarios, both in the central characters and in the group, a sense of mystery and awe, describable in poetic rather than in psychological terms, although an orthodox Freudian might identify it with the "oceanic feeling" that goes back to the baby's sense of blissful union with the mother.

This awesome and uncanny feeling can perhaps be understood if we again think in terms of Jung's collective unconscious, which certainly must include the age-old, world-wide belief in the possibility of true communication with the dead. On some deep level, the protagonists and the group felt that there was contact with the spirits of the dead, not in a literal but in a mythic sense, in the sense of right-brain activity, of the "Clairvoyant Reality"

*Taken from four different marathons.

LeShan describes[6] and which in various terms has been described as the mystical experience, perhaps best summarized and evaluated by William James.[7]

This by no means implies that the "ghosts" or spirits of the deceased persons return from death in a personal visit to the bereaved, in the naive sense that a fake medium produces "ectoplasm" or spirit rappings or a voice from a trumpet. It does, however, perhaps suggest an idea that can be neither proved nor disproved—that under these special circumstances there was contact with the loving and well-wishing aspects of the beloved person, which (according to the mystical way of thinking, difficult and even embarrassing as the concept is to most of our Western minds) has now become part of the Cosmos, the All, the Infinite, God.

This experience, I believe, is made possible by the atmosphere of deep warmth and goodwill created when a marathon goes well. In psychoanalytic terms, the group itself provides a benevolent introject to replace the reproachful introject that had been haunting our four protagonists. In metaphysical terms, if we accept the possibility that these four people underwent transcendental experiences, it seems to me that this could happen because in the group it was *safe* to accept such an experience. The group is sane; it is realistic; it is supportive; it provides an anchor that makes it safe to voyage into the depths and heights of the transpersonal. At the same time, the group accepts fantasized communication with the dead as an *emotional* reality. I have never known a marathon participant to be frightened by these transpersonal scenarios, or to be facetious about them, or to have any difficulty in returning to what LeShan terms the Sensory Reality.* Nor has anyone with whom I have used this technique ever reported any negative aftereffects; the spirits of the departed did not create any psychotic "manifestations," but instead, the bereaved individuals tended to think much less about the loss and to accept the bereavement as part of the past.

Regardless of whether one accepts the hypothesis of "alter-

*As noted in Footnote 9, it should be reiterated that I would not use this particular approach with anyone whose perception of reality, in the common sense meaning of the term, was fragile.

nate realities" (or, more accurately, alternate ways of perceiving a Reality beyond our intellectual and sensory ability), it is clinically certain that there is great therapeutic power in the myths that have been universal to mankind, even though they have been partially rejected by industrial Western civilization. The Oedipus legend, for example, long preceded Freud's formulation of the sexual attraction which, consciously or unconsciously, exists between parents and children. In contemporary thinking, many distinguished psychotherapists, beginning with Jung and later represented by such clinicians as Assagioli,[4] Grof,[8] and Perry,[9] have made brilliant therapeutic use of the relationship between individual experience and the great human myths. When I am able to approach an individual problem presented by a marathon participant in a way that taps the energies bound up in our unconscious contact with these myths, the therapeutic results can be spectacular.

"Lloyd" and "Julie" were attending a five-day country marathon. They had been lovers for some years and shared a home although they were not legally married, ostensibly because one of them had difficulty in finalizing a divorce from a former spouse. They came from another part of the country and I knew little about them, but it was soon possible to see that they were deeply in love and that there was also great tension between them.

Both were in their late thirties. Both were dynamic, attractive, successful, and self-assertive. Lloyd especially carried self-assertiveness to a point that could have been described as macho; for example, one morning he terrified us all by swimming alone across and back a nearby mountain lake, half a mile each way.

After three days during which Lloyd had said little that was personal, Julie approached me privately. She and Lloyd had a problem. It was embarrassing for Lloyd to speak about it. Should she bring it to the attention of the group, or ask him to talk about it?

The problem was Lloyd's impotence. He had been impotent with her from the beginning. Since he had also been impotent with his wife, Julie did not think it was a function of their relationship. Medical examinations showed nothing physically wrong. She loved him, Julie said, and for her the sexual frustration was far more bearable than her awareness of how frustrated *he* must feel.

It seemed to me that Lloyd, with his macho quality, would find it intolerable to discuss this problem in the group. I advised Julie to say nothing and to give him no advice. I had not the faintest notion of what to do.

But the next day in the group I found it possible to say to Lloyd, "You know, we really don't know much about you. What kind of family did you have, for instance?" This was the blandest question I could find, but to my great relief Lloyd poured out the whole story of his childhood.

Lloyd's father had been a powerful, domineering man, who actually required his children to address him as "Sir." An uncle had been equally overpowering. Completing the picture, Lloyd had an older brother who—doubtless visiting upon Lloyd the treatment his father visited upon him—had constantly snubbed Lloyd, teased him, and sometimes humiliated him.

It was easy to understand why Lloyd had developed his macho quality. His choice, he must have felt, was to be exaggeratedly masculine or to be a total cipher.

It was also easy to understand why Lloyd had developed impotence. Unconsciously, he must have believed that if he proved himself to be a man, he would be punished by the powerful older males who had surrounded him in childhood. It was impossible not to think in classical psychoanalytic terms: Lloyd must feel castrated.

Usually I avoid psychoanalytic jargon, but *castrated* seemed the only word to use. A member of the group came to my rescue.

"My God, Lloyd," he said, "those fellows really cut your balls off!"

In retrospect, the therapeutic stratagem that occurred to me then seems so daring that it surprises me that, having had less awareness then of the value of using mythic material in therapy than I have now, I possessed the courage to suggest it. Indeed, for years I avoided reporting this episode to colleagues, partly because of the difficulty in describing the extreme solemnity of a scenario that might seem farcical, and partly because I feared that this approach might be picked up and turned into a routine "encounter game."

I said, as nearly as I can remember, "I agree. You must have felt castrated. How about getting even? Let's have a ceremony."

A marathon group usually develops an intuitive sense of the theatrical. Somehow or other, the men arranged themselves in a semicircle. A young woman, walking like a priestess, went into the kitchen and returned with a dull table knife.* She gave it to Lloyd. Two pillows were arranged in such a way as to suggest an altar, before which Lloyd knelt, knife in hand.

The men were terrified. The women were totally silent. The primitive, atavistic fear of castration was alive in the room.

Finally, my co-therapist, a vigorous younger man, took responsibility. He advanced and knelt before the pillow altar, arms behind him. Lloyd, without actually touching his "victim" at all, slashed the air in front of his crotch, then slowly picked up an imaginary set of testicles, went to the window, and tossed them out. My co-therapist, looking pale, returned to his place.

After several long minutes another man approached the pillow altar and the same scene was repeated. Then another, then another. A few of the men chose to remain seated, and nobody tried to persuade them to the imagined sacrifice. All the "victims" remained clothed, none were exposed, none were actually touched. The whole scene was conducted in pantomine. And each time, after the dull knife slashed the air, Lloyd once more rose and slowly tossed the imagined genitalia out the window.

We never discussed this scene directly. The powerful symbol of castration had been used to express loss of manly confidence, but it remained a symbol. We had enacted one of the great primitive myths, in such a way as to partially drain it of its terror. After the ceremony, there was a long silence. Then, spontaneously, the group broke for a swim.

*Only in retrospect does it occur to me that there were sound reasons for my nodding to a young and attractive woman to perform this part of the rite, rather than getting the knife myself. In transference terms, I was a mother figure and did not wish to become a castrating agent for the other men in the group. In mythic terms, because of my age and my leadership, I was the senior witch. The implicit permission for Lloyd to be sexual and powerful had to come not only from me, but from a pretty young woman.

That evening and for part of the next day, the men talked freely about the difficulties of manhood; all of them sometimes felt inadequate. Several women remarked thoughtfully that they could better understand that being a man was not necessarily easy. Actual physical castration, as a primitive symbol of the loss of manhood, was never mentioned. Nor did Lloyd mention his potency problem. The group ended two days later without a direct word about Lloyd's problem.

The following weekend I had an enraptured phone call from Julie. She and Lloyd had spent some days, as planned, at a seaside resort. Lloyd had regained his potency. They were, Julie said, deliriously happy.

In psychoanalytic terms, this episode may be conceptualized as an experience in which Lloyd released the unconscious fear of castration that had rendered him impotent by symbolically taking the position of the dominant male in the group, without retaliation from either of his two symbolic parent figures (my co-therapist and myself) or from his siblings (the other group members). He also symbolically castrated his father (my co-therapist) and received the permission of his mother to be sexual (by my intuitive choice of a pretty young woman to bring him the dull table knife). Yet I do not believe that the efficacy of this scenario can be explained entirely in terms of Lloyd's repressed unconscious fear of castration. It was an enactment of a mythic ritual, a primitive ceremony, which tapped the deep levels of the collective unconscious; it was a transpersonal experience.

Technically speaking, after a symbolic episode of such intensity, I would usually take some time in the group for cognitive integration of the experience. In this instance, I was honor bound to secrecy because Lloyd had never revealed his problem. As I had no further contact with Lloyd and Julie, I do not know their future history, except that I received a happy and appreciative Christmas card. It was my hope that Lloyd, and perhaps Julie also, would seek individual treatment to deal on a conscious and rational level with what happened in the marathon. It cannot be assumed that a symbolic experience, however intense and meaningful, could completely and permanently correct a long-standing symptom without arousing various related anxieties.

The concluding phases of a marathon are of special interest

in several ways. During the last few hours, I make a deliberate effort to help participants think about what they will do when they return to their homes, families, work. They are warned that although they may retain some of the joyfulness and exhilaration marathon participants usually (but not always) feel toward the end of the experience, some of these feelings will prove ephemeral. Sometimes depression and separation anxiety occur and must be dealt with. We return, in other words, to the world of the Sensory Reality.

But in the last half hour, there is sometimes a symbolic farewell experience. Nearly always, the participants sit in a circle and clasp hands as a gesture of shared humanity and support. Occasionally, if a member of the clergy is present, he will ask the group's permission to invoke a nonsectarian blessing, which is accepted even by agnostics as an expression of goodwill. We sometimes go through a ritual of sharing a farewell glass of wine, in which each person receives a glass, holds it without tasting, and pours it back into the decanter; the wine is thus mingled, and each participant again receives and drinks a glass of wine. It is a ceremony in which no specific religious statements are ever made, but which obviously has a deep resemblance to Christian communion, in turn preceded by centuries of belief in the sharing of wine as a symbol of fellowship.

*Chapter 8*

# MYSTICISM AND MADNESS

*If you talk to God, that's prayer. If you talk to God and he answers back, that's schizophrenia.*

"Old joke"—quoted by Hampden-Turner

*The schizophrenic is drowning in the same waters in which the mystic swims with delight.*

—Joseph Campbell

Some years ago, in a seminar at a psychoanalytic training institute, we were taught how to establish a tentative diagnosis in the initial interview. Among the exploratory questions suggested was, "Have you had any strange experiences?" If the prospective patient recounted experiences we would now call paranormal or transpersonal, there was a possibility of schizophrenia.

Resemblances between some aspects of the schizoprenic experience and the mystical experience are so striking that some clinicians actually regard mysticism as a manifestation of schizophrenia, others see schizophrenia as mysticism gone wrong or misunderstood by society. Before grappling with these possibilities, let me describe two patients, both seriously disturbed, both obsessed by mystical ideas in a distorted form: with "Breck," the idea of universal unity and universal love; with "Amy" the longing to help and save humanity.

Breck was the son of a family whom I know well enough to be sure that he was raised with normal affection and understanding. As a child he had suffered from nightmares and was somewhat shy, but he had friends, did well in school and at sports, and generally seemed fairly "well-adjusted." At sixteen he became morose and anxious, had a return of the nightmares, sometimes talked disjointedly although he was able to attend school. The family was ethnically Jewish, but Breck believed he was in touch with Christ. He also stated that he could read minds and foresee events; for example, he had "foreseen" the murder of John Lennon. At times he felt terrified, at other times blissful and full of love. To allay the terror or to express the love, he would go to the local supermarket and embrace strangers. Since he was a burly six-foot-three, the strangers were understandably alarmed, although nothing aggressive or sexual was ever reported. Reluctant to hospitalize him, his parents sent him to two psychiatrists. The first put him on a stiff regime of antipsychotic drugs and instructed him to tell himself "And that's crazy" when he experienced such feelings as his sense of universal love. The second psychiatrist, with whom he remained in treatment for several years while living at home, gave him minimal drug dosage and semi-analytic treatment in which his breakdown was regarded as a reaction to adolescent sexual drives; both psychiatrists diagnosed him as schizophrenic. His florid symptoms eventually disappeared and he could function, although at a slightly lower level than before, both socially and intellectually.

The case of "Amy" was told to me by a colleague, "Mrs. M." Amy's childhood had been deprived and somewhat traumatic, and in her mid-twenties she was living alone in a small apartment, almost entirely isolated socially, but able to support herself. Ever since she could remember, Amy had been obsessed by the world's tragedies—the mistreated animals, the hungry and sick children, the threat of a nuclear holocaust. She spent many hours alone in her room, praying for everyone who was sick or hungry or unhappy. In a revelation, it came to her that she must cut off her right hand. This sacrifice would appease God, and he would spare us.

Almost on the verge of this self-mutilation, Amy suddenly found herself pushing the doorbell of Mrs. M., who lived in the building and whom she knew to be a therapist in private practice, although they had barely spoken. Mrs. M., fortunately, was a deeply dedicated therapist who saw Amy through her acute psychotic episode, and over a period of several years helped her function outside a hospital. Although Mrs. M. had been advised by a supervisor to interpret Amy's intended self-mutilation as a defense against sexuality and hostility and her concern for the world's victims as a defense against own aggressiveness, Mrs. M. focused instead on Amy's wish to be helpful, and constantly reminded her that as a mutilated person she would be able to do little for others. In fact, she was persuaded to do volunteer work for a reputable organization set up to help undernourished children in other countries; she attained a minimal level of social functioning slightly higher than before her crisis.*

Unquestionably, some relationship exists between mysticism and schizophrenia, but even a speculative approach to this relationship must begin with some hypothesis as to the underlying cause of the socially irrational behavior, the confused thinking, and the personal misery we call schizophrenia. Here we run into incredible differences of opinion.†

*Some special institutions exist to serve patients in such crises (technically, acute schizophrenic reaction in the early stages). They use no drugs, provide a warm and accepting atmosphere, and are staffed by counselors who (as did Mrs. M. with Amy) recognize the possibly constructive aspect of the crises, often within a Jungian theoretical framework. These programs, which frequently have difficulty in obtaining funds to survive, have included R. D. Laing's Kingsley Hall in London, John Weir Perry's Diabasis in California, and Esalen's "blow-out center." Their rate of discharge is higher than that of conventional mental hospitals, but they typically limit admission to intelligent young people whose disturbance is acute, not chronic.

†It has been said that the number of theories about the cause and treatment of schizophrenia is approximately equal to the number of clinicians in the field. Some clinicians bypass the problem by stating unequivocally that if an illness can be helped by psychotherapy or other nonphysical treatments, it is by definition not schizophrenia, a diagnosis they limit to a specific biochemical condition. Clearly, this is a question for Humpty Dumpty, who insisted that a word must mean whatever he chose it to mean.

Schizophrenia may be regarded as a purely biological condition caused by neurological and chemical anomalies, treatable by drugs, by a low-stress regime, and (according to some clinicians) massive doses of vitamins. It may be a functional disorder caused by maternal deprivation in infancy or by contradictory messages from a "double-binding" or "schizophrenogenic" mother. It may involve a combination of constitutional predisposition and traumatic life events. Indeed, it may not be a disease at all; it may simply represent society's rejection of misfits and rebels or it may represent a crisis in which an individual is seeking to break through the boundaries of habit and repression and reach a higher stage of often-spiritual personal development. According to these last theories, the tragic burned-out "long-term chronics" in back wards are people who have been stupefied by drugs, electroshock, regimentation, and neglect, to the point that they can no longer function. It is even possible that schizophrenia is not a specific pathological condition, but simply a wide spectrum of behavior and feelings that may be evoked by an even wider range of inner and outer conditions. All these viewpoints, with innumerable variations and combinations, are advanced by specialists whose sincerity, ability, and experience cannot be questioned.*

Acute schizophrenia, in addition to the bizarre behavior and noncommunicative speech that frequently lead to hospitalization, often involves experiences that resemble the experiences of mystics. Several clinicians have pointed out that it is often difficult to

*References on the etiology and treatment of schizophrenia could fill several volumes. Bellak [1] offers a current overview of current conventional work. Arieti [2] gives a classical description of schizophrenic psychodynamics and in another more recent book[3] explicitly recognizes "the nobility and greatness that are at times hidden within mental illness." A readable presentation of the strictly biological viewpoint is offered by Pfeiffer.[4] Sechehaye's classic account of intensive psychotherapy with a schizophrenic adolescent is still worth reading.[5] Szasz[6] maintains that mental illness involves a refusal to take moral responsibility for life's demands. Laing[7] and Perry[8] maintain that acute schizophrenia may represent a basically healthy effort to break with the "false self." Wilber[9] offers a reconciliation of mysticism and schizophrenia that is difficult to read but highly worthwhile, with comprehensive references.

discriminate between statements made by mystics and descriptions of the schizophrenic experience.[10, 11, 14]

> The whole system rose up before me like a vague destiny looming from the abyss . . . The whole room seemed to me to be full of God. The air seemed to waver to and fro with the presence of Something I knew not what.

> I spent the later part of the night in ecstasies of joy, praising and adoring the Ancient of Days for his free and unbounded grace . . . then the devil stepped in and told me if I went to sleep I should lose it all.

> God actually touched my heart. The next day was horror and ecstacy. I began to feel that I might be on the quest of some spiritual awakening.

> (I had) a sense of communion, in the first place with God, and in the second place with all mankind, indeed with all creation.

> I had a great awareness of life, truth and God . . . I had the feeling I loved everybody in the world.

> . . . From a tiny glow the awareness in me became a large radiating pool of light, the "I" immersed in it yet fully cognizant of the radiantly blissful volume of consciousness all around, both near and far. Speaking more precisely, there was ego consciousness as well as a vastly extended field of awareness, existing side by side, both distinct yet one.

The first of these quotations is by James Russell Lowell, the American poet, who experienced a conversion but who is not usually thought of as a mystic. The second is from a young man, never hospitalized, who later became a minister. The next three are from patients who subsequently became increasingly confused, sometimes suicidal, delusional, and required hospitalization. The final quotation is from the Yoga mystic, Gopi Krishna, who went through a long and painful period he regarded as the awakening of Kundalini, a period during which (as he acknowledges) he would have been diagnosed as psychotic even in a culture that accepts such experiences; from this experience he emerged happy, well-balanced, and with a sense of enhanced physical and spiritual power that was also perceived by some Western scientists who studied him.*

Theoretical Category I. Acute schizophrenia is a spiritual crisis in which the individual is in the process of attaining valid mystical knowledge, such as the awareness of deep kinship with mankind, with nature, and with God, the final stage of which is the awareness "All is One." Sometimes the individual lacks the ego strength to handle this growth process, which can be terrible and painful.[12,13,15] He may therefore speak incoherently and show bizarre behavior, for which he is usually hospitalized and may be treated with drugs and shock that effectively bring about repression of the mystical experience. He then either returns to society or eventually ends up as a back-ward chronic patient.

A number of clinicians whose orientation is toward transpersonal psychology believe that such people can achieve a level of

*The first two quotations in this series are provided by William James,[10] the next three by Bowers and Freedman,[11] who give excellent references for those who wish to explore the inner experience of schizophrenia. The last quotation, from Krishna's autobiography,[12] is a paradigm example of the mystic's sense of being one with the universe while retaining his selfhood. Krishna describes the awakening of Kundalini, "the serpent power," seen as an evolutionary potential in man; this awakening involves the movement of a force at once physical and psychic upward through the various chakras (energy centers) of the body. I regard myself as unqualified to evaluate this Eastern concept, but some reputable Western scientists consider it valid.[9] It is interesting to compare Krishna's autobiography with that of Boisen, a Western mystic who was highly influential in developing pastoral psychology as a profession and who also underwent psychotic episodes.[13]

personal and social integraton higher than the prepsychotic level if they receive appropriate guidance. At Esalen, the psychiatrist Stanislav Grof and his wife, Christina, are training counselors to work with acute psychotics who may be undergoing a spiritual crisis. A workshop at the 1978 meeting of the Association for Humanistic Psychology, offered by the psychiatrist Jack Nelson, is described as follows.

> Schizophrenia is an altered state of consciousness, which exposes the ego to powerful forces from the deepest realms of human consciousness. The same may be said for states of mystical exaltation . . .

A variation of this position is taken by Wilber,[9] who suggests that the ego's normal barriers against its invasion by unconscious forces may be broken down by external stress, endogenous biochemical factors, or spiritual strivings. The ego is then *simultaneously* invaded by regressive impulses (from the archaic personal unconscious) and by transpersonal, mystical visions and ideas (from the superconscious or the Jungian "collective unconscious").

This theory accounts for the fantastic juxtaposition of infantile behavior (such as smearing feces) with garbled expressions of some of the highest human ideals ("I am love, God is love, I am God").* It enables us to recognize schizophrenia as a pathological condition, while continuing to see the mystical experience as representing contact with great alternate realities beyond our ordinary senses.

*Assagioli observes that the not infrequent delusion of being Christ or God represents a confused awareness that all men participate in the divine nature. Such patients "are dazzled by contact with truths which are too powerful for their mental capacities to grasp and assimilate.[16, p. 45] A delightful and pathetic account of three hospitalized patients who shared the delusion of being Christ [17] suggests fragments of wisdom and insight that have survived the schizophrenic process. An alternative perspective, quite different from that of Assagioli, is that these delusional patients suffer essentially from a sense of total worthlessness which leads to compensation through identification with a revered figure.

The implication for treatment, I think, is that the schizophrenic's spiritual aspirations, even if expressed in bizarre form, should be explicitly recognized and respected, as in the work of Laing and Perry. Perhaps one reason for Amy's recovery was that her therapist acknowledged the genuineness of her desire to be of service to humanity, rather than emphasizing the self-punitive aspect of her mutilation fantasy, while the psychiatrist who taught Breck to tell himself "And that's a crazy idea" was certainly not respecting the validity of his lovingness, even though his unawareness of the feelings of other people did certainly indicate a schizophrenic condition.

Category II. Mystical experiences are seen as normal events treated in our culture as abnormal. The behavior of shamans in nonindustrial cultures, such as trances and physical seizures [18,19] would probably lead to hospitalizaton here, and the visions of medieval mystics, accepted as a sign of divine grace, would be regarded as alarming hallucinations.*

But it is not unusual for the practicing clinician in this country to see occasional patients who might well be diagnosed as schizophrenic by an inexperienced practitioner, even though they are actually caught between two cultures. The family culture may be Hispanic, West Indian, or (more rarely) Native American, and the patient half believes in concepts that older family members take for granted (spiritism, possession, hauntings, the power to curse.). These young patients are often highly intelligent and upwardly mobile, yet it is difficult for them to reconcile their two sets of ethnic values. I have seen several of these patients who were half afraid of being actually psychotic, half afraid of possessing powers they saw as fearsome and even diabolic. In each case, I was fortunate enough to be able to relieve their anxieties in a few sessions, and none of them wished for extended treatment.

*Although this may be offensive to traditionalist believers, we must acknowledge that if the doctrine of transubstantiation occurred in a nonindustrial culture, and if it were taken literally rather than as a beautiful symbol of the union of God and man, we would regard it as archaic and regressive. The philosopher Haldane defined superstition as "somebody else's religion."

"Dolores" came to my office at the suggestion of a psychology professor.* But the professor was worried. Dolores was deeply upset about her seriously ill father and even more upset by a series of what she called "funny experiences", which caused her to think that perhaps she herself had brought about his illness.

She was a plump, attractive twenty-one-year-old whose behavior was appropriate despite her great anxiety and who quickly made good personal contact. Once we were at ease together, she told me that some weeks before her father was taken ill, when he seemed in normal health, she'd had continuous premonitions that he might die. Then she went on to something that had bothered her for years. As a tiny child, she had looked at a picture of President John Kennedy and said, "Mommy, he gonna die." Could she have *caused* Kennedy's death? Could she have *caused* her father's illness? Did she possess some terrible power? Or was she crazy to even think so?

Now I had various alternatives. I could try to persuade her that, as a child, she had overheard adults discussing the possibility of Kennedy's death (a possibility for any strong public figure) and had unconsciously remembered this conversation. Or I could try to persuade her that the whole thing was imagination. The third alternative, which I selected, was to tell her that a number of people had experienced premonitions about Kennedy's death, that I knew at least two youngsters who believed they had foreseen John Lennon's murder,† and that "science was now studying" such premonitions, which were interesting but had no practical effects. As for her father, she had probably noticed subtle indications of failing health; after all, she must have keen powers of observation, since she was an artist. By convincing Dolores that premonitory knowledge was neither bad nor crazy, but rather a matter for scientific study, I succeeded in relieving her anxiety.

But we had just begun.

There was also Dolores's grandfather. He had died a few

---

*"Carmen," in Chapter 2, is another example of such a person.

†I do indeed know people who claim to have foreseen both murders, but do not know whether they are documented premonitions or pure fantasy. Since my purpose was to be useful to Dolores, I left these alternatives vague.

years before. Once again, she had foreseen his death and feared that she had caused it. Several times, she had seen his "ghost"— his apparition. Most frightening of all, her family told her that while she was asleep, she would sometimes give a characteristic whistle that had been a signal between them. She was deathly afraid of spirit possession.

This time there seemed no alternative choices. Dolores would go into real panic if she believed completely that she saw her grandfather's ghost and that his spirit came to her at night and whistled through her lips in demonic possession. I told Dolores very firmly that she had a wonderful imagination and that, like all artistic people, she had strong visual imagery (a phrase she could understand) and had imagined the apparition. I disposed of the noctural whistle by explaining that she probably missed her grandfather and was dreaming about him, comparing the whistle to sleepwalking and sleeptalking, which people seldom remember. By accepting the possibility of Dolores's premonition about Kennedy, I had already established myself as someone who would not ridicule her ideas as superstitious nonsense, and it was therefore easy for her to accept my explanation, especially since it was mingled with implied praise.

Now came inspiration. I asked Dolores whether her grandfather had really loved her.

"Oh, yes, I was his favorite. Always his favorite."
"Then why would he want to scare you? Wouldn't he want you to feel safe and happy?"

We reviewed our conversation. I repeated that Dolores might well have precognitive ability; there was scientific evidence that such powers might exist, but they did not imply causation. The appearance of her grandfather was almost certainly imagination; if not, all she had to do was say, "Grandfather, you scare me, if you love me please go away!" This last point, of course, was a precaution lest I had not quite convinced her, perhaps also a precaution against the (to me) infinitely remote possibility that the apparition might actually *be* an apparition.* Dolores went

*The folklore of apparitions indicates that if a "ghost" is seriously requested to go away it usually complies.

away relaxed and happy, with a promise to come back if she "got upset" again.

This young woman might have been regarded as mentally ill by someone who did not take her cultural background into account. Continued therapy might well have helped her reconcile her two sets of cultural values, but antipsychotic drugs would certainly have been worse than useless.

Category III. Mysticism is totally pathological and akin to schizophrenia. One version of this viewpoint is the reduction of all human experience to biochemical and neurological conditions; consciousness is thus merely an epiphenomenon of matter. Since both mental illness and mysticism are caused by abnormal biological conditions, the treatment is pharmacological.*

Without necessarily adopting biochemistry as the basis for all human experience, there are some highly distinguished clinicians who view mysticism as totally pathological. Their opinions, presented by a writer thoroughly in sympathy with the transpersonal viewpoint, who goes on to present the opposing position, are as follows:[21]

> Many psychoanalytic writers . . . have labelled meditation a regression to primary process thinking. Alexander (1931) saw meditation as "a sort of artifical schizophrenia with complete withdrawal of libidinal interest from the outside world;" [p. 130]; the outcome is a masochistic (ascetic) and systematic undoing of the entire development of ego capacities which leaves the adept catatonic. Federn (1982) viewed mystical union as a return to primary narcissism. Becker (1961) sees meditation as "imbibing in magical, omnipotent, self-hypnotic trance experiences" [p. 646] which produce diffuse body experiences, depersonalization, loss of ego-functioning and conversion to a magical belief system that views all this pathology as positive. Prince and Savage (1966) elaborately compare the phenomena of mystical states with similar ones in infancy, psychosis and psychedelic states.

*An excellent current summary of this tendency to reductionism, with a temperate presentation of the alternate viewpoint, is found in reference 20.

Motives for these states have been stated to be a reaction to intense hatred of the Oedipal parent; a struggle with irrational authority (Freud, 1928; Salzman, 1953); a defense against libidinal or, more rarely, aggressive impulses (Dickes, 1965, Hartocollis, 1976); or a soothing transitional object that relieves stress, much like a child's blanket (Horton, 1974).*

Clearly, mystics and meditators are very sick indeed, and should be treated by drugs, psychotherapy, and any other available methods. To those who agree, these opinions will seem a fine example of clear realistic thinking; to those who view the capacity for mysticism as a valuable and precious human ability, they will seem reductionistic to the point of absurdity.

Category IV: Mysticism is essentially a defensive adjustment that "serves certain psychic needs or constitutes an attempt to resolve certain ubiquitious problems."[22, p. 715] The reference here is to a monograph prepared by the Group for the Advancement of Psychiatry, consisting of three hundred psychiatrists whose combined opinion is presumably represented by this much quoted publication. They write further that "the mystic is motivated in his search by disappointment with society, by the need to escape from unacceptable external realities, or by the need to rid himself of depression and the feeling of being a rejected outsider . . . in reaching this goal, the mystic at last achieves a sense of belonging, and the mystical union symbolizes union with a parental figure from whom he felt estranged."[22, p. 790]

Many similarities are drawn between certain phases of schizophrenia and the mystical experience: ordinary people and events are seen as representatives of a supernal world; there is a sense of ecstacy; there is a feeling of ineffable communion with the Divine Being. Religious activities, such as abstinence, confession, and penitence are seen as neurotic efforts to ward off depression by obtaining the love and forgiveness of the parents. In fact, the mystics's conviction that he is merging with God is

*Reprinted by permission, *Journal of Transpersonal Psychology*, 1978, Vol. 10, #2, 159–60. References to dates, authors and pages are given in the original source article.

actually a return of the infant's longing for a blissful oceanic merging with the parents.

The mystic "is generally not mentally ill," but his condition is of special interest because " mystical phenomena . . . can demonstrate forms of behavior intermediate between normality and frank psychosis . . . the paradox of the return of repressed aggression in unconventional expressions of love." While "the mystical defense" remains effective, the mystic is unlikely to seek psychotherapeutic help, and for this reason (as the authors acknowledge) there are not many in-depth psychological studies of "mystics who show unmistakable psychopathology." *Ibid,* p. 731.*

Although they regard mysticism as a borderline pathological condition, these writers point out two important specific differences between mysticism and mental illness. First, the mystic deliberately seeks his experience through such self-disciplines as abstinence, meditation, and constant prayer, whereas the schizophrenic is overwhelmed by his unexpected breakdown. Second, the mystic usually does not retreat completely from the world, but maintains ties with others, while the schizophrenic is likely to let go of his human relationships. Treatment, presumably, would involve an attempt to strengthen the patient's reality testing and his ties with the external world.

In hospitals or on an out-patient basis, the psychotherapist may see two types of patients whose difficulties are related to the mystical experience: those described under Category I, with whom mysticism and schizophrenia are entangled; and those who are undergoing the terrible despair and depression that has often been described as a phase on the journey toward fully realized mysticism.[10] With both types, it seems to me that the therapist cannot be especially helpful by arguing about what the therapist perceives as delusions, but does better to uncover and recognize the needs and feelings that lie beneath the possibly

---

*A similar point is made by Grof,[23] a psychiatrist who does accept the mystical experience as valid. He believes that treatment is sought by people who undergo mystical experiences by which they feel confused and overwhelmed, while other individuals pass through personality changes and attain a higher stage of spiritual development without professional help.

delusional material. Indeed, I know of few instances in which either ridicule, confrontation, or rational arguments convinced anyone to give up an emotionally rooted delusional belief. The best single criterion by which we can discriminate between mysticism and mental illness is probably to consider the extent to which a patient is capable of recognizing the reality of and caring about other people.*

Even though the personal development of the mystic may entail phases during which psythotherapeutic help is useful or even necessary, it seems that there are cogent reasons against identifying mysticism with pathology. As James has pointed out,[10] mystics are often capable, vigorous, socially active people; we need think only of Schweitzer, Gandhi, and Mother Theresa. Although the "peak experiences" described by Maslow[24] do not usually equal the mystical experience in intensity, there are clear similarities, and we must note that Maslow's "peakers" were usually happy, self-actualizing individuals.

*My account of various approaches to the possible relationships between mysticism and schizophrenia is probably colored by my personal preference for the viewpoint given in Category I, especially as seen by Wilber and Assagioli.

*Chapter 9*

# THERAPEUTIC PATHWAYS TOWARD
# THE TRANSPERSONAL

*The most beautiful, the most profound emotion we can experience is
the sensation of the mystical. It is the fundamental emotion that
stands at the cradle of true art and science.*

—Albert Einstein

Transpersonal psychotherapy is sometimes termed the Fourth
Force. The First Force is psychoanalysis, with its primary emphasis on the elucidation and integration of unconscious drives
although it increasingly recognizes the importance of object-
relations (that is, relationships between people). The Second
Force is behavior modification, with its emphasis on the relief of
symptoms. The Third Force is humanistic psychology, also*

---

*The term *Third Force* was coined by Maslow, a key figure (with Carl
Rogers) in the development of humanistic psychology.[1,2] There is a
distinction between *secular humanism,* which is sharply criticized by such
religious traditionalists as the Moral Majority as essentially atheistic and
materialistic, and *humanistic psychology,* which is also concerned with
human welfare (as, indeed, are psychoanalysis and behaviorism) but
which is by no means inconsistent with the recognition of spiritual values.

termed the *human potential movement,* which focuses upon the individual's ability to change and grow, in contrast to the earlier two "Forces," which have been criticized as viewing man as a robotic creature of instinct and habit.

Transpersonal psychology, as a philosophy and as a method of psychotherapy, is closest to humanistic psychology, of which it is an historical outgrowth.\* It also has commonalities with various other approaches. Among Western thinkers, the most powerful influence is Jung, who postulates a "collective unconscious" that enfolds the "archetypes," symbolic representations of man's relationships with mankind and the cosmos. It emphasizes the here and now as do Gestalt psychologists. It is akin to mysticism in the assumption that each individual is part of a network that includes not only mankind, but nature, the cosmos, and ultimately God (as a nonsectarian concept). Findings from parapsychological research are often cited in support of their viewpoint by transpersonal psychologists, although it is logically possible to accept *psi* as a little understood physical phenomenon without taking a transpersonal perspective. It has been deeply influenced by Eastern philosophy, especially Zen Buddhism, which has attracted many clinicians originally trained in the traditional Western approach to therapy.†

The term *transpersonal* is probably best understood if we take it literally, to mean "beyond the personal." It denotes a sense of deep relatedness to other persons, which goes beyond their ability to gratify our needs. Most transpersonal psychologists also believe that higher and further realms of reality exist beyond the familiar realms of sensory data; in this higher realm each human being is part of what is variously termed God, the Cosmos, the

---

\*Relevant literature includes the *Journal of Transpersonal Psychology* and references 3 and 4. Relationships between Eastern thought and Western psychotherapy are discussed in 5, and 6 describes conversion to Eastern mysticism by a former Harvard psychology professor.

†For example, over a thousand psychiatrists, psychologists, and social workers attended an all-day conference given by Baba Muktananda in June of 1979 in South Fallsburg, New York. Two thousand attended a Sufi-sponsored conference on healing in Washington, D.C., in November 1981.

Universal Mind. A slightly different approach is that all reality is One, but that we can usually perceive only a limited aspect of it. Since conventional science accepts only sensory data and its cognitive interpretation, the transpersonal approach, unlike parapsychological research, cannot be evaluated in objective, scientific terms.

Yet individuals of many cultures and many ages have maintained that they have had direct, intuitive experiences of alternate reality, which to them carry a sense of absolute conviction. Such experiences typically occur in altered states of consciousness, which can sometimes be facilitated by meditation; by drugs; by nearness to death (see following chapter); possibly by psychosis (see preceeding chapter); and by natural human activities (childbirth, music, dancing) that suddenly take on extraordinary intensity. The altered state may also have religious implications; in Western theology it may be termed *conversion*; in Eastern philosophy, *enlightenment*. It bears striking similarities to the "peak experiences" described by Maslow, which sometimes are described as having spiritual overtones. In many instances, people who have undergone peak experiences, or who feel that they have been in touch with another, higher form of reality, report an enduring sense of joy, serenity, and closeness to others. Transpersonal psychology is concerned with the study of these altered states.

The transpersonal experience, with its quality of mysticism, is by some scholars seen as intrinsically pathological. Others, "including Bergson, Toynbee, James, Schopenhauer, Nietzsche, and Maslow, have suggested that the world's greatest mystics and sages represent some of the highest, if not the highest, stage of human development."[7, p.3] Mysticism has even been seen as a tremendous evolutionary step forward.[8,9,10] This is a philosophical issue that most of us will decide on the basis of temperament and preference. Therefore, it seems to be both personally arrogant and therapeutically counterproductive if a therapist seeks to impose his personal value system upon his patients.

"Is it all right if I talk about God?" asked a new patient rather shyly—and somewhat surprisingly, for he was a successful middle-aged executive. His previous therapist, he told me, had interpreted any reaching out toward religious experience as an infantile wish for an all-powerful father or for the "oceanic bliss" of the primitive mother-baby union.* Another highly accredited therapist has described goals for his patients as: "1. Health—long life. 2. Sexuality. 3. Economic success."† Both of these therapists clearly believe that transpersonal values have no place in therapy, yet I have seen many people professionally who have already reached the three goals established by my colleague and who are wretched because they feel that life is without meaning or purpose.‡ Let me share two experiences of my own with such people, experiences dating back to a time when I was relatively unacquainted with certain approaches to transpersonal psychotherapy (such as meditation and guided imagery), which I would now attempt to use with "Clare."

"Clare" was in her late twenties, very attractive, with an interesting job and an income generously augmented by wealthy parents. She had left her husband, mostly because his income and prestige did not satisfy her. She lived well and dated often but suffered from the typical "narcissistic" sense of hollowness, and was interested only in dates, clothes, and prospects of a better marriage. In a blundering attempt to widen Clare's horizons, I suggested that she might attend a local synagogue (her background was strongly Jewish). Her immediate reply was "But I wouldn't meet good men that way!" Clare left therapy after a few months, her self-image slightly improved, but with no real change.

"Pamela" also came from a wealthy, materialistic family. She was married, with two young children and no apparent interest in life except sex. Her record of infidelity, apparently unsuspected

*Such infantile wishes may well have contributed to the patient's longing for the transpersonal, but it is reductionistic to assume that this longing was *nothing but* infantile wishes.

†In *Voices,* the official publication of the highly respected American Academy of Psychotherapists.

‡This patient population, technically described as "narcissistic character disorder," is extremely large. They often respond favorably to a prolonged, intensive course of modified psychoanalysis. Certainly, few or none of them would respond to a direct attempt to inculcate transpersonal values, an attempt that would be naive on the therapist's part.

by her husband, was spectacular. Yet she did not enjoy sex. It was merely "something to do."

As we worked together, it transpired that Pam had always been valued for her unusual beauty.* Her parents had dressed her up, showed her off, treated her like a doll. Her husband did the same. As we were beginning to understand this, Pam had a dream in which she and I were having sexual relations.

She looked at me coquettishly. "Maybe I'm really a lesbian?" The strategem was obvious. Firmly I told Pam that this did not seem to be her problem. She believed she could be esteemed only for her appearance and sexuality. Her dream was a product of this belief, not of a homosexual drive.

We worked on this theme for some months, then were interrupted by vacation. In the fall Pam came in for a farewell thank-you visit. She was dressed less flirtatiously and she was happy. She had become intensely interested in the women's peace movement; now the children were in school, and the movement took all her free time. She had stopped having affairs—"there simply isn't time, besides I never really liked it." Her marriage was better. She could give more to her children. Except for two appreciative Christmas cards, I never heard from Pam again.

Never had I recommended to Pam that she find some outside interest, nor had I shared my passionate concern for world peace. In analytic terms, energy became available when she no longer needed compulsive promiscuity to build up self-esteem, and this energy had now turned outward. Why this occurred with Pam and not with Clare could be explained only by extensive case histories; the significant point is that humanistic-transpersonal growth occurred spontaneously as therapy progressed, without any special effort on my part.

Pushing the patient toward humanistic or transpersonal goals seems to me contrary to the therapist's basic function, which

---

*Pam had worked previously with two male therapists. With one, she had sexual relations, and the other had terminated because, he told her frankly, he was tempted by her seductiveness. Although I am generally impatient with male therapists who claim "the patient lured me on," I am inclined to believe that in this instance Pam had really been very provocative.

I regard as assisting the patient to grow according to his own internal guidelines. People who consciously wish for spiritual growth, if they do not find it in Western religious traditions, usually seek it in mystically oriented workshops or ashrams (although, of course, this may be an avoidance of inner conflicts and external challenges).

Yet there are people entering therapy who seem to long for a deeper dimension of living without quite knowing how to define it. Certain techniques, which fall well within the scope of conventional psychotherapy,[11] including psychoanalytically oriented therapy and Gestalt work, often lead toward the transpersonal: dreamwork, guided imagery, meditation, and (in the past) carefully supervised use of psychedelic drugs. Other forms of therapy offer a specifically transpersonal approach, such as psychosynthesis, meditative therapy, and the Fischer-Hoffman method. Still others fall outside the rubric of conventional psychotherapy altogether: psychic healing, the mind-training methods of Arica and Silva, EST, and workshops conducted by Eastern mystics. All these approaches will be surveyed in an overview of contemporary trends, which will be greatly condensed and simplified, since ample references are available.

I. *Dreamwork.* A transpersonal approach to dreams does not *exclude* the Freudian search for disguised wish-fulfillment through free association, nor the Gestalt technique of asking the dreamer to identify in turn with each dream element, seen as representing various aspects of the self. But a deeper meaning may be sought. The dream may carry a message not from the Freudian individual unconscious, in which specifically personal material resides, but from the Jungian collective unconscious, where archetypal symbols common to all mankind reside.* Jungians maintain that a dream often indicates some aspect of the dreamer's personality, frequently a spiritual aspect, that needs to be developed.

When a mysterious symbol appears in a dream (a closed door, a wall, a road receding into the far distance) its exploration

---

*Anyone interested in transpersonal psychology will find in Jung a treasure house of information and ideas. Perhaps the best beginning for someone unfamiliar with Jung is with his autobiography.[12]

often leads toward the transpersonal. Here is a dream brought to me by a supervisee.

"Gracia," a well-functioning woman in her early forties, entered therapy with a presenting symptom of feeling "rootless, not exactly lonely, but as if I don't belong anywhere." She had a satisfying social and professional life and was almost apologetic for entering therapy. The dream that occurred after about four months of treatment was one in which she faced a closed door and could not open it because of a vague fear of what might lie beyond.

Trained in the classic analytic method, my supervisee had asked Gracia for free associations. Nothing emerged. Since the dream still seemed important, I suggested that Gracia should be asked to relax, return to the dream, and imagine opening the door.

When the therapist requests visual and kinetic imagery, the guardian intellect often seems less vigilant than if the therapist asks for free associations. Gracia was able to get back into the dream and see the door. It was a heavy door of dark wood, carved with figures reminiscent of a procession.*

In fantasy, eyes closed, Gracia could finally open the door, and found herself facing an altar. Above the altar was a statue of Christ crucified, not the conventional statue, but highly modernistic, suggestive rather than representational, and made of luminous material.

It was a beautiful statue; Gracia was very moved. Wisely, the therapist said little. Throughout several sessions, the meaning of the symbol emerged.

Gracia had grown up in a family which, although loving, was heavily restricted by Fundamentalist religious beliefs. Pleasure was almost sinful. Jewelry was never worn. Religion was a duty. Gracia had remained on good terms with her family, but she rejected their values entirely (or so she thought) and was an agnostic. In discussing the dream, however, she began to see that

---

*It is interesting to note that the door eventually turned out to remind Gracia of the carved doors to the Duomo Baptistry in Florence, Italy.

some of her family's values, such as high ethical standards, were still meaningful to her. The statue symbolized, very beautifully, the concept that she could retain some of their beliefs, while rejecting their philosophy of self-denial. The eventual outcome was not only that Gracia could now feel closer to her parents, but also that she could allow herself more enjoyment.

II. *Symbols and Fantasy*. The exploration of symbols through fantasy and visualization may help to clarify and solve a personal conflict and may also help to establish contact with the wider and deeper realm of human experience we call transpersonal.*

Imagery may be used to explore the meaning of a symbol, such as Gracia's statue, introduced spontaneously by the patient. Alternatively, the therapist may conduct the patient through an entire fantasy journey.

In Assagioli's exercise "Blossoming of the Rose,"[13, pp. 213–15] the therapist slowly describes, in detail, the unfolding of a rosebud while the patient, with closed eyes, visualizes the process. Assagioli regards the rose as a symbol of the soul, or the spiritual self, and believes that this exercise may stimulate spiritual development, although he does not claim that this invariably takes place. The choice of the symbol seems arbitrary, and the patient's role in the process seems entirely passive. My own preference, if the patient does not spontaneously produce a symbol such as Gracia's statue, is to suggest the *beginning* of a fantasy journey, then allow or encourage the patient to continue in his own direction. Examples follow.

"Christine," in her late twenties, was so unhappy and depressed that her ability to function socially and vocationally was rather a miracle, although she was seriously neurotic. As a child she had lived in an atmosphere of melancholy and deprivation. Her mother had been semi-alcoholic, her father withdrawn.

---

*Imagery has other therapeutic uses; for instance, it may help recovery from traumatic experiences, it may assist the emergence of important memories, and it gives emotional depth and meaning to the therapeutic processes. Pertinent references include Assagioli, [13] the journal *Synthesis*, and the *Journal of Mental Imagery*, published by the recently founded International Imagery Association.

Moreover, he was an undertaker, and the funeral parlor adjoined the house, so that the little girl lived constantly in the presence of death and mourning.

Christine could enjoy almost nothing. She was haunted by memories of her dark and gloomy childhood. A previous therapist, whose work with Christine had been terminated by external circumstances, had been effective in helping Christine get in touch with her natural anger at her early deprivation; this had considerably relieved Christine's tension. But she was still unhappy.

Without much optimism I tried an experiment for which Christine gave me an opening by telling me that she could not recall one happy childhood memory.

In archetypal symbolism, the meadow is generally considered to represent the world of the child.[13, p.307] I asked Christine to visualize a beautiful meadow, with flowers and fresh grass, and to imagine herself as a small girl wandering through it. Rather to my surprise, Christine was able to do this. She took over the fantasy eagerly, describing the colors of the flowers (mostly yellow) and adding a soft breeze. She remained in her imaginary meadow during the rest of the session and left without comment or questions.

In our next session, Christine wished to return to the meadow, and described what she saw there. She spontaneously imagined a brief meeting with an aunt whom whe recalled as warmer and more cheerful than the other family members. Thenceforward, Christine told me, she could often dispel the wretched memories of childhood by getting back into "my meadow."

This fantasy seemed a turning point in a long, complex, and generally successful course of therapy. By this fantasy, Christine had either recovered happier childhood feelings than she had been able to remember, or else had actually been able to create for herself a happier childhood through the archetypal symbol of the flowering meadow.

Contact with an archetypal symbol may also be made spontaneously if the therapist suggests the beginning of a fantasy. One of my favorite procedures, "The Figure on the Path," is used when a patient faces a problem to which his own inner wisdom, his unconscious self-knowledge, may be assumed to have the answer. Thus the question "Do I want to change my profession?" would be appropriate because the patient somewhere knows the answer. A question such as "Will I be more successful in another city?" would be inappropriate, because the answer depends upon unknown future circumstances.

"Curt," a science teacher in his early thirties, told us in a marathon group that although he functioned well and enjoyed his girl friend he often felt depressed. Moreover, he suffered from breathlessness, although he did not smoke and no medical problem could be discovered. He was asked to formulate his problem as a question, and responded simply with "Why do I feel so bad?"

I now asked Curt to close his eyes, breathe deeply, and imagine himself in a safe, secluded place—a beach, a meadow, a pine forest. There was a path winding into the distance, its ending lost in perspective. As he gazed along the path, a figure would appear, at first unrecognizable. Gradually, as it approached, he would see it more clearly. At last it would be close enough for him to ask the question. These instructions were delivered softly and slowly, Curt following the visualization with closed eyes, until my final words, "Now ask the question—listen for the answer."

As Curt listened, tears rolled down his cheeks (he told us later that it had been many years since he had wept). After some time, he told us what he had seen—a woman robed in white, who did not resemble anyone he knew. Her answer to his question was "You think too much—you should pay more attention to your feelings."

Obvious advice. Anyone in the group would have agreed that Curt was too cerebral and repressed. Yet in visualizing the white-robed woman, Curt had apparently reached his own inner wisdom, his anima (in Jungian terms, the feeling-intuitive part of himself that had been undeveloped). I advised Curt to enter individual therapy to work further on this problem, but never found out whether he took my advice. However, I did receive a letter saying that he could still visualize the white-robed figure, that his depressions were less noticeable, and that the symptom of breathlessness, apparently associated with repressed emotion, was ameliorated.

Having conducted this exercise perhaps a hundred times, I am impressed by the frequency with which the figure of a white-robed woman, representing feminine wisdom, or an old, white-bearded man, Jung's Wise Old Man, appear to people who cannot be expected to know about these archetypes, thus lending credence to Jung's contention that the archetypes are common to mankind. Other figures that may appear include a respected teacher or older relative or (more rarely) someone currently important in the patient's life. Usually, the figure, although its message may be cryptic, is kindly and compassionate; rarely, it is malevolent, in which case it represents a self-destructive inner force and must be dealt with therapeutically as if it were a toxic introject.

The opportunities for symbolic fantasy in therapy are rich and varied. I have been asked whether some patients may not use fantasy as an escape from reality; this risk can easily be avoided by asking, "How will you translate this insight into daily living?"

III. *Meditation.* Meditation may be used to relieve stress, to develop the ability to concentrate, and for problem solving. As an adjunct to therapy, meditation may permit the emergence of new memories and feelings that can then be brought to the next session.[14] It may be used to facilitate self-healing, or for the healing of others (as discussed in the following chapter). As a part of various Eastern disciplines, it may be used as a pathway to spiritual enlightenment.*

But the procedure is variable. Meditation has been defined as an effort to communicate with a greater Being, a process that clearly resembles prayer in the Western sense; or as total concentration on "doing one thing at a time" as a discipline that strengthens the entire personality structure;[15] or as "a series of mental exercises designed to effect certain changes in how a person sees

---

*The literature on meditation is extraordinarily rich. Carrington[14] offers the best overall book for the practicing clinician because of the flexibility and sophistication with which she approaches the values and pitfalls of meditation. LeShan[15] discusses a wide variety of techniques open to the Western meditator. Goleman[16] describes various approaches to meditation, primarily Eastern. There is a vast proliferation of research, summarized in reference 17.

or relates to the world."[18, p.51] Some methods, such as "sitting Zazen," are strenuous; others, such as Transcendental Meditation (TM) are permissive and relaxing.* TM involves the repetition of a "mantra," a Sanscrit word chosen by the TM instructor, which is soothing to many meditators and possesses the special magic of an exotic, unknown language. Meditation may involve counting of the breath, gazing into a candle flame, or pondering upon such a phrase as "All is One," "God is good," or the Buddhist "Om mani padme hum." Meditators may be instructed to take the lotus position, difficult for most Westerners, or may be advised to assume any comfortable position. TM specifies twenty-minute meditations, one before breakfast and one before dinner; other schools require longer meditations. Carrington finds (as I do) that under stress a meditation of even a few minutes may be helpful. Perhaps the most satisfactory hypothesis to account for these diversities is that "the intention of the meditator may be a prime determinant of the outcome."[19, p.6]

The therapist's approach to meditation will depend upon his personal experience. Some therapists ask their patients to desist from meditation, if they are already practicing it, on the grounds that feelings and thoughts from the unconscious should be sought only during the therapeutic session. Therapists who have personal experiences with meditation are usually more favorably disposed and may even wish to use it as an adjunct to therapy. Since there is scant literature on this topic, except for Carrington,

---

*TM is criticized by some psychologists because its methods are kept secret, thus preventing their evaluation through research. For example, the TM instructor apparently selects a mantra on the basis of the candidate's age rather than on personality characteristics, but this is not officially acknowledged. A rigid schedule of twenty minutes twice a day is insisted upon, although clinical experience suggests that this might be too much for some meditators, not enough for others. TM students must also promise never to teach the TM method (without undergoing the special prolonged training required from TM instructors) or to reveal their mantra. Most psychotherapists will find Carrington's approach, which she terms Clinically Standardized Meditation and which is based on research and experience rather than on authoritarian dogma, more congenial.

let me share my own approach to meditation as a therapeutic adjunct.

Because of the rigidity of the TM method, I prefer not to suggest a TM course to patients; if they wish to take this course I encourage it but suggest using individual judgment as to the most desirable duration of the initial meditations. For a new meditator, twenty minutes may be too long, especially if anxiety is provoked. Indeed, there is some clinical evidence[17] that long meditations, or over-frequent meditations, may be unwise for some borderline schizophrenics, since meditation definitely involves withdrawal from the outside world.

Under special circumstances I may actually suggest meditation, for example, for a middle-aged woman returning to college who found it difficult to study; a young singer who suffered from stage fright; a man with tachycardia for which no medical reason could be found—in short, conditions of tension and anxiety. If the patient likes the idea, I do not hesitate to give instructions along the lines of Carrington's Clinically Standardized Meditation, which gives the patient a choice of several procedures (breath counting, use of a mantra, contemplation of a candle flame) and in which duration depends upon the comfort of the meditator.*

Meditation may be used as part of a self-healing effort. A patient who followed the TM meditation procedures diligently was suffering from chronic ileitis, for which he had undergone extensive and repeated surgery and for which no hope of a medical cure was offered. At the end of a routine TM meditation,

---

*No therapist should attempt to give even the simplest instruction in meditation without personal experience, any more than he should conduct therapy without experience as a patient. I regard myself as qualified to give simple meditation instructions because I have taken a TM course (although I did not adhere to the instructions); several seminars with Goodrich under the auspices of the Consciousness Research and Training Project; and various other meditation seminars. I do *not* regard myself as qualified to teach meditation to those who wish to use it for spiritual development, and would refer such seekers to a recognized teacher. However, I have at times meditated with a patient for healing purposes as described in the following chapter.

when he felt relaxed, he decided spontaneously to visualize his body as whole and well. He liked the feeling, continued the procedure, and believes that the effects were beneficial.* Since his experience, I may sometimes suggest to a physically ill patient who is already meditating that he conclude the meditation by visualizing his body as perfectly well, although *not* as a substitute for appropriate medical attention.

Meditation may also be of help in problem solving. The procedure is to ask oneself the relevant question, then proceed with meditation. Surprisingly often, a satisfactory answer "pops into the mind" within a few hours. Using this technique, I have often asked myself what is blocking a particular patient or why we have difficulty making contact, and often the procedure is effective. Occasionally, I have suggested this procedure to a patient, explaining that the answer comes from his own unconscious, not from an occult source.

Most patients to whom I have taught meditation report increased calmness and energy; two have learned to forestall headaches *most* of the time; several have reported temporary relief from mild depression. None have described a sense of depersonalization, and none have reported the semi-hallucinatory visions described in the literature which, according to LeShan, should be viewed as a distraction or even a trap rather than as an achievement. On the other hand, none have reported the bliss sometimes described in the transpersonal literature.[19] Probably it is not by chance that the experience of my patients almost exactly parallels my own experiences during some six years of fairly regular meditation.

IV. *Psychedelic Drugs.*† Use of LSD and other powerful

*Ten years after his physicians were inclined to predict a life span of only a year or two, this man, (although still ill), is still enjoying life. In addition to meditation, he underwent considerable psychotherapy and a fortunate life change. Of course, a sample of one is scientifically worthless.

†Most of the material in this section is based on data kindly provided by Dr. Richard Yensen, currently conducting research on the use of LSD with cancer patients at the University of Maryland.

psychoactive drugs, such a psilocybin and mescaline, is legally controlled in the United States, with the exception of a few government approved research studies. Consequently, their interest for psychotherapy lies in contributions from earlier research to our understanding of personality.

The history of LSD in the United States is tragic. In the early forties this drug, synthesized in a laboratory, was recognized almost by chance as probably the most powerful psychoactive substance known.* Within a few years, literature on LSD was escalating and was filled with conflicting claims. In some doses it was regarded as *psychotomimetic* (mimicking psychosis) in its chemical effects, thus giving support to those who regard psychosis as caused by biochemical abnormality. Administered in a therapeutic setting, it was found to be *psycholytic* (mind dissolving) and dissolved the barriers of repression, thus deepening and facilitating psychotherapy. Finally, it could be *psychedelic* (mind manifesting), since it frequently brought about mystical experiences.[20,21,22] Especially remarkable was the extent to which the subject's expectations, the purpose for which the drug was administered, the relationship between subject and therapist or experimenter, and the physical setting were all crucial in determining the effects.

Yet even this finding was inconsistent. Alcoholics were given LSD in the hope that they would be frightened away from alcohol by an artificial delirium tremens. Instead, many had intense mystical experiences, leaving them without further interest in alcohol.[23]

Tragedy came in the 1960s when LSD became a street drug, and the Harvard professor Timothy Leary publicly advised the nation's youth to "turn on, tune in, and drop out." Tens of thousands of young men and women were drawn to LSD by sensation-seeking, a wish for group affiliation, and undoubtedly in many instances a search for transcendental experience. Many

*Psychoactive substances from native plants are used by nonindustrialized tribes throughout the globe for worship and healing, and perhaps were also used by highly developed past civilizations such as ancient Greece. See references 20 to 24.

ended in mental hospitals, at least temporarily.* Although few or no instances of lastingly adverse effects were reported from adequately supervised LSD experiences, the government responded with strict legislation.

The data that meanwhile accumulated is of considerable interest. Under LSD, people recalled experiences going back to earliest childhood with hallucinatory vividness. Other experiences, termed "perinatal,"[22] are apparently related to biological birth, not literally but symbolically, for example, a feeling of being trapped endlessly in a dark tunnel and at last emerging ecstatically into light. Some subjects went through experiences in ancient cultures, with vivid details of architecture and ritual that archaeologists subsequently validated. These details could have come from books or pictures once seen and consciously forgotten, but stored deep in memory; they could also be viewed as representing access to the history of mankind through the collective unconscious. Other experiences included encounters with figures such as the Jungian archetypes; with other universes and their inhabitants; with "blissful or wrathful deities;" and finally, an ineffable sense of "consciousness of the Universal Mind."[22]

Few of us will believe that under LSD a subject may leave his body and actually meet "blissful or wrathful deities." But the intensity of the LSD experience, and the extraordinary similarity of the reports of hundreds of carefully supervised subjects, cannot but deepen our respect and awe for the complexities of the human mind.

*Although I never utilized LSD as a therapeutic tool, during those years I did see several patients on "bad trips." Anyone who has witnessed this agony can understand the motives of those who restricted the use of LSD. I recall one young woman who had taken LSD on her own repeating over and over in absolute horror the phrase "Three oranges and an artichoke" as I was being guided on a professional visitor's tour through a disturbed ward. She was calmed down by thorazine. If an empathic therapist had remained with her and helped her to explore the meaning of her fearful hallucination, her experience might have been therapeutic.

V. *Specific Therapeutic Systems.* The techniques just described can often be integrated with such therapeutic approaches as psychoanalytic psychotherapy and Gestalt. Various other systems use transpersonal concepts as their basic approach, with the goal to be attained that of spiritual and transpersonal development.

The great name in Western transpersonal psychology is, of course, C. G. Jung.* His contributions include the concept of a "collective unconscious" common to all men, containing the "archetypes" that are universal superhuman symbols of man's relationship to humanity and to the cosmos; emphasis on spiritual development, especially in the last third of the life span; and the necessity of remaining in touch with myths and dreams, seen as linking man to the spiritual world. It is said of Jung that when asked whether he believed in an afterlife, he replied firmly, "I do not *believe. I know.*"

Institutes in the United States and Europe train Jungian therapists, whom Jung terms "analytical psychologists," presumably to distinguish them from Freudian psychoanalysts. But Jung's influence pervades the entire field of transpersonal psychology. It is especially evident in the theory and methods of psychosynthesis developed by the Italian psychiatrist Roberto Assagioli and taught in various centers in Europe, the United States, and Canada.[13]

Assagioli's central idea is that the "repression of the sublime," man's higher nature or the superconscious, is as dangerous to psychological growth and health as is the repression of sexual impulses in Freudian thinking. His work therefore included deliberate stimulation of spiritual thoughts, feelings, and actions through meditation and guided imagery. For example, he used the Grail Legend and Dante's Divine Comedy to provide themes for structured exercises.†

---

*For comtemporary work in the Jungian tradition, see the *Journal of Analytic Psychology.*

†Every method of therapy, obviously, has its specific pitfalls. Just as overly traditional Freudians may emphasize repressed sexual drives to the exclusion of other aspects of human life, and behaviorists may

Assagioli postulated the existence of a "Higher Self" in each man, a concept by no means equivalent to Freud's superego, but rather "a center of self-awareness and will," which is specifically compared to the Christian idea of Christ and the Hindu idea of Atman, the spirit within. Part of Assagioli's method involves the strengthening of the will through a series of exercises. He also recommends detachment of the "Higher Self," a "point of pure consciousness," from the physical self, through repetition of such phrases as "I am not this body," and detachment from unruly emotion by such phrases as "Anger is going on." Many American psychologists would see these techniques as fostering depersonalization, and Assagioli himself recognized their riskiness with any patient who "has the feeling that his body does not belong to him.[13 p.123] In fairness, it should also be noted that Assagioli was flexible; for example, he anticipated a classical bioenergetic technique by suggesting to an adolescent with an unruly temper that he tear telephone books apart when he felt his rages coming on.[Ibid, pp. 105–6]

Several innovative approaches to therapy* also make use of transpersonal concepts. An example is Emmons' meditative

---

disregard the unconscious, so psychosynthesists may focus upon spiritual growth and neglect practical realities. In the seminar with Assagioli which I attended in Italy in 1968, participants were asked to report any disturbance following a guided fantasy led by Assagioli's assistant, another psychiatrist. One participant, a young man, reported a frightening image of a great eye staring from the sky. The assistant asked him to find in his pocket a "magic pill" that would relieve his anxiety, presumably in order to convey the idea that he himself possessed self-healing wisdom. Not only was the paranoid ideation disregarded, but the assistant was apparently unaware of what most of us knew in the seminar— that this participant was suffering an untreatable visual deterioration that would end in blindness.

*The methods described here merely offer a sample of various contemporary approaches to transpersonal psychology; there are many others, including Masters' and Houston's Mind Games;[26] Vaughan's training in intuition;[27] Progoff's dialogues;[28] and Yensen's perceptual-affective therapy.[29]

therapy,[30] which consists almost entirely of helping the patient find his "Inner Source," described as a "wisdom . . . given many names . . .: the deep self, the overself, the superconscious, the higher self, the biological wisdom. . . . The tendency in the United States is to hypnotize the Inner Source, to biofeedback it, mind control it, seminar train it, guide its imagery, stimulate it with mantras, with music, with dance, with machines, with psychedelic drugs. . . . There is an entirely *natural* way of getting in touch with the Inner Source."[30, p. 4] This seems less fantastic if one remembers homeostasis and the body's immunological systems.

The "natural way" consists of first explaining the procedure, then asking the patient to lie down, eyes closed, and describe every experience, including bodily sensations, the inner visual field, and thought processes. This procedure is distinguished from free association by closed eyes; explicit recognition and trust of the Inner Source; minimal therapeutic interpretation; and flexible time limits. Patients are reported to improve through catharsis, spontaneous insights, intense reliving of traumatic childhood experiences, improved self-acceptance, and often "a greater awareness of God or an Ultimate Reality." The efficacy of this procedure may lie partly in Emmons's confidence; his book does not report its use by other therapists. Nevertheless, it is interesting to find an approach that reminds us of the patient's own intrinsic self-healing power.

In contrast, Fischer-Hoffman, in the "Quadrinity Method" (body, mind, spirit, emotion)[31] requires us to accept the concept, not necessarily implied either by parapsychology or by the transpersonal viewpoint, that discarnate spirits exist and may take an active, benevolent interest in human affairs.* The basic idea of the Quadrinity approach is psychologically sound in that it requires the patient to express fully his fury and resentment first at his mother, then at his father, then to become reconciled with both by understanding that they, like himself, were also victims of

---

*Hoffman's book has been issued by a well-established publishing house and endorsed by several respected professionals including Virginia Satir.

circumstance.* This procedure, which is extremely dramatic and highly structured, is conducted with the help of a "spirit guide" whom the patients meet in a fantasized "sanctuary" and who apparently is seen not as a creation of the patient's unconscious mind, but as an actual spiritual entity. Hoffman writes:<sup></sup>*Ibid.*, p. 69

> Some people find false guides that are projections of their current concerns or problems. Your real guide is never someone you know or a famous person. Often negative spirits masquerade as Jesus, Buddha, or other religious teachers.

A central technique of this method involves a conversation between the client as he or she was at puberty, and the father or mother at the same age. Hoffman again emphasizes that "The dialogue is *not* a fantasy or guided imagery. It is a mind revelation employing natural sensory perception abilities† in order to receive and tune into the emotional experiences of mother's past.*Ibid.*, p.126

On an *a priori* basis, it is quite possible to accept Hoffman's claims of cure, since his system is based not only on catharsis followed by forgiveness but on the widely accepted finding that parents, knowingly or unknowingly, may convey to their children unhappy and destructive "scripts" or "programs." The method itself, if it is eventually substantiated by objective research, should

*Nearly every school of psychotherapy, as far as I know, maintains that it is beneficial for us to experience rage, or at least resentment, in varying degrees, toward our parents, and then accept and forgive them as similar victims of circumstances. This concept is found in such diverse sources as Oriental mysticism, which holds that our parents, like ourselves, are affected by *karma*, and the philosopher-psychoanalyst Erich Fromm, who held that our parents, like ourselves, are victims of society.

†"Natural sensory perception abilities" is Hoffman's term for ESP; he means that the patient is using ESP to contact his parent at the age of puberty.

not be judged by Hoffman's account of its origin, which also involves communications from discarnate spirits.

As he tells us, Hoffman was the proprietor of a men's clothing store and a part-time psychic. In a clairvoyant vision he was visited by his friend, Dr. Fischer, who had been dead for six months, and who in life had been a neuropsychiatrist skeptical about parapsychology and psychic phenomena. Fischer taught Hoffman the Quadrinity Process, instructing him in how to use the Process to help others. At this time, Hoffman is training professionals to use what was originally called the Fischer-Hoffman method, and he states that "Dr. Fischer, through me, continues to improve and refine the Process."*Ibid.*, p. 220

Although I am disposed to accept many concepts of transpersonal psychology, it is difficult to write of Hoffman's claims, sincere though I believe them, without irony. Reality is certainly stranger than it seems, and it may indeed be that Dr. Fischer returned from the dead to transmit a new and better method of psychotherapy. The alternative explanation, which is less spectacular, is perhaps equally awesome: that Hoffman's unconscious mind synthesized the Process from his reading and observation.

VI. *Mind-Training Systems.* Various institutes offer highly structured "mind training" sessions to groups of several hundred people over a period of days, for fees ranging from $300 to $700. People may take these courses in a genuine search for personal growth, from a need for social contacts, or because they are seeking a quick, relatively easy cure for emotional problems. Indeed, the promotional literature of Silva Mind Control actually quotes a journalist who took the course and described it as "the perfect therapy for this fast-moving age; it's quick, it's enjoyable, and it works."

These institutes typically deny that they offer therapy. Nonetheless, they use techniques that elicit strong emotions, they offer guidance in successful living, and they encourage ventilation of intense feeling. Although the leaders usually lack professional training and do not take legal or ethical responsibility as therapists, it is difficult to distinguish their procedures from psychotherapy. Other criticisms of these institutes include: frank commercialism; the possible risk of using powerful psychological techniques with unscreened people; and, with some institutes, an effort to develop "psychic powers" such as telepathy in all candidates, regardless of their personal stability.

Silva Mind Control and EST (Erhard Seminars Training) are representative of these institutes, although there are many others. EST vigorously challenges the accepted self-image of participants; Silva tries to give participants greater respect for their potential psychic functioning. EST emphasizes challenge, Silva emphasizes support. Both induce altered states of consciousness (probably light hypnosis) through guided imagery and meditation; both attempt to develop mental control of physical states; both regard reality as affected strongly by our expectations. Although EST has been described as having "a strongly Buddhist orientation in Western format,"[33, p.141] it does not specifically emphasize the spiritual dimension of human experience. Silva, on the other hand, strongly emphasizes the transpersonal; participants are instructed to seek and find male and female "helpers" within themselves while at the level of deep relaxation and are deliberately trained to use their psychic powers in various ways, including psychic healing. However, impartial, carefully controlled research[36] has found no evidence of the promised clairvoyant ability in Silva graduates except under conditions that could have allowed the experimenter to give unconscious subliminal cues.

Most of the mind-training institutes present "research," usually a tabulation of replies to questionnaires by satisfied participants. Professional evaluation is variable.* A laudatory study of EST is offered by a psychiatrist who referred 67 of his patients;[33] others report serious psychiatric disturbances as a result of participation.[34] An EST participant already in psychotherapy is probably in the best position to utilize the experience positively.

Reports on Silva are also contradictory. Two respected biofeedback experts who identify strongly with transpersonal psychology regard Silva as dangerous, believing that it may train unstable people to develop psychic powers they are not equipped to handle.[35] They quote the case of a Silva graduate who began to

*Fenwick,[32] a clinical psychologist who took the EST training, offers a readable description and evaluation of her experience.

hear one of his "imaginary psychic advisors" speaking to him without being invited to do so.* On the other hand, two psychiatrists sent 189 patients, including 75 who were seriously disturbed, to Silva and concluded that it is "relatively safe and highly beneficial for the disturbed individual (*at least, while under the care of a psychiatrist familiar with the program*)."[37, p. 64] (Italics mine).

Silva is helpful for some people because it recognizes and respects paranormal experiences and mystical aspirations often associated with the fear of insanity and thereby may alleviate anxiety or even expand consciousness.

VII. *Eastern Mystical Teachers.* Transpersonal psychology is far more profoundly influenced by the various schools of Eastern thought than by Jewish or Christian mysticism, although there are some strong mystical Christian movements in the United States.† Hardly an issue of the *Journal of Transpersonal Psychology* lacks one or more articles on the theory, research, or practice of Zen or other varieties of Buddhism, Taoism, Sufism, or other Eastern traditions. Anyone known to be interested in transpersonal psychology finds his mailbox crammed with announcements of courses, lectures, and seminars given by swamis, yogis, and lamas whose credentials are all but impossible for the average Westerner to evaluate. Moreover, some of these announcements seem tainted with an advertising approach; they use such phrases as "Ascended Being of Pure Light," "age-old secrets of happiness

*Clinically speaking, Silva is not necessarily responsible for this disaster. Auditory hallucinations may be precipitated by a wide variety of circumstances.

†Notably the Association for Research and Enlightenment (A.R.E.), a nondemoninational Christian association founded on the teachings of the mystic and trance healer, Edgar Cayce. A.R.E. has extensive headquarters at Virginia Beach, Va., maintains a large resident and travelling staff, and has nearly 2,000 study groups around the country. My impression is that it is not open to the accusations of commercialism that have been levelled against the TM organization and some of the mind-training institutes. It is my further impression (statistically unverified) that A.R.E. tends to attract conventional American families, while the Oriental teachers attract intellectuals and young members of the counterculture.

and powers," "the attainment of perfect inner bliss." Yet upon investigation, it appears that many of these teachers are highly trained representatives of their traditions and that they are enthusiastically endorsed by many of our own respected M.D.'s and Ph.D.'s.

LeShan thinks that the active effort of the mystical Eastern schools to find students is a sign of threatening world holocaust. He points out that in the past it might have taken years for a student to find a serious teacher of Zen or Sufism; today they may advertise in newspapers. He sees this not as commercialism, but as an effort by the Eastern masters to communicate their wisdom in the hope of avoiding global disaster, and he summarizes their position as, "If our carefully hoarded knowledge is not used now, it will be too late. It is now or never for the human race . . . to find and live the unused side of itself."[15, p. 135]

LeShan may be correct about the motives of the Eastern mystical teachers. Yet it seems no wiser to assume that anyone who calls himself an Eastern mystic is qualified to teach than to assume that anyone who calls himself a psychotherapist (at least in states where the profession is not regulated by law) is qualified to treat patients. There are perhaps three general attributes that might lead to justifiable suspicion of a guru, as indeed they would lead to justifiable suspicion of a Western specialist: 1) financial greed; 2) rigid authoritarianism, for example, the insistence that there is only one "right way" to meditate; 3) an attitude that the guru alone knows ultimate secrets that he will share only with a chosen few.

Like the mind-training courses, these teachers probably attract not only people who are genuinely seeking spiritual growth, but also people who would like a fast trip to happiness. Their approach differs sharply from psychotherapy in that no attention is usually paid to the individual's past traumas or present conflicts. The personal Freudian unconscious is bypassed. The approach, which typically includes meditation, chanting, and the guru's teachings, is focused on the relinquishment of such negative emotions as fear, anger, and greed, and on the attainment of a serene mystical conviction that *all is one*.

It is fairly easy to play the game of identifying the Eastern mystical approach with psychopathology. Thus the mindfulness meditation, "Vipassana," which consists in watching thoughts come and go without getting involved with them, can be compared to obsessive-compulsive rumination. Emotional detachment can be compared to depersonalization. A sense of communion with the universe can be seen as loss of ego boundaries.

Yet it seems erroneous to regard the mystical experience as entailing a loss of individuality. Jung, our great Western mystic, regarded "individuation" as a prime goal of analysis. Maslow found that "self-actualizing individuals" were most likely to have peak experiences. Anyone who has been fortunate enough to experience, even momentarily, complete absorption in music, beauty, or love knows that these experiences do not involve the loss of selfhood but rather its transcendence. However, the meditative life style is so alien to the active Western temperament that the effects of Eastern teachings will probably be felt principally through their influence on transpersonal psychology.

VIII. *Psychic Healing.* Medical treatment depends upon at least two basic factors: the treatment itself, and the physician-patient relationship. Even the most conservative physicians today recognize that the patient's confidence in the physician not only alleviates stress, but probably creates conditions favorable to the mobilization of the patient's natural healing system. Thus the term "placebo effect"* need not imply a deceptive physician and a gullible patient, but rather the stimulation of a basic self-healing process.

Beyond the placebo effect, there is some solid experimental

---

*The placebo effect was investigated two decades ago in an experiment which, although brilliant, seems ethically horrendous. An operation for anginal pain, which entailed tying off a chest artery, had brought symptomatic relief and greater exercise tolerance for about 40 percent of the patients treated. A group of patients was utilized for research by performing this operation on half the cases, but only giving anesthesia and opening the chest, without tying the artery, on the other half. Results were identical—still 40 percent—and the operation was abandoned, leaving open for consideration the question of how often radical surgical or pharmacological treatment is helpful because patient and physician believe in it rather than because of the actual procedure.[38]

evidence[39] and considerable anecdotal evidence[40, 41] that there is such a thing as psychic healing,* in which the healer brings about positive physical changes through such methods as prayer, concentration, and the laying on of hands. Some physicians may be natural healers, although there also exists evidence that psychic healing can be taught and learned, primarily through meditative techniques.[42] Some healers believe that they bring about God's intervention through prayer; others that they are the agency for benevolent spirits; still others that a transfer of psychic energy is involved. LeShan holds that healing may occur when the healer is able to enter an altered state of consciousness in which he merges lovingly with the healee who responds with accelerated functioning of his self-reparative systems.[40, 42].† This phenomenon may take place when healer and healee are barely acquainted, or even when the healer is at a distance and knows only the healee's name.

A highly respected psychiatrist suggests that psychic ability, telepathy in particular, may well be a factor in therapeutic

*The evidence for psychic healing is less impressive than the evidence for psi and other paranormal phenomena, probably because experimental data is more difficult to obtain. The integrity of LeShan, who has reported some striking personal experiences,[40] has never been questioned, but his data can be regarded as inconclusive by skeptics, since the possibility of coincidental spontaneous remission of disease in his healees cannot be ruled out. Reports about the famous Philippine surgical healers have been seriously questioned. References [39,41,43] give widely different interpretations by trained investigators who observed these psychic surgeons at work.

†In 1969, LeShan began training healers in his method, principally by teaching them arduous and undramatic ways of meditation. The training has been continued in recent years by Joyce Goodrich, a clinical psychologist, under the aegis of the Consciousness Research and Healing Project in New York. Trainees are instructed to accept no remuneration, and to work only with healees who are concomitantly under conventional medical care. The Project is planning a carefully designed series of double-blind experiments in distance healing with patients undergoing gall bladder surgery.

effectiveness.* It is also possible that psychic healing ability may play a part in effective psychotherapy. However, it is dismaying that many psychics who consider themselves healers offer services as paid psychotherapists without theoretical or technical training.

A colleague tells of her patient, "Della," who came for treatment because she felt that her whole life was "gradually falling apart." Within a few months it became apparent that Della lost jobs and friends because of her irritability and self-centeredness. My colleague was working hard to help Della understand this, when Della decided that therapy was "too slow" and consulted a psychic advisor. The psychic told Della that her problems arose from bad karma carried over from previous incarnations,† karma that could be dispelled by further sessions with the psychic. Della decided nevertheless to remain with my colleague, but it now became considerably more difficult to help Della see her part in creating her own troubles.

Some psychic entrepreneurs offer themselves as advisors to therapists who may request "readings" on difficult patients.[45] These psychics possibly possess telepathic ability that enables them to pick up the therapist's unconscious or unformulated knowledge of the patient; they then feed it back in a way that can clarify the therapist's problem. However (as described in an earlier chapter), there are supervisory methods, such as asking the therapist to role-play the patient, which can also bring to light the therapist's unconscious knowledge. A therapist who is so dubious about his ability that he must consult a psychic might well consider further training.

We all know that even a highly accredited physician or psychologist may be incompetent. Yet in selecting a specialist, it is possible to evaluate credentials and then make a choice on the basis of personal trust and congeniality. With psychics there are no established standards of training and credentials and evaluation is difficult. The danger signals of charlatanry here are

---

*Jerome Frank, in his Master Lecture at the 1981 convention of the American Psychological Association in Los Angeles.

†The concept of karma and reincarnation can readily be misused to avoid taking personal responsibility.

similar to those suggested in the preceding section: frank commercialism, as shown in the attempt to "sell" the client on further paid sessions; an overly directive attitude; and the promise of miracles.*

In general, transpersonal techniques (particularly dreamwork, guided imagery, and meditation) may well be used to deepen and enrich the therapeutic experience. Like all techniques, they should be applied according to the needs of the indi-

---

*Since research in psychic healing is still at the point where anecdotal data may be of interest, let me present my personal experiences.

Some years ago, I had a broken leg that did not knit for well over a year, and my orthopedist recommended a bone graft. Reluctant about the operation, I decided to try unorthodox treatment, and persuaded my orthopedist to grant a month's delay. During that month I had four acupuncture treatments and five treatments from a husband-wife team of psychic healers who "transmitted energy" through their hands, prayed, and also recommended certain herb teas. My leg healed completely, with no residual effects. It *may* have been coincidence.

I did *not* "have faith," as I informed the psychic healers. I did, however, perceive upon meeting them that they were sincere. They did not charge; I gave them a "donation," but it is my impression that they would have worked without fee.

Later, in the course of preparing this book, I saw two psychics recommended by colleagues. To the first psychic I brought a personal problem which was bona fide although not severe enough to send me back to psychotherapy. She picked up the problem almost accurately (probably through a combination of telepathy and subliminal cues), gave me advice which seemed irrelevant, and recommended three additional sessions "for clearing" at a fee comparable to that of a prestigious therapist.

With the next psychic, I asked for help with a patient about whom I was genuinely worried. This one did not give advice, but closed her eyes, "beamed energy" at the patient, told me confidently that he would now improve rapidly, and again charged a surprisingly high fee. The patient did indeed get slowly better, but at the rate which might reasonably have been expected in therapy. It is only fair to emphasize that with the first healers, I was actually in need of help, whereas with the other two healers, I was conducting an investigation.

vidual. For some patients, they may help bring about a joyous widening of horizons; others may use preoccupation with mystical experiences as a dreamy way of avoiding the world of taxes, automobiles, and alarm clocks in which we all must function.

*Chapter 10*

# DEATH, MOURNING, AND THE PSYCHOTHERAPIST

*If we cannot face death with equanimity, how can we be of assistance to our patients?*

—Kübler-Ross

In ordinary practice, every psychotherapist faces patients who, with varying seriousness, consider suicide, and others preoccupied by fear of death. We see patients mourning for the loss of a beloved, or perhaps we must help someone through an immediate bereavement. Sometimes a patient in treatment learns that he has a life-threatening illness; sometimes, indeed, the patient *enters* treatment to cope with the threat of impending death.

Formerly, these situations were the responsibility of religious guides who provided comfort through prayer, offered absolution from sin, held out hope for survival, and/or tried to instill acceptance of the will of God. Today, although many people still turn to church or synagogue for help, psychotherapists are increasingly faced with situations involving death for which their ordinary therapeutic skills are not always sufficient.

The individual philosophy of different therapists is not necessarily based upon theoretical orientation. On a personal level, therapists may be traditionally religious, uncompromisingly materialistic, humanistic, or transpersonally oriented. Some regard themselves as skilled technicians; others, overtly or covertly, regard themselves as spiritual advisors. In private conversation, I have heard a respected classical analyst say that he considers no psychoanalysis really complete until the analysand has relinquished "superstitions" such as belief in God and immortality. I have heard another equally respected analyst maintain that genuine emotional maturity must involve spiritual development. But regardless of theoretical orientation or personal belief, it is difficult for a therapist to work effectively with death-related problems until he has come to terms with the certainty of his own eventual death and its meaning to him.*

Transpersonal psychology is making a significant contribution through its attention to the experience of dying.[2,3,4] Nevertheless, it is possible to obtain an advanced degree and even go through a post-doctoral training institute without learning how to work with death-related emotional problems. And, although several recent books deal with the meaning of death to the individual, the topic is still often treated as taboo.† Thus the clinician may be quite unprepared for such problems.

"Lew" was in his first year of private practice, and he was one of my first supervisees; we were learning together. For some months he had been working with"Janet," a middle-aged woman who had sought help for periodic mild depressions as well as for marital problems, for which her husband was concurrently seeing another therapist.

*An eminent psychologist specializing in thanatology holds that the specific belief or value system of the therapist is less important than the clarity and firmness of that belief.[1] My own conviction is that it is even more important for the therapist to regard the *patient's* belief, or lack of belief, with genuine respect.

†Many theologians, as well as many psychotherapists, seem to share this taboo. As I recall various funeral or commemorative services, the speakers devoted their time exclusively to eulogy and/or exhortation. Perhaps they were correct in gauging what their listeners wanted—an avoidance of death.

Lew was justifiably proud; Janet's depressions had grown lighter and her marriage had become more satisfying. Then, entering my office one day, Lew looked so distressed that I immediately forgot supervision and inquired, "What's wrong?"

Very wrong, indeed. In a routine checkup, Janet's physician had discovered a tumor that seemed malignant, in a location making a biopsy difficult and an operation almost impossible. He had suggested drastic chemotherapy, but was obviously pessimistic.

Janet, Lew told me, had opened her session with "I won't be coming any more," explaining that her natural anxiety, along with the debilitation the treatment would inevitably entail, would deprive her of the energy to "face up to her problems." She thanked Lew for his help and they said a friendly good-bye. Lew was in distress not only because of his personal feeling for Janet but because "all his good work had gone for nothing," as he expressed it ruefully.

After this session, devoted partly to helping Lew work through his own feelings, something felt wrong. I thought about it, consulted a senior colleague, and telephoned Lew with specific suggestions.

Janet, I thought, must feel very much alone despite her improved marriage. She was not a religious woman, hence could not turn naturally to a pastoral counselor. She must have many feelings—anger, bewilderment, fear.* Therefore I suggested that Lew should phone Janet and inform her that he had been mistaken in accepting her termination. He would like to continue

*Kübler-Ross's description of the five stages typical of the person who faces death, described in reference 2, are denial, anger, bargaining, depression, and acceptance. They offer an excellent guideline as to what the dying person may experience. However, another leading thanatologist[1] does not view them as necessarily typical.

Kübler-Ross's work has been highly influential in calling attention to our cultural difficulties in dealing with death and dying. She has been sharply criticized in the lay press because of some questionable professional associations, but such associations in no way detract from the value of her observations.

seeing her. If she was not well enough during her difficult treatment to come to his office, he would visit her home. Did Lew feel able to do this, I asked him.*

Lew responded with enormous relief. He had been haunted by the sense that he'd deserted Janet. He also felt anxiety. In his own analysis, he had never worked through feelings about death. Spontaneously he decided to return for further analytic work in this area. Meanwhile, he called Janet.

She was delighted. Although she had taken the initiative in termination she had felt deserted. She had also felt she "did not wish to burden him" with her tragic situation. They continued to work together for several months, dealing with an unconscious fantasy of Janet's that her illness was somehow a punishment for various misdeeds, real or fantasized. Their final interview was in the terminal wing of a hospital (her cancer had metastasized) and her last words to him were, "You've helped a lot." She had been able to accept her death. Later, Lew received a letter from her husband, also expressing warm appreciation. Lew grew by this experience, and so did I.

Recently I was consulted by "Ruth," a warm and mature psychologist, about her twenty-one-year-old patient, "Lisa." There were tragic similarities between Lisa and Janet, both of whom were just beginning to enjoy life as a result of psychotherapy, but Lisa's case presented special problems.

Lisa's physician had diagnosed an ovarian tumor that proved malignant and necessitated intensive postoperative chemotherapy under hospitalization because there was extensive tissue involvement. The prognosis was uncertain; Lisa might die soon or live for several years. Each week Ruth visited her patient for a session in the hospital, where Lisa confided that she feared she was "going crazy." When her pain became acute, Lisa would drift off into a bluish haze in which she seemed to separate from her body, float around the room, and sometimes even visit her

---

*Since no therapist can help a patient by offering more support than he can give ungrudgingly, let me note that Lew was young, vigorous, and without family obligations. If today I were faced by a patient in Janet's situation, with my physical energies somewhat limited by age, I would offer telephone appointments rather than house visits.

sweetheart, whom she usually "saw" in his room reading. At these times the pain would disappear. These experiences were usually blissful, but they had also been terrifying. Twice, Lisa had felt herself pursued by the devil. There were no indications of incoherence or bizarre behavior, nor did the hospital staff see any psychiatric problems.

Lisa was clearly undergoing "out-of-body" experiences, which are not uncommon for people close to death. Luckily, Ruth was familiar with this phenomenon, and could convince Lisa that it did not indicate insanity. Somewhat uncertain of her own spiritual convictions, Ruth nevertheless utilized her knowledge of Lisa's orthodox Catholic background and suggested that these "dreams while I'm awake," as Lisa called them, might "be God's way of helping Lisa bear her pain."*

In discussing the devil experiences, Ruth was more at home, since much of her previous work had been devoted to relieving Lisa of lifelong guilt about her father's incestuous attacks during her childhood. This work continued in the hospital. My only contribution to Ruth's admirable handling of the case was that if Lisa again found herself pursued by the devil, she might say to him firmly, "I belong to God, you cannot hurt me." Ruth agreed that Lisa would find strength in this suggestion, not only as a defense against her inner devil, but as a further indication that the therapist respected her experiences.

It was more difficult for Ruth to decide how best to work with Lisa's denial that her life span was probably limited. A well-meaning physician had congratulated Lisa on her "recovery;" another physician said that chemotherapy could give her only a year or two. Now Lisa was happily making plans for the future, marriage to her sweetheart, raising a family. Again, Ruth handled the problem appropriately by accepting Lisa's thoughts about the future, but at the same time pointing out that each present day could be enjoyed—which was quite true since Lisa was usually able to take pleasure in music, flowers, and visiting friends. We

*This would not have been Ruth's natural phrasing; she adopted Lisa's Catholic perspective with appropriate clinical skill. Similarly, my suggestion of what Lisa might say to her visionary devil was meant to be in line with Lisa's religious approach, not mine or Ruth's.

agreed that it was not Ruth's responsibility to persuade Lisa to face death prematurely, but that she should instead listen for later indications that Lisa might be ready to discuss what death meant to her.

Patients such as Lisa and Janet challenge the psychotherapist's personal maturity as well as his technical skills. My conviction is that every clinical training program should include mandatory courses on the management of death-related situations, and that every clinician's personal therapy should include work on facing death. If the therapist has not accepted his own eventual death, he may be uneasy and perhaps inept in working with a seriously ill patient, and may tend to support denial by the implied message "Just cheer up and don't think about it."

Yet a significant distinction must be made between collusion with the patient's pretense that no illness exists and the support of hope. Even with cancer patients, unexpected remissions may occur, and hope may be a factor in such remissions. No responsible psychotherapist would advise a patient who has accepted standard medical treatment to *abandon* such treatment in favor of prayer, meditation, psychic healing, or positive imagery, yet considerable data suggests that these supplementary approaches are often associated with remissions or improvement of life-threatening illness.[7,8,9,10,11,12] Such procedures may be effective because they mobilize the body's natural abilities to fight disease, a process that requires no mystical explanation. An alternative explanation, which would be held by many theologians and transpersonal psychologists, is that these procedures facilitate contact with the cosmic healing forces of the universe (or God). If these alternative explanations were fully understood, in a way our present state of knowledge does not enable us to understand, they might not after all be contradictory. This question involves an understanding of the ultimate nature of reality, which thinkers from various disciplines are *exploring*.[14,15,16,17,18,19,20]

Fortunately, the clinician who may wish to use such techniques as LeShan's psychic healing meditation or Simonton's positive imagery need not grapple with their philosophical implications. It is usually sufficient to discuss briefly the well-accepted fact of the relationship between mind and body. These techniques, well-described in the references cited, are entirely com-

patible with standard medical treatment and ongoing psychotherapy.*

With bereaved patients, the therapist's personal belief in the
possibility of an afterlife may be equally important as with the
patient who is seriously ill. From my practice I recall "Bertha,"
who entered treatment with a depression so serious that electroshock had been recommended. She chose psychotherapy instead, and worked with me intensively, although it was over a year
before the depression lightened. Among other etiological factors,
we found that she had never completed her mourning for a lovely
five-year-old daughter who had drowned some years before. As
often in repressed grief or incomplete mourning, Bertha was still
tormented by thoughts of "times when I wasn't nice enough" and
"if only I'd been more careful!" Bertha's unrealistic guilt was
considerably relieved after a year and a half of treatment, and her
depression began to fall within the range of ordinary "blue
spells." Then came the question.

Did I, Bertha's therapist, think that "Pixie was still alive
somewhere?" Or was she nothing, bones in a coffin? This image,
earlier in treatment, had been a melancholic obsession.

It seemed unfair, after our intense work together, to reply
with a variation of "What do *you* think?" I therefore told Bertha

*Although by no means do I consider myself a psychic healer, I have
attended several seminars in psychic healing (given by Joyce Goodrich
along the lines developed by LeShan and under the auspices of the
Consciousness Research and Training Project in New York City) and
have occasionally meditated with a patient who is physically ill. The
patient, who sits facing me, is asked to close his eyes and visualize himself
as well while I imagine healing energy streaming through me toward the
patient. Almost always, the patient feels refreshed, and occasionally
there are such follow-up reports as "The doctor says I'm improving
faster than he thought I would;" nothing spectacular has occurred, nor
have I ever had occasion to use this approach with terminal illness. I do
not include these meditations as part of the regular paid therapy session,
but add fifteen minutes before or afterward, without fee. The clinically
interesting point is that this procedure does not seem to interfere with
ongoing therapy or even with expressions of the negative transference in
later sessions.

openly that my own mind was divided. Part of me believes that death is a transitional stage toward growth and experience on another plane of development that is almost unimaginable to our present state of knowledge, while part of me regards death as a passage to nothingness.*

Despite my inconclusiveness, Bertha was comforted. My own split belief, apparently, gave her strength to endure a similar division of thinking within herself. She was finally able to regard Pixie's death as a mystery that must be accepted, and go on with the business of life. It seems far better for a therapist to share his own confusion or uncertainty (if the patient is ready for this) rather than to pretend a belief that is not quite sincere in the hope that it will offer reassurance.

On the other hand, it is important for the therapist not to influence the patient by his own personal belief, whatever it may be. No therapist, I am sure, would try to deprive a seriously ill patient of belief in God and the afterlife, even if the therapist himself considers them childish delusions. Yet there is abundant evidence that the therapist's own value system comes through, however he may try to be impartial. Perhaps a therapist who views transpersonal beliefs as nonsense should not try to work on death or bereavement with a patient whose orientation is religious or spiritual. Similarly, if the patient is comfortable with a mechanistic view of the universe, it is not the therapist's place to become an evangelical guru for religious or transpersonal ways of thought, for the patient may depend upon his "realistic" philosophy to maintain his sense of personal identity.

A wise and mature pastoral counselor told me the following story. Minister of a Protestant church, he had for years known "Jim," who with his family attended services regularly. Jim was

---

*I am aware that most traditional psychologists would regard this split as a sign of emotional immaturity, or even as an indication of conflict and wishful thinking, while transpersonal psychologists might see it as a stuck point in my spiritual development. Oddly enough, I do not find this split distressing. However, it is not an *even* split. On the whole, I regard the mystical view of life as closer to the ultimate reality (whatever that may be) than the materialistic and reductionistic view.

now in his eighties, with many grandchildren and a fine record of service to the community. Hearing that Jim had returned from a hospital with only a few months to live, the pastor paid him a home visit to offer the consolation of prayer and hope for a life hereafter, according to the tenets of the religion in which the pastor firmly believed.

Politely and appreciatively, Jim refused these consolations. Jim believed that death was final, a complete end of consciousness. He would live on in his fine children and grandchildren and in the contributions he had made to society. He had attended church because he believed that it was a socially useful institution and because he enjoyed the friendly contacts.

It would have been absurd to challenge the philosophy by which Jim had lived well and with which he was dying contentedly. Wisely, the pastor spoke of Jim's family, shook hands, and departed.*

In one specific situation I have made use of a transpersonal concept in a shamelessly manipulative way—when a patient threatens suicide. Every trained therapist is familiar with suicide's various underlying dynamics, such as self-punishment and/or the wish to punish someone else, but while these dynamics are being clarified an emergency must sometimes be met. With a patient who feels consciously that he yearns only for oblivion, I may speak musingly of the Eastern religious doctrine that inability to handle problems in this incarnation results in a karmic repetition of the same problem after death, perhaps under even more difficult circumstances.

"Do you really believe that?" asks the amazed patient.

"I don't know . . . it's an interesting idea . . . millions of people do believe it." The patient, of course, is not convinced, but he may

---

*Pastoral psychology, which represents an attempt on the part of organized religion to meet the psychological needs of troubled people, has some overlap with transpersonal mysticism but in general seems closer to conventional psychotherapy. Readers who wish to explore this area are referred to the journals *Pastoral Psychology, Journal of Pastoral Care, Psychology and Religion,* and to such contemporary writing as Wise's effort to synthesize Freudian insights with Christian theology.[21]

be shaken into a reevaluation of his life and death, and I suspect that several suicide attempts have been prevented partly by this approach.*

In contrast, patients obsessed with the fear of death often avoid discussing it in therapy, an avoidance with which the therapist may collude. When the fear does emerge, it may turn out to be associated with a sense that life has been incompletely lived; death is feared as total isolation; or there is sometimes an intense horror of the death experience itself. One patient said, "I don't mind the thought of *being* dead, but I am terrified of *dying*." This horror can sometimes be partially alleviated by a discussion of the prototypical near-death experience (conventionally abbreviated as NDE), which has been widely reported and discussed† in transpersonal and parapsychological literature.[22,23,24,25,26] These experiences, coming from persons of widely divergent cultures, ethnic groups, ages, and educational level, bear striking similarities, although a given individual may have only *one* or *several* or *all* of the experiences. They may include a sense of departure from the body, possibly including a vision from above of the unconscious physical self being attended by medical personnel; passage through a long, dark tunnel, often frightening; emergence into light, with a sense of bliss or even ecstacy; being met by a deceased relative or friend who acts as a guide; glimpses of beautiful gardens or luminous towers; and often confrontation with a dazzling white light that may be seen as a celestial being. Persons who have undergone this experience report that they have lost their fear of death and feel better prepared to enjoy their remaining lifespan.

There is solid documentation that, as subjective experiences, these events do occur; they have been described in the most conservative medical journals.[27,28,29] The majority of academic psychologists probably hold that these experiences represent a

---

*I use this Eastern teaching partly because it startles the patient, catching him off guard, and partly because it is actually more acceptable to me than the Western concept of hell.

†Reference 30, an article in the *American Psychologist*, provides an excellent bibliography on this subject and an interesting overview, although the author's position is skeptical and even satirical.

state of consciousness altered by near-death neural and biochemical reactions interpreted as wish-fulfilling visions. Others, including clinicians of wide experience,[2,3,26,31] point out the striking similarities of NDE's among a wide population, the strong subjective conviction that these experiences are valid, and the fact that they are by no means associated with psychiatric symptomatology; the tentative conclusion, then, is that they are genuine glimpses of an afterlife.

Research parapsychologists, in keeping with their traditional caution, in general take a middle ground between total skepticism and uncritical belief, as exemplified particularly well by Grosso,[32] who points out that the vigorous "debunking" of aggressive skeptics is well-matched by "the fiery . . . tendency to believe" of some dedicated mystics (in his example, drawn not from the ranks of clinicians but from students at a yoga ashram). The choice of how to interpret NDE's and other possible evidence of survival after death is clearly determined by individual philosophy and values. Luckily, the practicing clinician is not required to make such a decision but need only regard the feelings and beliefs of his patient with open-mindedness and respect.

# REFERENCES

## INTRODUCTION

1. Tornatore, N. "The Paranormal Event in Psychotherapy: a Survey of 609 Psychiatrists." *Psychic* 7 (1977): 34–37.

2. Vaughan, F. Transpersonal Psychotherapy. *Journal of Transpersonal Psychology.* Vol. II, 9. L979, pp. 101110.

3. Rush, J. H. Physical Aspects of Psi Phenomena. In Schmeidler, G. (ed.) *Parapsychology.* Metuchen, New Jersey. 1976.

4. James, W. *Varieties of Religious Experience.* New York: Random House, 1929.

5. LeShan, L. *The Medium, the Mystic and the Physicist.* New York: Random House, 1966.

## CHAPTER 1

1. Ellis, A. "Reanalysis of an Alleged Telepathic Dream." *Psychoanalysis and the Occult.* Edited by G. Devereaux. New York: Int. U. Press, 1953.

2. Rhine, J. B. *The Reach of the Mind* New York: Farrar, Straus, 1960.

3. Rhine, Louisa. *ESP in Life and Lab* New York: Macmillan, 1965.

4. Schmeidler, Gertrude R. & McConnell. *ESP and Personality Patterns* New Haven: Yale University Press, 1958.

5. Hansel, C. E. M. *ESP, a Scientific Evaluation* New York: Charles Scribners' Sons, 1966.

6. Gurney, E., & Myers, F. W. H. *Phantasms of the Living.* London: Kegan Paul, 1918.

7. Tyrrell, G. N. M. *Apparitions.* New York: MacMillan, 1963.

8. Rhine, Louisa. *The Invisible Picture.* Jefferson, N.C.: McFarland & Co., 1960.

9. Schmeidler, Gertrude R. "Separating the Sheep from the Goats." *Jl. Amer. Soc. for Psychical Research* 39 (1943): 47–49.

10. Tart. C. C. *Altered States of Consciousness.* New York: John Wiley & Sons, 1969.

11. Heywood, Rosalind. *Beyond the Reach of Sense.* New York: S. P. Dutton, 1974.

12. Pratt, J., Rhine, J. B.; and Stuart, C. *Extrasensory Perception after Sixty Years.* New York: Holt, 1940.

13. Ullman, M., and Krippner, S. *Dream Telepathy.* New York: Macmillan, 1974.

14. Cox, W. E. "Precognition: An Analysis, II." *Jl. Amer. Soc. for Psychical Research* 50 (1956): 99–107.

15. Fodor, N. *On the Trail of the Poltergeist.* London: Arco, 1959.

16. Roll, W. G. *The Poltergeist.* New York: Nelson Doubleday, 1972.

17. Owen, A. R. G. *Can we Explain the Poltergeist?* New York: Garrett, 1964.

18. "Symposium: Psychokinesis on Stable Systems." *Research in Parapsychology.* Metuchen, N.J.: Scarecrow Press, 1974.

19. Schrager, Elaine. *The Effect of Sender-Receiver Relationships and Associated Personality Variables on ESP Scores in Young Children.* Unpublished doctoral dissertation, New York University.

20. Gaddis, V. and M. *The Curious World of Twins.* New York: Hawthorne, 1972.

21. Schmeidler, Gertrude R. "Evidence for Two Kinds of Telepathy." *Int. Jl. Parapsychology* 3 (1961): 5–48.

22.  Freud, S. *New Introductory Lectures in Psychology.* London: Hogarth Press, 1934.

23.  Ehrenwald, J. *New Dimensions of Deep Analysis.* New York: Grune & Stratton, 1952.

24.  Schwartz, B. *Psychic-Nexus.* New York: Van Nostrand Reinhold, 1980.

25.  Tannous, A., and Donnelly, Katherine F. *Is Your Child Psychic?* New York: Macmillan, 1979.

26.  Pearce, J. C. *The Magical Child.* New York: Dutton, 1977.

27.  Karagulla, Shafica. *Breakthrough to Creativity.* Marina del Rey, California: Devorss & Co., 1967.

28.  Joy, W. B. *Joy's Way.* Los Angeles: J. P. Tarcher, 1978.

29.  Sugrue, T. *There is a River.* New York: Holt, Reinhart & Winston, 1942.

30.  Dykshoorn, M. B. *My Passport Says Clairvoyant.* New York: Hawthorne Books, 1974.

31.  Dean, D., and Mihalasky, J. *Executive ESP.* New York: Prentice-Hall, 1974.

32.  Eisenbud, J. *The World of Ted Serios.* New York: Morrow, 1967.

33.  Rogo, D. S. *Exploring Psychic Phenomena.* Wheaton, Ill.: Theosophical Publishing House, 1976.

34.  Garrett, Eileen. *Many Voices: The Autobiography of a Medium.* New York: G. P. Putnam's Sons, 1968.

35.  LeShan, L. *The Medium, the Mystic, and the Physicist.* New York: Ballantine, 1966.

36.  Hilton, C. *Be My Guest.* Englewood Cliffs, N.J.: Prentice-Hall, 1957.

## CHAPTER 2

1.  Reik, Theodor. *Listening with the Third Ear.* New York: Farrar, Straus, 1948.

2.  Eisenbud, Jule. "Use of the Telepathy Hypothesis in Psychotherapy." *Specialized Techniques in Psychotherapy.* Ed. Gustav Bychowski and J. Louise Despert. New York: Grove Press, 1952.

3.   Eisenbud, Jule. *Psi and Psychoanalysis.* New York: Grune & Stratton, 1970.

4.   Freud, Sigmund. "Dreams and the Occult." *New Introductory Lectures on Psychoanalysis.* New York: W. W. Norton, 1933.


### CHAPTER 3


1.   Freud, S. "Dreams and the Occult." *New Introductory Lectures on Psychoanalysis.* New York: W. W. Norton, 1933.

2.   Ehrenwald, J. *The ESP Experience.* New York: Basic Books, 1978.

3.   Eisenbud, J. *Psi and Psychoanalysis.* New York: Grune & Stratton, 1970.

4.   Ullman, M., and Krippner, S. *Dream Telepathy.* Baltimore, Md.,: Penguin, 1974.

5.   Fodor, N. *New Approaches to Dream Interpretation.* New York: Citadel Press, 1951.

6.   Schwartz, B. E. *Psychic Nexus.* New York: Van Nostrand Reinhold, 1980.

7.   Schmeidler, Gertrude, and McConnell, R. S. *Esp and Personality Patterns.* New Haven: Yale University Press, 1958.

8.   Pederson-Krag, Geraldine. "Telepathy and Repression." *Psychoanalysis and the Occult.* Edited by G. Devereaux. New York: International Universities Press, 1970.

9.   LeShan, L. *The Medium, the Mystic and the Physicist.* New York: Viking, 1974.


### CHAPTER 4


1.   Mintz, Elizabeth E. *Marathon Groups: Reality and Symbol* New York: Appleton-Century, 1971.

2.   Schwartz, B. E. *Psychic-Nexus.* New York: Van Nostrand Reinhold, 1980.

3. Rogo, E. S. *Exploring Psychic Phenomena*. Wheaton, Ill., Theosophical Publishing House: 1976.

4. Schutz, W. *Joy*. New York: Grove Press, 1967.

5. Reik, T. *Listening with the Third Ear*. New York: Pyramid Edition, 1964.

6. Mintz, E. E. Transpersonal Events in Traditional Psychotherapy? *Psychotherapy: Theory, Research and Practice*, 15, 1, Spring, 1978.

7. Erickson, M. H. *Collected Papers*. Halstead Press, 1979.

8. Schmeidler, Gertrude R. Separating the Sheep from the Goats. *Jl. Am. Soc. Psychical Research*, 40 (1946): 36–64.

## CHAPTER 5

1. Dean, S., Plyler, C. O., and Dean, M. L. "Should Psychic Studies be Included in Psychiatric Education?" *Am. Jl. Psychiatry* 137-10 (October 1980): 1247–9.

2. Tornatore, N. "The Paranormal Event in Psychotherapy: a Survey of 609 Psychiatrists." *Psychic* 7 (1977): 34–37.

3. Schmeidler, Gertrude R., and McConnell, R. A. *ESP and Personality Patterns*. New Haven: Yale University Press, 1958.

4. Hansel, C. E. M. *ESP, a Scientific Evaluation*. New York: Scribners, 1966.

5. Eisenbud, J. *Psi and Psychoanalysis*. New York: Grune & Stratton, 1970.

6. Ullman, M., and Krippner, S. *Dream Telepathy*. New York: Macmillan, 1973.

7. Spotnitz, H. "The Need for Insulation in the Schizophrenic Personality." *Psychoanalysis and the Psychoanalytic Review* 49, 3 (Fall 1962): 3–25.

8. Bates, K. E., and Newton, M. "An Experimental Study of ESP in Mental Patients." *JL. Parapsychology* 15 (1951): 271–277.

9.  Gurney, E., Myers, F. W. H., and Podmore, F. *Phantasms of the Living*. New Hyde Park: University Books, 1962.

10.  Mintz, E. E. "Obsession with the Rejecting Beloved." *Psychoanalytic Review* 67, 4 (Winter 1980–81): 479–492.

11.  Dean, E. D., and Mihalsky, J. *Executive ESP*. New York: Prentice-Hall, 1974.

12.  Krippner, S., and Murphy, G. "Humanistic Psychology and Parapsychology." *Jl. Humanistic Psychology* 13, 4 (Fall 1973): 3–24.

13.  Morrow, R. *Journeys Out of the Body*. New York: Doubleday, 1971.

## CHAPTER 6

1.  Maslow, A. H. *Toward a Psychology of Being*. Princeton: Van Nostrand-Reinhold, 1968.

2.  Mintz, Elizabeth. *Marathon Groups, Reality and Symbol*. New York: Appleton-Century-Crofts, 1971.

3.  Bach, G. R. "The Marathon Group: Intensive Practice of Intimate Interaction." *Psychol. Reports* 18 (1966):995–1002.

4.  Owen, Iris with Sparrow, Margaret. *Conjuring up Philip*. New York: Harper & Row, 1976.

5.  Perls, F. *Gestalt Therapy Verbatim*. Lafayette, Cal.: Real People Press, 1969.

6.  Freud, Anna. *The Ego and its Mechanisms of Defense*. New York: International Universities Press, 1966.

7.  Mintz, Elizabeth E. "Group Supervision: An Experiential Approach." *International Journal of Group Psychotherapy* 28, 4: 467–479.

8.  Nelson, Marie C. "The Paranormal Triangle in Analytic Supervision." *Psychoanalysis and the Psychoanalytic Review* 25, 3, (1958): 73–84.

9.  Nelson, Marie C., and Strean, H. "Further Clinical Illustration of the Paranormal Triangle Hypothesis." *Psychoanalysis and the Psychoanalytic Review* 49, 3 (1962): 61–74.

## CHAPTER 7

1. Greeley, A. *Ecstacy, a Way of Knowing.* Englewood Cliffs, N.J.: Prentice-Hall, 1974.

2. Wilson, C. *New Pathways in Psychology.* New York: Taplinger, 1972.

3. Mintz, Elizabeth E. "A Look in the Box." *Psychotherapy: Theory, Research and Practice,* 16, 3, Fall, 1979.

4. Assagioli, R. *Psychosynthesis.* New York: Viking, 1971.

5. Mintz, Elizabeth E. "On the Dramatization of Psychoanalytic Interpretations." *Group Therapy 1974.* Edited by Wolberg and Aronson. New York: Grune & Stratton, 1974.

6. LeShan, L. *The Medium, the Mystic and the Physicist.* New York: Viking, 1966.

7. James, W. *Varieties of Religious Experience.* New York: Random House, 1929.

8. Grof, S. *Realms of the Human Unconscious.* New York: Viking, 1975.

9. Perry, J. W. *Roots of Renewal in Myth and Madness.* San Francisco: Jossey Bass, 1976.

## CHAPTER 8

1. Bellak, L. *Disorders of the Schizophrenic Syndrome.* New York: Basic Books, 1979

2. Arieti, S. *Interpretation of Schizophrenia.* New York: Brunner, 1955.

3. Arieti, S. *The Parnas.* NewYork: Basic Books, 1979.

4. Pfeiffer, C. C. *et. al. The Schizophrenias: Yours and Mine.* New York: Pyramid, 1970.

5. Sechehaye, M. A. *Symbolic Realization.* New York: Int. U. Press, 1951.

6. Szasz, T. S. *The Myth of Mental Illness.* New York: Dell, 1961.

7. Laing, R. D. *The Divided Self.* Baltimore, M.d: Penguin, 1960.

8. Perry, J. W. *The Far Side of Madness.* Englewood Cliffs, N.J.: Prentice-Hall, 1974.

9. Wilber, K. *The Atman Project.* Wheaton, Ill: Theosophical Pub. House, 1980.

10. James, W. *Varieties of Religious Experience.* New York: Collier, 1961.

11. Bowes, M. B. and Freedman, D. X. "Psychedelic Experiences in Acute Psychoses." *Psychiatry and Mysticism.* Edited by S. Dean. New York: Nelson Hall, 1975.

12. Krishna, Gopi. *Kundalini.* Berkeley, Cal.: Shambala, 1970.

13. Boison, A. *Exploration of the Inner World.* New York: Harper, 1962.

14. Bernstein, C. *"A Transpersonal Approach to Schizophrenia."* Master's thesis, Lone Mountain College, 1976.

15. Kaplan, B., ed. *The Inner World of Mental Illness.* New York: Harper, 1964.

16. Assagioli, R. *Psychosynthesis.* New York: Viking, 1971.

17. Rokeach, M. *The Three Christs of Ypsilanti.* New York: Columbia, 1981.

18. Roheim, G. *Magic and Schizophrenia.* Bloomington, In: Indiana U. Presss, 1955.

19. Dean, S. R., and Thong, D. "Transcultural Aspects of Metapsychiatry." *Psychiatry and Mysticism.* Edited by S. Dean. New York: Nelson Hall, 1975.

20. Peele, S. "Reductionism in the Psychology of the Eighties." *American Psychologist* 36, 8 (Spring 1981): 807–18.

21. Boals, G. P. "Toward a Cognitive Reconceptualization of Mysticism." *Jl. Trans. Psycho.* X, 2, (1978).

22. Group for the Advancement of Psychiatry. *Mysticism: Spiritual Quest or Psychic Disorder?* Vol. IX, Publication 97, November, 1976, New York.

23. Grof, S. *Realms of the Human Unconscious.* New York: Viking, 1975.

24. Maslow, A. *Religions, Values and Peak-Experiences.* Columbus, Oh: Columbus State University Press, 1964.

## CHAPTER 9

1. Maslow, A. *Toward A Psychology of Being.* New York: Van Nostrand, 1962.

2. Maslow, A. *Religions, Values and Peak Experiences.* Columbus, Oh: Ohio State U. Press, 1964.

3. Boorstein, S., *ed. Transpersonal Psychotherapy.* Palo Alto, Cal: Science & Behavior Books, 1980.

4. Tart, C., *ed. Transpersonal Psychologies.* New York: Harper & Row, 1975.

5. Watts, A. *Psychotherapy East and West.* New York: Pantheon Books, 1961.

6. Ram Dass. *Journey of Awakening.* New York: Bantam Books, 1978.

7. Wilbur, K. *The Atman Project.* Wheaton, Ill.: Theosophical, 1980.

8. Teilhard de Chardin, P. *The Appearance of Man.* Translated by J. M. Cohen. New York: Harper & Row, 1965.

9. Krishna, Gopi. *Kundalini.* Berkeley, Cal: Shambala, 1970.

10. Bentov, I. *Stalking the Wild Pendulum.* New York: Dutton, 1977.

11. Mintz, E. E. "Transpersonal Events in Conventional Psychotherapy?" *Psychotherapy: Theory, Research & Practice* XV, 1 (1978).

12. Jung, C. G. *Memories, Dreams, Reflections.* New York: Random House, 1961.

13. Assagioli, R. *Psychosynthesis.* New York: Viking, 1965.

14. Carrington, Patricia. *Freedom in Meditation.* New York: Doubleday, 1978.

15. LeShan, L. *How to Meditate.* New York: Little, Brown, 1974.

16. Goleman, D. *Varieties of the Meditative Experience.* New York: Dutton, 1977.

17. Shapiro, D. & Walsh, R., eds. *The Science of Meditation: Research, Theory and Experience.* New York: Aldine, 1980.

18. Kornfield, J. "Intensive Insight Meditation." *Jl. Trans. Psycho.* XI, 1, (1979): 41–58.

19. Walsh, R. N. "The Initial Meditative Experience." *Jl. Trans. Psycho.* X, 1 (1978): 1–28.

20. Huxley, A. *The Doors of Perception, and Heaven and Hell.* New York: Harper & Row, 1954.

21. Grof, S. *Realms of the Human Unconscious: Observations from LSD Research.* New York: Viking Press, 1975.

22. Grof, S. "Varieties of Transpersonal Experiences: Observations from LSD Psychotherapy." *Psychiatry and Mysticism.* Edited by S. Dean. Chicago: Nelson-Hall, 1975.

23. Hoffer, A., and Osmond, H. *The Hallucinogens.* New York: Academic Press, 1967.

24. Eliade, M. *Shamanism—Archaic Techniques of Ecstacy.* Princeton: Princeton University Press, 1964.

25. Miller, S. "Dialogue With the Higher Self." *Synthesis 2.* Redwood City, Cal: Synthesis Press, 1978.

26. Masters, R., and Houston, Jean. *Mind Games.* New York: Viking, 1972.

27. Vaughn, Frances. *Awakening Intuition.* New York: Doubleday, 1979.

28. Progoff, I. *Depth Psychology and Modern Man.* New York: Julian, 1969.

29. Yensen, R. "Perceptual Affective Therapy." *Transpersonal Psychotherapy.* Edited by S. Bookstein. Palo Alto, Cal: Science and Behavior Books, 1980.

30. Emmons, M. *The Inner Source.* San Luis Obispo, Cal: Impact, 1978.

31. Hoffman, B. *No One is to Blame.* Palo Alto, Cal: Science & Behavior, 1979.

32. Fenwick, S. *Getting It.* New York: Lippincott, 1976.

33. Simon, J. "Observations on Patients Who Took EST." *Transpersonal Psychotherapy.* Edited by S. Boorstein. Palo Alto, Cal: Science & Behavior Books, 1980.

34. Glass, L., Kirsch, J., and Parris, F. "Psychiatric Disturbances Associated with Erhard Seminars Training." *Am. J1. Psychiatry* 134 (1977): 245–247.

35. Green, E., and Green, A. *Beyond Biofeedback.* New York: Dell, 1977.

36. Brier, B., Schmeidler, G. R., and Savits, H. "Three Experiments in Clairvoyant Diagnosis with Silva Mind Control Graduates." *Jl Am. Soc. Psychical Res.* 69 (July 1975).

37. McKenzie, C. D., and Wright, L. S. "The Consciousness Movement." *Voices* 17 (Spring 1981).

38. Frank, J. "Psychotherapy and the Healing Arts." *Healing*. Edited by J. L. Fossage and P. Olsen. New York: Human Sciences, 1978.

39. Krippner, S., and Villoldo, A. *Realms of Healing*. Millbrae, Cal: Celestial Arts, 1976.

40. LeShan L. A. "Toward a General Theory of Psychic Healing." *Psychiatry and Mysticism*. Edited by S. Dean. Chicago: Nelson-Hall, 1975.

41. Meek, G. W. *Healers and the Healing Process*. Wheaton, Ill: Theosophical House, 1977.

42. Goodrich, Joyce. "The Psychic Healing Training and Research Project." *Healing*. Edited by J. L. Fossage and P. Olsen. New York: Human Sciences, 1978.

43. Nolen, W. A. *A Doctor in Search of a Miracle*. New York: Random House, 1974.

44. Truax, C. B., and Carkhuff, R. R. *Toward Effective Counseling and Psychotherapy*. Chicago: Aldine, 1967.

45. Brothers, Barbara J. "Psychics and Hypnosis: A Skeptic's View." *Voices* 17, 1 (1981).

## CHAPTER 10

1. Schneidmann, E. *Voices of Death*. New York: Harper & Row, 1980.

2. Kübler-Ross, Elisabeth. *On Death and Dying*. New York: Macmillan, 1969.

3. Kübler-Ross, Elisabeth. *Death: The Final Stage of Growth*. Englewood Cliffs, N. J.: Prentice-Hall, 1975.

4. Grollman, E. A. *Explaining Death to Children*. Boston: Beacon Press, 1967.

5. Yalom, I. *Existential Psychotherapy*. New York: Basic Books, 1980.

6.   Grof, Stanislav, and Grof, Christina. *Beyond Death: The Gates of Consciousness.* London: Thames & Hudson, 1980.

7.   Oyle, I. *The Healing Mind.* New York: Simon & Schuster, 1976.

8.   LeShan, L. *You Can Fight for Your Life.* New York: Evans, 1977.

9.   Simonton, G. C.; Matthews-Simonton, O. S.; and Creighton, J. *Getting Well Again.* New York: J. P. Tarcher, 1978.

10.  Mahrer, A. R. "Treatment of Cancer through Experiential Psychotherapy." *Psychotherapy: Theory, Research & Practice* 17, 3 (Fall 1980).

11.  Torrey, E. F. "Psychic Healing and Psychotherapy." *Psychiatry and Mysticism,* Edited by S. Dean. Chicago: Nelson Hall, 1975.

12.  Simonton, C. The Role of the Mind in Cancer Therapy. *Ibid,* 293–308.

13.  Frank, J. D. *Persuasion and Healing.* Baltimore: Johns Hopkins Press, 1973.

14.  LeShan, L. *Alternate Realities.* New York: M. Evans, 1976.

15.  Wilbur, K. *The Spectrum of Consciousness.* Wheaton, Ill: Theosophical Publishing House, 1977.

16.  Wilbur, K. *The Atman Project.* Wheaton, Ill: Theosophical Publishing House, 1980.

17.  Pearce, J. G. *The Crack in the Cosmic Egg.* New York: Julian, 1971.

18.  Pearce, J. G. *Exploring the Crack in the Cosmic Egg.* New York: Julian, 1974.

19.  Zukav, G. *The Dancing Wu Li Masters.* New York: Morrow, 1979.

20.  Needleman, J. *A Sense of the Cosmos.* New York: Dutton, 1965.

21.  Wise, C. A. *Pastoral Psychology.* New York: Aronson, 1981.

22.  Siegel, R. K. "The Psychology of Life after Death." *American Psychology* 55, 10:911–931.

23.  Ring, K. *Life at Death.* New York: Coward, McCann & Geoghegan, 1980.

24.  Grosso, M. "Life at Death" (a review of the above). *Jl. Amer. Ass'n. for Psychical Research* Vol. 75, 2 (April 1981): 172–176.

25.  Lewis, H. D. *Persons and Life after Death.* New York: Harper & Row, 1978.

26. Grof, S., and Halifax, J. *The Human Encounter with Death*. New York: Dutton, 1977.

27. Sabom, M. B., and Kreutziger, S. "Near-death Experiences." *New England Jl. of Med.* 297, 1071 (1977).

28. Stevenson, I. "Research into the Evidence of Man's Survival after Death." *Jl. Nerv. & Mental Disease* 165: 152–170.

29. Stevenson, I., and Grayson, B. Near-Death Experiences. *Jl. Amer. Med. Ass'n.* 242 (1979); 265–267.

30. Siegel, R. K. "Accounting for 'Afterlife' Experiences." *Psychology Today* (January 1961): 65–75.

31. Moody, R. *Reflections on Life after Life*. New York: Bantam, 1977.

32. Grosso, M. "Psi, Survival and the Religious Outlook." *Jl. Amer. Soc. for Psychical Research* 74, 2 (April 1980): 227–238.

# INDEX

# INDEX